Scotland and America

A Study of Cultural Relations
1750–1835

Scotland and America

A Study of Cultural Relations
1750–1835

ANDREW HOOK

BLACKIE

Glasgow and London

Published by
Blackie and Son Limited
Bishopbriggs, Glasgow G64 2NZ
5 Fitzhardinge Street, London W1H 0DL

ISBN 0 216 90041 7

Printed by Thomson Litho Ltd., East Kilbride, Scotland

For Judith

In memoriam
W. T. Hook
1898–1964

Contents

Preface

My concern is with the impact upon America of the literary and intellectual movement which distinguished Scotland in the eighteenth and early nineteenth centuries. Bringing to Scotland an international reputation as a centre of culture and learning, that movement was a many-sided one. Its scope was reflected in its impact upon America, and therein lies the explanation of the variety of materials brought together in the following pages. In their relationships to America, Scottish literature, Scottish literary theory, Scottish philosophy, and Scottish medical and scientific studies are all clearly worthy of independent consideration. Douglas Sloan's *The Scottish Enlightenment and the American College Ideal* (1971) provides a useful model for such specialised studies. But the provision of a basic and widely-ranging account of Scottish literary and intellectual influence upon America, particularly in the period after the American Revolution, seems to me at this time equally useful and perhaps more necessary.

For purposes of organisation I have separated the diverse material considered into two main categories, reflecting an internal division within Scotland's cultural renaissance in the eighteenth century. That division is represented on the one hand by David Hume, Adam Smith, William Robertson and Hugh Blair, looking outward from Scotland to England and Europe generally, and on the other by Allan Ramsay, Robert Fergusson and Robert Burns, looking inward to Scotland's own national traditions and past. It was to Hume and the other 'North Britons' that Scotland owed her intellectual reputation, but it was Burns and his predecessors that brought her literary fame.

After briefly surveying the general cultural situation involving Scotland and America in the years before the Revolution; and after considering the effect of the Revolution upon that situation, I discuss Scotland's impact upon America after 1783 in terms of this division between the intellectual and literary aspects of her cultural renaissance. The division was responsible for the creation of a double image of Scotland in American eyes: Scotland on the one hand as the land of learning and on the other as the land of romance. Early in the nineteenth century that double image, the development of which I have traced, represented what Scotland had finally come to suggest to the American mind and imagination. How America looked upon Scotland tells us something about both countries. My primary concern has been with America, but I should like to think that by considering the American perspective upon Scotland from 1750 to 1835 or thereabouts I have helped to clarify Scotland's own cultural history in that crucial period.

Most of the research for this study was carried out at Princeton University. With its own long and fruitful history of intellectual kinship with Scotland, Princeton was an ideal centre for the investigation of the Scottish impact upon America. In the shadow of such great Scottish Princetonians as John Witherspoon and James McCosh I can only hope that my work is not entirely unworthy of the great tradition which they so brilliantly embody.

For his advising and encouraging me to undertake a study of this kind I owe a large debt of gratitude to Professor Willard Thorp formerly of the English department at Princeton. To Owen Dudley Edwards, too, of the University of Edinburgh, I am deeply indebted for constant and generous help and advice. A special word of thanks is due to my wife, at once my severest and most loving critic.

Purposing a visit to Kaleedoni, a country integrally united to Dominora, our course now lay northward along the western white cliffs of the isle. But finding the wind ahead, and the current too strong for our paddlers, we were fain to forego our destination. . . .

And now, some conversation ensued concerning the country we were prevented from visiting. Our chronicler narrated many fine things of its people; extolling their bravery in war, their amiability in peace, their devotion in religion, their penetration in philosophy, their simplicity and sweetness in song, their loving-kindness and frugality in all things domestic:—running over a long catalogue of heroes, metaphysicians, bards, and good men. . . .

In Kaleedoni was much to awaken the fervor of its bards. Upland and lowland were full of the picturesque; and many unsung lyrics yet lurked in her glens.

(Herman Melville, *Mardi*)

-I-

Introduction

You would wonder to hear how exactly they know the geography of North America, how distinctly they can speak of
its lakes, its rivers, and the extent and richness of the soil in
the respective territories where British colonies are settled: for
my part, did I not know the contrary, I would be tempted
to think they had lived for some time in that country...[1]

They who are so well acquainted with North America, according
to this author, are the common people of western Scotland, particularly those living in and around the thriving city of Glasgow, and
the other counties and towns in the south and west. The date is
some time in the early 1770s.[2] Almost exactly a century before,
certain ancestors of these people had also come to know America.
Covenanters in arms against the religious policy of the government
of Charles II, defeated and imprisoned, they had been punished by
banishment to the American colonies. For them America could have
meant no more than the prospect of permanent separation from their
homeland and kinspeople. What had happened in the succeeding
hundred years to make the unknown known? To make the America
of ultimate exile a familiar territory, its geography a commonplace?
In a broad sense the answer is to be found in the pattern of change
and growth in the eighteenth century which lies behind the emergence of what may be broadly described as the Scottish Enlightenment. What that process of enlightenment involved was a
progressive widening of horizons in all directions, economic,
intellectual, and cultural in particular. In the notion of Scotland's

I

western horizon extending out across the Atlantic to include the continent of North America one may discover an image not at all inappropriate to the nature of the changes occurring in so many aspects of Scottish life in the eighteenth century.

Of course the sole justification for the writing of this book is the fact of the Scottish Enlightenment. Without it there would have been no reason why any country, new or old, should have shown any kind of interest in what the *Edinburgh Review* once called 'a little shabby scraggy corner of a remote island, with a climate which cannot ripen an apple.'[3] But by the end of the eighteenth century, and in the early decades of the nineteenth, Scotland was universally seen as offering an intellectual and cultural richness which more than compensated for her physical barrenness. (And, as we shall see, in time that barrenness too came to have its value.) Scotland's men of science and letters had won for her an international reputation for intellectual and artistic achievement. Significant Scottish contributions had been made, or were being made, to an astonishing range of subjects: literature, history, philosophy, theology, painting, architecture, literary criticism, sociology, economics, mathematics, medicine, chemistry, geology, and engineering. Along with some of her people, these were the goods that formed the staple of Scotland's trade with the world, and with the New World in particular.

Trade is a two-way process, however, and as far as Scotland and America were concerned, a system of exchange was already operating when the first signs of Scotland's cultural development in the eighteenth century were beginning to appear. But before turning to a fuller consideration of the part America played in helping to create the conditions in which change and growth could occur in eighteenth century Scotland, I wish first briefly to stress a particular aspect of Scotland's developing cultural life the significance of which, at least in relation to Scotland's influence abroad, has been insufficiently recognised.

The intellectual and artistic life of eighteenth century Scotland is marked by two apparently contradictory impulses or emphases; one is exclusively native or national, the other more English or European or international. Allan Ramsay, Robert Fergusson, Robert Burns looked inward to Scotland herself, to the rediscovery and revitalisation of her enduring folk and literary traditions; Francis Hutcheson,

Adam Smith, and David Hume looked outward to the wider intellectual world, bringing Scotland to the forefront of European philosophical and scientific thought.[4]

Where the difference between the two groups is made clearest is over the question of language. Many Scotsmen in the eighteenth century seem to have sensed the connection between national identity and a national language. But for the 'North Britons'—the Hutcheson, Smith, Hume group—because there had never been a firmly established tradition of prose-writing in Scots, there was no alternative to English. Scots, a vigorous, energetic, spoken language in the eighteenth century—the language spoken by all the people of Scotland of all classes outside the Gaelic area of the north and west—was entirely deficient in the formal, learned, technical vocabulary required by philosophers and historians like Robertson, Hume, and Smith. English was for them the natural choice, even as Latin had been for their medieval predecessors.

When this has been said, however, it remains true that the North Britons' endorsement of English as their own language, both by the example of their work and by more direct comment, does reflect a considerable concern for English interest and critical approval. That they in fact consciously experienced some sense of inferiority in face of the established literary culture of London and the south is certainly true. How conscious they were of the recentness of their arrival upon the general cultural scene is made clear for example by the preface to the first, short-lived *Edinburgh Review* (1755), whose contributors included Blair, Robertson, and Smith. The preface suggests that 'If countries have their ages with respect to improvement, North-Britain may be considered as in a state of early youth, guided and supported by the more mature strength of her kindred country', and further compelling evidence of their longing for English approbation may be seen in the North Britons' nervous desire to purge their writing of anything suggesting their Scottish vernacular background.[5] Hume's characteristic anxiety to have every Scotticism removed from his work before publication is well known.[6]

A particular respect for English standards is hardly typical of those who made up the other side of Scotland's eighteenth century revival. Nor were they specially concerned about English literary models. Interested in older Scottish traditions, they naturally took their stand on the vernacular. The first example of reviving interest occurred in

1706, a year before the Union, and eighteen years before Hutcheson's *Inquiry into the Original of our Ideas of Beauty and Virtue* may be said to have launched the North British movement: James Watson's *A Choice Collection of Comic and Serious Scots Poems Both Ancient and Modern,* additional volumes of which were published in 1709 and 1711. Allan Ramsay followed Watson's lead. The first volume of *The Tea-Table Miscellany,* which contained a mixed collection of old and new songs and ballads, including many edited specimens of old Scots folk poems, appeared in 1724. In the same year, Ramsay produced *The Ever-Green,* another collection this time mainly based on the contents of the Bannatyne MS., a collection made in 1568 of the poetry of Scotland's first golden age. In introducing their collections both Watson and Ramsay emphasise the essential Scottishness of their material.

The renewed interest in Scots popular literature, which the collections of Watson and Ramsay demonstrate, was manifested in other ways during the same period. Poems and songs began to be written again in Scots by men such as Robert Crawford and William Hamilton of Gilbertfield, and also by some of the first of Scotland's literary ladies: Lady Wardlaw, whose 'Hardyknute' was the most successful ballad imitation of the eighteenth century, Lady Grizel Baillie, and later in the century, Jane Elliott, Mrs Cockburn and Lady Anne Barnard.[7] Meanwhile, the main vernacular tradition was carried on in the Scots poems of Ramsay himself, and later, in the work of a greater poet, Edinburgh's own short-lived poet laureate— Robert Fergusson. In the poetry of Burns, who owed a great deal to Fergusson, the strengths, and the weaknesses, of that tradition were finally summed up. In the nineteenth century it lost its vitality, though in the early decades its creative influence is still strong in the work of James Hogg, John Galt, 'Christopher North' (John Wilson), and in the Scottish novels of Sir Walter Scott.

This native Scottish emphasis, central to one side of Scotland's eighteenth century revival—and perhaps not even entirely absent from the other[8]—has been insufficiently recognised in terms of Scottish influence abroad. In Scotland's relations with America only the impact of the North Britons has even been considered. I shall show that, especially in the period after the American Revolution, such an emphasis provides only a very partial picture.[9]

In Scotland too, the position after the American War was somewhat different. A new generation of writers and thinkers, who were to maintain for Scotland the international reputation that their predecessors had so ably won for her, was emerging. Henry Mackenzie (1745–1831), of *Man of Feeling* fame, straddles both generations, but most of the new generation did not come of age until well after the war with America. They may be said to have finally established themselves with the founding of the *Edinburgh Review* in 1802.[10]

Writing of this second generation period, Dr Daiches has said: 'When in 1822 George IV, dressed in what he had been told was the Royal Stuart tartan, visited Edinburgh and was proudly greeted by Sir Walter arrayed in the tartan of the Campbells, Scotland had become British in a sense that neither Whigs nor Tories could have foreseen in 1707.'[11] This is no doubt true, but it had at the same time become more assertively and proudly Scottish; and assuredly so in fields much more significant than that of Sir Walter's attire. When the *Edinburgh* was founded there was no need for an apologetic preface such as we have seen introducing its eponymous ancestor in 1755. Scotland has by now come of age in no uncertain manner; a cultural and intellectual equality with England is taken for granted; an assured confidence in their own independent worth and value characterises the new Scottish intellectuals just as clearly as a comparable uncertainty had characterised the old. Without that calm assurance, neither the *Edinburgh Review,* nor *Blackwood's Magazine* later, could have adopted and maintained the positions they did.

In 1819, *Blackwood's* in fact feels called upon to rebuke the Scots for their arrogant attitude towards England and English achievement:

> We are disposed to think that, upon the whole, the national pride of Scotsmen is manly and enlightened. Within the last hundred years Scotland has produced more men of genius than during all her previous history. . . . But we are greatly mistaken, if along with a proper pride in the achievements of our own genius, Scotsmen do not too generally entertain an unreasonable impatience of the ascendancy of the genius of England, and, since we must say so, a very unjust and illiberal determination to undervalue certain excellencies to which they themselves have never yet been able to attain.[12]

Looking back from the standpoint of 1828, the *Edinburgh Review* notes exactly the change I wish to draw attention to. It mentions the 'remarkable increase of nationality' in British, particularly

Scottish literature, and contrasts this position with that of the eighteenth century revival about which 'there was nothing truly Scottish, nothing indigenous. . . .' Scottish culture was rather 'almost exclusively French'. 'Never, perhaps,' says the *Review*, 'was there a class of writers, so clear and well ordered, yet so totally destitute, to all appearances, of any patriotic affection, nay, of any human affection whatever.'[13]

The *Review* itself is full of evidence of the spirit of resurgent nationalism. There is, for example, Jeffrey's famous review of *Marmion* in which one of the faults he points to is 'the neglect of Scotish feelings and Scotish character that is manifested throughout.' In relation to Flodden, 'no picture is drawn of the national feeling before or after that fatal encounter; and the day that broke for ever the pride and the splendour of his country, is only commemorated by a Scotish poet as the period when an English warrior was beaten to the ground. There is scarcely one trait of true Scotish nationality or patriotism entroduced into the whole poem. . . .'[14]

As in the eighteenth century, however, the decisive attitude is shown on the question of the Scottish vernacular. Here too a complete reversal has occurred. One wonders what the members of the 'Select Society for promoting the Reading and Speaking of the English Language in Scotland' would have thought of sentiments such as these:

> After having given this just and attractive description of the book, we have a sort of malicious pleasure in announcing to our Southern readers, that it is a sealed book to them; and that, until they take the trouble thoroughly to familiarise themselves with our antient and venerable dialect, they will not be able to understand three pages of it.[15]

But for a full statement of the *Review's* attitude towards Scots one must turn to an essay on Burns. Writing in 1809, the reviewer immediately makes the point that all modern evaluations of Burns endorse: all his best work is written in Scots.

> We beg leave too, (he continues) in passing, to observe that this Scotch is not to be considered as a provincial dialect,—the vehicle only of rustic vulgarity and rude local humour. It is the language of a whole country,—long an independent kingdom, and still separate in laws, character and manners. It is by no

means peculiar to the vulgar . . . it is the language of a great body
of poetry, with which almost all Scotchmen are familiar; and,
in particular, of a great multitude of songs, written with more
tenderness, nature, and feeling, than any other lyric compositions that are extant, and we may perhaps be allowed to say, that
the Scotch is, in reality, a highly poetical language; and that it
is an ignorant, as well as an illiberal prejudice, which would
seek to confound it with the barbarous dialects of Yorkshire or
Devon.[16]

In these passages it is difficult to discover any sense of inferiority
before the higher culture of those whom *Blackwood's* described as
'our enlightened neighbours, the Transtweeddalecarlians'.[17]

Finally, for an account of the distinctively Scottish quality of life
in Edinburgh at the opening of the nineteenth century one turns
inevitably to the nostalgic description by Lord Cockburn of his own
and Jeffrey's early days in the city:

Many of the curious characters and habits of the receding age,
the last purely Scotch age that Scotland was destined to see, still
lingered among us. Several were then to be met with who had
seen the Pretender, with his court and his wild followers, in the
palace of Holyrood. Almost the whole official state, as settled at
the union, survived; and all graced the capital, unconscious of
the economical scythe which has since mowed it down. All our
nobility had then not fled. A few had sense not to feel degraded
by being happy at home. The old town was not quite
deserted. . . .[18]

Lord Cockburn goes on to list the individuals in the university, in
the Church, and in the Law, who adorned the intellectual and social
life of the city and concludes that 'all this was still a Scotch scene.
The whole country had not begun to be absorbed in the ocean of
London.'[19] According to the 'modern' rate of travelling, London and
Edinburgh were still about 2,400 miles apart, with the result that
Edinburgh 'had then its own independent tastes, and ideas, and
pursuits. Enough of the generation that was retiring survived to cast
an antiquarian air over the city, and the generation that was
advancing was still a Scotch production'.[20]

Clearly the intellectual development of the eighteenth century,
while establishing the country's reputation on a European, international level, helped to focus Scotland's sense of national identity and

encouraged an awareness of her traditional, national literature and culture. In the decades after the American Revolution, when great successes were won precisely in the literary fields where the North Britons had failed, this sharpened awareness reached its highest point. Thus the Scottish intellectuals of the early nineteenth century were certainly less inhibited by their sense of Scottishness than their eighteenth century predecessors had been. Influences emanating from Scotland in this second period therefore cannot be legitimately regarded as indistinguishable from a wider English or 'British' pattern.

Scotland's cultural development from the early eighteenth century through to the first decades of the nineteenth is then characterised by impulses both national and international, local and cosmopolitan; in the generation prior to the American Revolution the division may be identified as one between poets and literary editors on the one hand, and broadly speaking men of the philosophical Enlightenment on the other. But in the subsequent generation, while neither impulse declines, no such clear division can be made. Such is the essential cultural pattern that has to be recognised in relation to Scotland's influence abroad during the period in question.

The relationship between economic growth and cultural development is not a simple one. But that improved economic conditions do stimulate or at least make possible an expansion of cultural activities seems reasonably certain. It was, then, by contributing to Scotland's economic development that America, from the earliest years of the eighteenth century, was already playing a part, if a silent one, in Scotland's cultural renaissance.

A consequence of the Navigation Act of 1661 had been the barring of the Scots from profitable overseas trade with England's colonies. The position was reversed, however, by the Treaty of Union of 1707 which opened all of England's colonies to Scottish trade. The promise of immediate economic expansion for Scotland which this change seemed to bring unfortunately proved to be illusory; in the years immediately after the Union, the trade of Edinburgh and Aberdeen, and so of most of the eastern half of the country, fell off rather than increased. It was only with regard to Glasgow and the west that the bright promise of the Union was fulfilled.

On his tour through Great Britain in 1722, during which his primary concern was with the economic and social conditions of the country, Defoe noted the great advantages that Glasgow possessed over London in the American trade. Basically the question was one of distance. Even though vessels cannot sail all the way up the Clyde to Glasgow, and goods must as a result be carried overland for a few miles, nonetheless the overall cost of transportation will be less because of the shorter voyage: '... even in Times of Peace, and take the Weather to happen in its usual Manner, there must always be allow'd one Time with another, at least fourteen to twenty Days Difference in the Voyage, either Out or Home....'[21] In time of war, Defoe observed, vessels sailing in and out of the Clyde would not be faced with the danger which arose from the presence of innumerable privateers in the English Channel.

In point of fact, the merchants of Glasgow and the towns to the south-west, had long been well aware of the advantages of their situation in terms of the American colonial trade. They had not even waited for the legalising Act of Union to begin to take part in it. Since the latter part of the seventeenth century the Clyde had been the centre of a profitable contraband trade with America—trade which was often carried on with Scots already resident in the tobacco colonies of Virginia, Maryland, and Delaware. Glasgow merchants too had early had considerable experience of speculation in tobacco; cargoes landed at Liverpool or Whitehaven were bought and re-exported to Holland and Sweden. In the years immediately subsequent to the Union, Glasgow's tobacco imports averaged 1,450,000 pounds (lb.) per annum. In 1722 the figure climbed to 6 million pounds. Until the 1740s there was no sizeable increase but then the really startling development began; 8 million pounds in 1741, 10 million in 1743, 13 million in 1745, 21 million in 1752, 24 million in 1753, 32 million in 1760, and finally, the record year, 47 million pounds in 1771. From 1740 on, the English tobacco trade had ceased to grow significantly. As late as 1738, the Scottish trade had accounted for only 10 per cent of the British total; but after 1740 this percentage, too, grew enormously until it reached the 51·8 per cent in 1769, when Glasgow had become the first tobacco port in the British Isles.[22]

This economic link between the Firth of Clyde and Chesapeake Bay played an important part in the material development of western Scotland. In Glasgow itself, it created the famous tobacco aristocracy, the real rulers of the city's destinies. The tobacco lords were proud men, aware of their power, remaining aloof from the rest of the society of the city, living in their splendid mansions on Virginia Street, and distinguished in the streets by their scarlet cloaks, cocked hats, and gold-headed canes.[23] But the trade did much more than create a handful of private fortunes:

> By this intercourse between Scotland and North America, which for more than half a century hath been rapidly encreasing, Scotland is in a situation which appeareth to be different from what it was in any former period: It may be considered as being, by means of its navigation and foreign commerce brought nearer to the Western continent than it was before. Good roads, you know, do, as it were, diminish the distance betwixt two cities; a long and continued intercourse, by safe and successful sailings, hath the like effect with respect to distant countries.[24]

Scottish merchants brought Scotland into familiar contact with the entire sweep of the seaboard of North America from Florida to Nova Scotia, and established in every port small but influential Scottish colonies within colonies: 'Their shipping routes stretched out from Glasgow like the ribs of a fan. At some of the extremities of these ribs, the year 1775 found the Scots merchants in a dominating position. Such was the case in the tobacco country and in Canada. Elsewhere, as at Charleston, Savannah, Wilmington, Philadelphia, and New York, they formed a powerful element in the trading community.'[25] When it is remembered that the trade which had brought America so close also had much to do with the fostering of emigration from Scotland, it becomes more than evident that the significance of this link between the countries extends far beyond its purely financial aspect.

The ribs of the trading fan were ideal paths for the conveying of Scottish cultural influences of all kinds—as students of the economic tie have noted. Price, for instance, says of the Scottish mercantile community in the Chesapeake Bay area: '...they were there, and twice a year their ships came to them from the Clyde—ships as numerous as those from all Britain besides. For many a Virginian, this must have meant that mail, news, reading matter, ideas, religion, politics came to him via Glasgow.'[26] He might have gone on to notice the effect in the reverse direction. There is no doubt that the strong trading link stimulated general Scottish interest in America, while the constant coming and going of ships provided the ideal means for satisfying it. *The Scots Magazine*, for example, the one conspicuously successful Scottish periodical in the eighteenth century, published continuously in Edinburgh from 1739 to 1826, even in its earliest numbers carried news from America. By 1750, 'Plantation News', a description soon to be changed to a monthly 'British North America' section, had become a regular feature of each issue, and once the war with the French and Indians broke out coverage became even fuller. In 1775, the magazine could claim with justice that 'the American dispute has been an object of our particular attention ever since its beginning. . . .'[27] As early as 1741 it had been printing opinions on the best way to handle the American colonies,[28] and from the time of the dispute over the Stamp Act to the outbreak of hostilities between Britain and her colonies the views of both sides were printed in the greatest detail, with real impartiality.[29]

What is of particular interest, in the reporting of these disputes, is the extent of the magazine's reprinting of American sources; extracts from American newspapers were a constant feature—indeed they formed the main source of information on what was actually taking place—as were other reports and letters from America. The practice of printing long extracts from the American press went on as late as 1776: a fact which suggests again the connection between this diffusion of American news and the existence of the tobacco trade between the Clyde and Chesapeake Bay, as it was of course in that year that the Revolution broke the trading link.[30]

The connection between commerce and emigration in Scottish–American relations has been referred to in passing above. But emigration, which has been traditionally regarded as the key to any accounting of the impact of other countries upon America, requires more than a passing reference. The scale of emigration from Scotland to America is not the determining factor in the question of cultural influence—obviously it is a very important one—but the fact of emigration unquestionably helped in itself to sharpen Scottish awareness of America throughout the eighteenth century. Usually because of a failure to distinguish between the native Scots and the Ulster Scots or Scotch-Irish, the total number of Scottish emigrants to America has often been greatly exaggerated. Recent estimates for the period 1763–75, the only period in which a 'spirit of emigration' was recognised as being widespread throughout the country, place the total number at something under 25,000.[31] In other words, by nineteenth century standards, or even by the standard of the contemporaneous Ulster Scot emigration, Scottish emigration to America was quite small.

However small the scale of emigration may now seem, it was nonetheless certainly large enough to make the whole question of emigration a very lively one at the time. In the 1763–75 period, the *Scots Magazine* continually reports the sailing of emigrant ships.[32] Discussion of the causes of this emigration became a popular topic. The reasons offered by the emigrants themselves—rack-renting by landlords, unemployment, the high price of meal, the turning of farms into sheep runs—were carefully noted.[33] Companies were formed to buy land in America; prospective emigrants met together, drew up rules, subscribed money, and sent company representatives over the Atlantic to make the necessary purchases.[34] But emigration also had its opponents who felt that the country's strength was being drained away, and attempts were made to discredit some of the proposed emigrant schemes.[35]

A potent influence in encouraging further emigrations and in disseminating knowledge about the American scene were the letters from America received by kinspeople and friends at home.[36] Such letters were sometimes published to refute the rumours spread by the opponents of emigration about the hard lot of emigrants and the unhealthiness of the climate of America. Few answers can have been as effective as one from Alexander Thomson, formerly a farmer near Paisley, who had sailed from Greenock in the ship *Friendship* with his wife and twelve children in July, 1771. He writes now on 16 August, 1773, to a gentleman near Glasgow of the land he has bought, the cost of living, and the advantages he has found in America. He goes on to describe the climate:

> Sir, I cannot express the beauty of the summer season, it is so fine, so pleasing, and healthy. While I and my sons are clearing ground, and go for a while to walk, or rest ourselves in the forest among the tall oaks on a summer day, the sight of the heavens and the smell of the air give me a pleasure which I cannot tell you how great it is. When we sit down to rest, the breezes of the south-west wind, and the whispering noise it makes on the top of the trees, together with the fine smell of the plants and flowers pleases us so exceedingly, that we are

almost enchanted and unwilling to part with such a pleasure.[37]

In such a description one can see the creation and diffusion of a Scottish version of the archetypal image of America as the New World; an image which may well sum up the Scottish awareness of America which the widely-discussed 'spirit of emigration' implies.

Taken together, then, the merchant link and the emigration movement provide a solid basis for the assertion that the most important and significant years in the history of Scottish–American relations were those immediately preceding the Revolution. 'Preceding', of course, because the outbreak of the American War meant the immediate severing of the commercial ties between Glasgow and the American colonies. After the war, trade was resumed but the Glasgow tobacco empire was never rebuilt; it was replaced by the West Indies trade and the cotton industry. But the war brought other changes. A writer in *Blackwood's Magazine* in 1825, in a discussion of travelling in America, touches upon one such:

> While the colonies remained attached to the mother-country, the constant interchange of civilities between officers of high connexions at home, and the inhabitants of the new settlements, tended to preserve a sentiment of reciprocal respect.... In a word, the war of the American independence broke off, between the two countries, the gentlemanly intercourse, which even yet cannot be said to have been renewed....[38]

In a rather wider context, and with fewer overtones of social caste, Graham adopts a similar view. 'The coming of the American Revolution', he writes, 'transformed Scotland's relations with America.... Although emigration and trade resumed after 1783, the Revolution had cut cleanly through the web of relationships between Scotland and North America.... The Revolution severed the numerous ties on both sides of the Atlantic.... After 1775 Scottish influence lost most of its force, a loss which was never made good.'[39] Obviously there is much here that is true. The coincidence of Scotland's merchant tie with America with a period of great intellectual vitality and vigour at home clearly establishes an almost ideal situation for the cultural influence of the one country upon the other. And there were other grounds on which Scotland and America might be expected to share some kind of sympathetic affinity. There was first of all the important similarity in religious life: the Church of Scotland had much more in common with the religious life of large and influential sections of America than the Church of England. Then Scotland's eighteenth century intellectual and economic expansion was paralleled by a similar development in America: although America produced no Hume or Adam Smith, Franklin, Jonathan Edwards, Jefferson and Madison, to name but a few, were men of no mean accomplishment.[40] Finally, it is possible to set up an identification of Scot and American on a deeper level: in relation to the dominant culture of England. In 1763, if hardly so remote as New York, Edinburgh was still a very long way from London. I have already made reference to Cockburn's estimate that in terms of 'modern' travel the Scottish and English capitals were 2,400 miles apart, and in 1763, according to William Creech, only one coach per month left Edinburgh for London, the journey taking from twelve to sixteen days. Before setting out on such a journey it was usual for people to make their wills presumably just as they would have done had they been sailing for London from Philadelphia or New York.[41] Before the cultural bar of London, then, the Scot and the American appeared as a distant provincial, and it is true that the standards of taste set in London were long accepted in New York and Philadelphia just as they were in Edinburgh.

Acknowledging these similarities in the positions of Scotland and America in the years before the Revolution, and fully recognising the favourableness of the situation in that period for all kinds of cultural exchange, one may nonetheless disagree that a dramatic and drastic change occurred as a result of the Revolution. To suggest that America was cut off from Scottish influence in 1775 is misleading except in so far as it may mean that the breaking of the commercial and political links prevented American reception of *new* Scottish influences: the impact of cultural and literary influences is rarely immediate. But in fact America did continue to be receptive of Scottish influence even after the Revolution; the subsequent developments in Scotland's cultural and intellectual life did have their effect upon America; the main period of influence of the more native and national aspect of the eighteenth century revival was to come after 1783; and the personal ties between the educated classes on both sides of the Atlantic, though temporarily loosened, were in the end to be renewed and in new ways made stronger than before. The Revolution, then, marked only a temporary break in Scottish–American cultural relations, and the continuity which marks the two generations of the Scottish revival is reflected in the continuity of Scottish influence upon America. Any changes in emphasis or appeal in the fifty years after 1783 are themselves the consequence of changes in the Scottish cultural pattern. To establish the context of that continuity, in the next chapter the pattern of Scottish–American cultural relations in the years preceding the American Revolution will be described.

NOTES AND REFERENCES

1. *A Candid Enquiry into the Causes of the Late and the Intended Migrations from Scotland. In a letter to J——— R———, Esq., Lanark-shire* (Glasgow, n.d.), p. 50.
2. The pamphlet contains a reference to John Millar's *The Origin of the Distinction of Ranks*, first published in 1771. It contains no reference to the American War.
3. *Edinburgh Review*, XL (1824), 432–3.
4. See David Daiches, *Robert Burns* (New York, 1950), pp. 8–9.
5. In 1761, Thomas Sheridan delivered a series of lectures in Edinburgh on the correct speaking of English. The lectures were attended by three hundred 'gentlemen'. The 'Select Society' of the city followed up Sheridan's visit by establishing 'The Society for promoting the Reading and Speaking of the English Language in Scotland'. See *The Scots Magazine*, XXIII (1761), 389–90, 440–1.
6. John Butt's essay 'The Revival of Vernacular Scottish Poetry in the Eighteenth Century' in F. W. Hilles and H. Bloom (Eds), *From Sensibility to Romanticism. Essays presented to Frederick A. Pottle* (New York, 1965), pp. 219–37, provides an excellent account of the linguistic situation of the North British writers.
7. See T. F. Henderson, *Scottish Vernacular Literature* (London, 1900), pp. 394–8, and cf. Henry Grey Graham, *Scottish Men of Letters in the Eighteenth Century* (London, 1908), pp. 321–47.
8. There is little to suggest that the North Britons desired only that their work should be subsumed within the dominant culture of England. A separate but equal status was their aim. Perhaps the best evidence of this is the uncritical eagerness with which, after eminently successful incursions had been made into the fields of philosophy, history, and criticism, they welcomed any Scottish literary production modelled in language and style on the works of the English Augustans: William Wilkie's *Epigoniad*, for example, which earned its author the title of 'The Scottish Homer', or the work of the blind poet, Dr Blacklock, which was ranked with that of Pope, or the *Douglas* of John Home, Scotland's Shakespeare.
9. The impact of Scott upon America has of course been widely studied. But the tendency has always been to treat him as an isolated phenomenon, in no way related to a wider Scottish tradition.
10. The originators of the *Review* were Francis Jeffrey (1773–1850), Sydney Smith (1771–1845) and Henry Brougham (1778–1868).
11. Daiches, *Robert Burns*, p. 15.
12. *Blackwood's Magazine*, V (1819), 3.
13. *Edinburgh Review*, XLVIII (1828), 288, 289.
14. Ibid., XII (1808), 12–13.
15. Ibid., 402. The book under discussion is *The Cottagers of Glenburnie*, by Mrs Elizabeth Hamilton.
16. Ibid., XIII (1808–9), 259.
17. *Blackwood's Magazine*, XXXI (1832), 984.
18. Lord (Henry) Cockburn, *Life of Lord Jeffrey, with a Selection from his Correspondence*, 2 vols in one (Philadelphia, 1856), I, 125–6.
19. Ibid., p. 127.
20. Ibid., pp. 127–8.
21. Daniel Defoe, *A Tour Thro' the whole Island of Great Britain*, with an Introduction by G. D. H. Cole (London, 1927), II, p. 749.
22. For a detailed account of Glasgow in the tobacco trade, see Jacob M. Price, 'The rise of

Glasgow in the Chesapeake Tobacco Trade, 1707–1775', *William and Mary College Quarterly*, 3rd Series, XI (April, 1954), 179–99.

23. John Strang, *Glasgow and its Clubs* (Glasgow and London, 1857), pp. 35–7.

24. *A Candid Enquiry into the Causes of the Late and the Intended Migrations from Scotland*, p. 52.

25. Ian Charles Cargill Graham, *Colonists from Scotland: Emigration to North America, 1707–1783* (Ithaca, 1956), p. 127.

26. Price, p. 198.

27. *The Scots Magazine*, XXXVII (1775), 229.

28. Ibid., III (1741), 361–4.

29. Impartiality, however, was the ideal of all the British press at this time. See Fred. J. Hinkhouse, *The Preliminaries of the American Revolution* (New York, 1926), pp. 12–16.

30. To quote a single example of such extracts: 'From the Essex Gazette, printed at Salem in New England. Salem, April 25. Last Wednesday, the 19th of April, the troops of his Britannic Majesty commenced hostilities upon the people of this province, attended with circumstances of cruelty not less brutal than what our venerable ancestors received from the vilest savages of the wilderness . . .' *The Scots Magazine*, XXXVII (1775), 229.

31. Graham, *Colonists from Scotland*, pp. 185–9.

32. *The Scots Magazine*, XXX (1768), 446; XXXI (1769), 602; XXXIII (1771), 325, 500.

33. Ibid., XXXIII (1771), 500; XXXIV (1772), 395; XXXV (1773), 557; XXXVII (1775), 690.

34. See, for example, 'A plan agreed upon by a great many Farmers and others, in the Shires of *Dumbarton*, *Clydesdale*, and *Renfrew*, etc. for creating a Company of Farmers . . . ,' (Paisley, 1772). And cf. *The Scots Magazine*, XXXVI (1774), 221; XXXVII (1775), 165.

35. See, for example, the debate over the scheme backed by John Witherspoon, the Scottish president of the College of New Jersey, for emigration to Nova Scotia: *The Scots Magazine*, XXXIV (1772), 482–3, 483–4, 587–8.

36. Margaret I. Adam, 'The Causes of the Highland Emigrations of 1783–1803,' *Scottish Historical Review*, XVII (January, 1920), 75.

37. *News from America. Letter 1. From Alexander Thomson, late Tenant at Corker-Hill in the Parish of Paisley, now Proprietor of a considerable Estate in Pensilvania. To a Gentleman near Glasgow* (Glasgow, 1774), p. 8.

38. *Blackwood's Magazine*, XVIII (1825), 423.

39. Graham, *Colonists from Scotland*, pp. 148–9.

40. See John Clive and Bernard Bailyn, 'England's Cultural Provinces: Scotland and America', *William and Mary College Quarterly*, 3rd Series, XI (April, 1954), 202.

41. William Creech, *Edinburgh Fugitive Pieces* (Edinburgh, 1815), pp. 68–9.

– II –

A Fruitful Harmony

One problem facing the student of cultural relationships is that of
definition: what precisely constitutes such a relationship? The
simplest answer, though a restrictive one, is that implied by all
students of the migrations of peoples: the culture of one country is
conveyed to, or imposed upon another, by large-scale movements
of population from the first country to the second. When this
definition, despite its disregard of the mind and imagination of both
countries, is accepted and applied to a particular relationship such as
that between Scotland and America, it produces works which, at
best, consist of brief biographies of great numbers of Scots or their
descendants in every aspect of American cultural, intellectual and
social history, and, at worst, of imposing lists of Americans from
generals to golfers, who somewhere in the past ten generations may
lay claim to Scottish blood.[1] What this reveals is the inadequacy of
the original definition; it describes a cultural debt, not a relationship.
Furthermore, the mere presence of an immigrant group in America,
even one with its own distinctive culture, proves nothing. In terms
of influence the position of such a group remains problematic, just
in the way that the significant volume on the shelves of a library
does; in the case of the book there is still the question of whether it is
taken off the shelf and read. Clearly availability is not to be
automatically identified with influence; as important as availability
is a receptive frame of mind, an openness to influence, on the part
of the potential reader. The argument applies equally to the possible
influence of immigrant groups in America or elsewhere. American
culture was in fact peculiarly receptive to Scottish influence, but

in addition there existed a group of Americans who meet whatever exacting standard is used to define the true bearers of cultural influence from one country to another. These are Americans who came to Scotland specifically to enter into and learn from Scottish cultural and intellectual life before carrying the fruits of their experiences home to their native land.

During the eighteenth century, there were in fact large numbers of Americans in Scotland. Almost all of them were there for strictly practical purposes; the desire for education of some kind accounts for a high percentage of the total. Why they should have chosen to come to Scotland will be considered below, but any answer to that question would be incomplete unless it took account of the influence of a single man—the key figure in personal relations between Scots and colonial Americans as well as in many other aspects of British-American relationships—Benjamin Franklin of Philadelphia. Franklin was in Scotland on two separate occasions; the first time as early as 1759, the second in 1771, and the first visit in particular was of high importance for the subsequent pattern of relations between Scotland and America. Important as they are in themselves, Franklin's two Scottish visits will be of rare value in helping us to trace that pattern in the years before the Revolution.[2]

Arriving in Scotland in the autumn of 1759, Franklin was not descending upon some foreign land entirely unknown to him. Even before coming to London in 1757, the Agent for Pennsylvania had had many friendly contacts with natives of the northern part of the mother country. William Strahan, for example, a Scot who had taken the high road south from Edinburgh to become one of London's principal printers and booksellers, had long been his friend and correspondent. Out to Philadelphia from Strahan's London office in 1744, had come David Hall, 'Edinburgh Davey', who had first been employed by Franklin, and in 1748 had become his partner in the printing business which Hall was eventually to take over altogether. Through Hall, if not in any other way, Franklin was very probably brought in contact with the whole Scottish colony in Philadelphia.

In 1747 had occurred an event which must have brought together all the Scots in the city: the founding of the St Andrew's Society of Philadelphia. Twenty-five natives of Scotland had met in a tavern in the winter of 1747 to consider the organisation of a society, the purpose of which would be the relief of needy fellow Scots. Of that original twenty-five, David Hall was one.[3] And Franklin was friendly with many other Scots among the Society's members. It is inconceivable that he should not have heard much of Scotland from these natives whose attachment to the land of their birth traditionally grew stronger when they were far away from it.

Even if Franklin had not made these Scottish connections in his home town, once he had arrived in London he would inevitably have been brought into contact with the Scots in the city. His friendship with the influential Strahan, who was a central figure in the Scottish circle in London, would have been sufficient to guarantee that, but he had other reasons for being interested in the Scots and Scotland. In February, 1759, he had been notified by the University of St Andrews that he had been awarded the honorary degree of Doctor of Laws in recognition of his work on electricity; as Nolan says, this gesture probably encouraged him to think of making a trip to Scotland. At the British Coffee House, kept by a Scotswoman, Mrs Anderson, and the favourite resort of all the Scottish intellectuals in London,[4] Franklin would have met his scientific friend, Sir John Pringle, one of the circle of North Britons in Edinburgh, later president of the Royal Society, and probably many other Scots: Smollett, John Home, Alexander Carlyle, Andrew and William Hunter, renowned in medical circles, Alexander Wedderburn, now rising at the bar, later to be one of Franklin's bitterest antagonists, and James Boswell. From all of these, if not from his English friends, most of whom would probably have actively discouraged him, Franklin would have received encouragement for the idea of a trip to Scotland.

Franklin and his son William, arrived in Edinburgh early in September, 1759. Almost immediately they were honoured with the freedom of the city. In the days that followed they entered fully into the lively social life of the North Britons. They stayed with Sir Alexander Dick; they met and were entertained by David Hume, Lord Kames, Adam Ferguson, the two Monros, Joseph Black, Doctors Cullen and Russell, William Robertson and Adam Smith. A little later they sampled in the same way the social and intellectual life of Glasgow, meeting Professor Simson, the mathematician in the university, Alexander Wilson, in 1760 made the first professor of astronomy at Glasgow, Andrew and Robert Foulis, the famous printers to the university, Adam Smith again, and Professor John Anderson, who was to be the Franklins' guide on their Highland tour. On his arrival at St Andrews Franklin was treated with great respect, he was made a Guild Brother of the town and the university faculty held a formal reception in his honour. He renewed his acquaintance with David Gregory, the professor of mathematics whom he had met the year before in London at Strahan's house, and with Dr Patrick Baird, the Scottish doctor who had practised for several years in Philadelphia before returning to St Andrews in 1743. In St Andrews too, Franklin helped to treat a young student called David Steuart Erskine. Later, as we shall see, as the Earl of Buchan, Erskine became a somewhat eccentric enthusiast for everything connected with America.

The Franklins returned to Edinburgh at the end of the first week in October, 1759. From Lord Kames they received an invitation to spend some days at Kames House in Berwickshire on their way south—an invitation which they gladly accepted. That they enjoyed their stay in the Borders is indicated by the letter of thanks which Franklin wrote to Lord and Lady Kames after his return to London. The letter also gives us some idea of the impression that Scotland had made on the American visitors:

> My Son joins with me in the most respectful Compliments to you, to Lady Kames, and your promising and amiable Son and Daughter. . . . Our Conversation till we came to York was chiefly a Recollection and Recapitulation of what we had seen and heard, the pleasure we had enjoy'd and the Kindnesses we had receiv'd in Scotland, and how far that Country had exceeded our Expectations. On the whole, I must say, I think the Time we spent there, was Six Weeks of the *densest* Happiness I have met with in any Part of my Life. And the agreeable and instructive Society we found there in such Plenty, has left so pleasing an Impression on my Memory, that did not strong Connections draw me elsewhere, I believe Scotland would be the Country I should chuse to spend the Remainder of my Days in.[5]

Franklin continued to correspond with Lord Kames, and in 1761 he received an invitation to return to Kames House. The letter he wrote in reply again suggests the deep impression that the visit to Scotland in 1759 had made upon him:

> Your Invitation to make another Jaunt to Scotland, and Offer to meet us halfway *en famille*, was extreamly obliging. Certainly

I never spent my Time anywhere more agreeably, nor have I been in any Place, where the Inhabitants and their Conversation left such lastingly pleasing Impressions on my mind, accompanied with the strongest Inclination once more to visit that hospitable friendly and sensible people.[6]

Although he maintained his correspondence with Lord Kames, Sir Alexander Dick and David Hume, Franklin did not return to Scotland until 1771, by which time a considerable change had come over relations between the American Colonies and the United Kingdom. In the twelve years that had intervened between his visits, no great changes had occurred in the make-up of Edinburgh's intellectual and social life. Franklin met again all his old friends; Hume, with whom he stayed, Principal Robertson, Lord Kames, Adam Ferguson, Drs Cullen, Monro and Black. Later, in Glasgow, with Henry Marchant, Attorney-General for Rhode Island, Franklin renewed old acquaintances with the Foulis brothers, Alexander Wilson, and Professor John Anderson. According to the diary kept by Marchant, at this time they also had supper with John Millar, professor of civil law at the university, formerly a tutor in Lord Kames's household and another stalwart friend of America.[7] During his last few days in Scotland, Franklin was once again lavishly entertained by his friends in Edinburgh: Hume gave a large dinner party in his honour—Lord Kames was present, along with Black, Russell, and Adam Ferguson. Next day, Franklin and Hume dined with Lord Kames, and the day after, with Ferguson: Kames, Russell, Black and Robertson were all present. So Franklin left Edinburgh in a private chaise for Preston in Lancashire to call at the home of a recently acquired son-in-law.

Franklin was an excellent ambassador for his country. When he was preparing to sail for America in 1762, he received a letter from Hume regretting his departure, and proceeding, 'America has sent us many good things, gold, silver, sugar, tobacco, indigo, etc., but you are the first philosopher and indeed the first great man of letters for whom we are beholden to her'.[8] Wherever he went in 1759, Franklin made a good impression, and even in the difficult days of 1771 he seems to have been able to maintain cordial relations with his Scottish hosts. Even if we choose to see in the letters written to

Lord Kames, quoted above, some good-natured exaggeration of the appeal of Scottish social life, there is plentiful evidence of a more material kind for the respect he had certainly come to hold for Scottish intellectual life. If, many years later, the pattern of Franklin's 1759 expedition to Scotland—the stay in Edinburgh, enjoying the city's close-knit social and intellectual life, followed by excursions to the west and into the Highlands—was to be followed by large numbers of American visitors, in the pre-Revolutionary years, it was Franklin's awareness of the vitality of Scotland's intellectual life and his personal ties with its leading figures, which were to produce tangible results.

Writing of the colonial tourist in Great Britain, William Sachse has said, '... if we except the medical students, Scotland remained a closed book for most Americans abroad.'[9] Franklin's connection with Sachse's exception is a real and decisive one. In the colonial period, essentially because of the fame of its medical school, the university of Edinburgh attracted many more American students than any other British university: approximately a hundred Americans studied there before the Revolution.[10] In the same period some twenty Americans studied at Glasgow university, while King's College and Marischal College, Aberdeen, attracted another sixteen. The first American to take a medical degree at Edinburgh was John Moultrie of South Carolina, who graduated in 1749, and Moultrie's example was undoubtedly followed by a handful of others in the years before 1759;[11] but it was the influence of Franklin that finally decided that the main flow of American students should be to Edinburgh rather than to the continent.

In the spring of 1760, John Morgan, later to play a key part in the development of medical education in North America, arrived in London from Philadelphia, undecided whether to pursue his medical education at Leyden or Edinburgh. Since Franklin was a friend of the family in Philadelphia, it was natural for him to seek advice from the most distinguished American in Europe. And Franklin, no doubt recalling his experiences of a few months earlier, advised him to go to Edinburgh. Morgan arrived in Edinburgh bearing letters from Franklin introducing him to Cullen and Lord Kames in the autumn of 1761, and Franklin went on to sponsor several other young American students in the same way: William Shippen, a graduate of the College of New Jersey; Adam Kuhn, of Pennsylvanian German origin, a botanist as well as a physician;

Benjamin Rush, another graduate of the College of New Jersey; Jonathan Potts, who came over from Philadelphia with Rush but had to return before qualifying for his degree; and Samuel Bard. On their return home all these students would play a central part in the development of medicine in America. The first American medical school was founded at the University of Pennsylvania in 1765; the school was modelled on that of Edinburgh, and Morgan, Shippen, Rush and Kuhn all became professors there.[12] They maintained their relations with the great Edinburgh teachers, and their influence was sufficient to ensure a continual flow of American students to Scotland, all of them armed with letters of introduction to the professors at Edinburgh. Such students were always warmly received. Cullen was reputed to have 'a special measure of esteem for Americans'.[13] The expectations and experience of Thomas Parke, for example, probably paralleled those of many of his compatriots. Parke arrived in Edinburgh in October, 1771, and on his second day in the city called to present his letters of introduction from Morgan and Rush, his teachers in Philadelphia, to, 'yt shining Oracle of Physic, which I have so long wish'd to see. I mean the great Dr. *Cullen*, who I found quite equalled my expectations.'[14]

The American students at Edinburgh seem on the whole to have been industrious and diligent, with a clear realisation of the purpose of their coming to Britain. The rather pedantic note of a letter Shippen wrote to his uncle in Lancaster, Pennsylvania, soon after his arrival in London, may not be quite untypical: 'I do not spend my time trifling about playhouses or operas or reading idle romantic tales or trifling newspapers at coffee-houses, as I find many have done before me, but rather in the rich improvement of those advantages which are not to be had in my own country.'[15] Certainly several of the Americans were disturbed by the levity some of their fellow students showed towards their teachers, while the founding of the Virginia Club in 1761 indicates the seriousness of their own intentions. The purpose of the club was strictly professional—the study of anatomy. One of its actions was to draw up a petition from the Virginian students at Edinburgh asking the Honorable Council of Virginia and House of Burgesses to make it unlawful for doctors to practice in the colony unless they held an academic degree.[16] The American students generally made a point of joining one or more of the medical societies which had become an important part of the medical education available at Edinburgh.[17]

However, it would be a mistake to leave the impression that to a man, the American medical students in the Scottish capital were inspired by an unremitting zeal for study. Many of them had both the time and the opportunity for other pursuits. Thomas Caw, of of South Carolina, for example, was admitted to the Speculative Society on 23 November 1764, that is, a few weeks after the institution of that famous body, which, in succeeding decades, was to have a profound effect on Scotland's intellectual and political development. In 1769, two other Americans, James McClung and Cyrus Griffin, both from Virginia, were admitted to the society.[18] Through the sponsorship of Franklin some American students were also able to move in Edinburgh's social and intellectual circles, both inside and outside the university. On the basis of the *Autobiography* which Benjamin Rush wrote in 1800, together with the letters written while he was studying in Edinburgh, we may reconstruct the experiences of such a student in some detail.

Rush and his friend Jonathan Potts had been preceded to Edinburgh by letters written on their behalf by Franklin to Sir Alexander Dick and others. As a matter of course they were already carrying letters from John Morgan, their professor in Philadelphia, to Dr Cullen. In a letter to Morgan, dated 16 November 1766, Rush described their reception by the great doctor. Dr Cullen had said that the demands on his time made by his academic duties and his practice prevented his treating his pupils with that hospitality he would have liked. ' "But however close my attention," said he, "may be to these necessary avocations, young gentlemen recommended to me from Dr. Morgan may always depend upon my immediate patronage and friendship." '[19]

Rush studied under Doctors Cullen, Monro secundus, Russell, Black and Gregory. He joined the Edinburgh Medical Society and possibly attended meetings of the Edinburgh Philosophical Society. He moved freely in North British circles. At least once, while dining with Sir Alexander Dick, he met David Hume. At Dr Gregory's he met William Robertson, then Principal of the University. He frequently met the blind poet, Dr Blacklock, probably while visiting other American medical students living in the poet's house.[20] Through Mrs Thomas Hogg, the wife of his Edinburgh banker, with whose family he was intimate, he was introduced to the family of the Earl of Leven. Another lasting friendship that Rush formed in Edinburgh was with the Revd Dr John Erskine, as we shall see, an indefatigable friend of America.[21] From the letters of introduction he gave to his son James, when he in turn came to study in Edinburgh, in 1809, it appears that Rush, apart from the members of the university faculty, had also come to know the Earl of Buchan, William Creech, the Edinburgh publisher and bookseller, and William Cullen's daughter, later married to a son of John Millar, the professor of civil law at Glasgow with whom Franklin and Henry Marchant supped in 1771.

Through Rush's letters and his *Autobiography*, we gain some insight into the impression that his Scottish experience made upon the young American medical student. Like all eighteenth century visitors to the city, he was shocked by the filthiness of the Old Town; in Rush's time the practice of throwing all kinds of household garbage out of the windows into the streets at eleven o'clock at night, preceded only by the warning cry of 'gardy-loo', still prevailed. In a letter written in December, 1766, Rush remarks that his friend Potts had already suffered the special kind of 'naturaliz- ation' that was the frequent consequence of such a habit, although he himself had so far successfully avoided it.[22] But despite drawbacks of this kind, we have Rush's own words in recognition of the importance in his life of his stay in Edinburgh. Writing to John Morgan in July 1768 at the end of his stay in Scotland, he said: 'the happiest period of my life is now near over. My halcyon days have been spent in Edinburgh.' Looking back over his life in 1800, he underlines and reinforces that sentiment: 'The two years I spent in Edinburgh I consider as the most important in their influence upon my character and conduct of any period of my life.'[23]

This is admittedly a very personal statement, but one may feel it is one with which many of the Americans who spent two or three years at the medical school in Edinburgh would have agreed.[24] For the Americans from South Carolina, or Virginia, or Pennsylvania— even from Franklin's Philadelphia—immersion in the active in- tellectual life of Edinburgh must inevitably have been a stimulating experience. Even if there was no encounter with any of the group of brilliant individuals who had won for Edinburgh her international reputation, simply the contact in classes and societies with so many other young students like themselves from England, Ireland, Scotland, Wales, most of the countries of Europe, the West Indies, and America, must have meant for many a significant widening of intellectual and cultural horizons.

That Franklin should have played any part even in the minor religious ties between Scotland and America may seem somewhat surprising: one whose religious convictions were so widely suspect hardly appears as a likely candidate for such a role. But here again Franklin did play a part. In the colonial period several American ministers felt the attraction of the prestige that went with the British honorary degree of Doctor of Divinity. The link between the Church of England and the Universities of Oxford and Cambridge presented a problem in this connection to which the Scottish universities were the obvious solution. It was here that Franklin's friendship with Principal William Robertson of Edinburgh became significant. In 1765, Franklin applied to Robertson for a degree for Ezra Stiles, later to be President of Yale; in 1767, Franklin applied again to Robertson, this time on behalf of Samuel Cooper of Boston, later a trustee of Harvard; and, within months, Franklin was embarrassed by requests for a similar favour from two other American ministers, Andrew Eliot of the North Church of Boston, and a New York clergyman named Rogers. In the end, these too received their degrees.[25] Earlier, in 1765, King's College, Aberdeen had awarded an Honorary D.D. to Mather Byles, a graduate of Harvard, 'Recommended in a very ample manner by the learned and ingenious Dr Benjamin Franklin.' Franklin also played an indirect part in the negotiations which finally brought to America, as President of the College of New Jersey, the Scottish clergyman, John Witherspoon.[26] But where Franklin's role in the history of the Scottish–American connection in medical education is of central importance, his contribution to the highly significant religious tie between the countries remains minor.

Historians have never agreed over the precise nature of the debt Presbyterianism in America owes to Presbyterianism in Scotland. One recent scholar has said that the American Presbyterian Church originally had closer ties with New England and London than with Scotland, and that, 'It was not, as has been asserted so often, largely a Scottish and Scotch-Irish Church patterned closely after the Scottish model.'[27] But if we choose to broaden the field somewhat, we may see that from an early date there had been close ties between the religious life of each country which cut across questions of sectarian allegiances. Scottish ministers, for example, regularly corresponded with their opposite numbers in America, and the tone of their letters often suggests a considerable familiarity with both the religious and wider cultural context of their correspondent's country. Such correspondence too often led to a regular exchange of books. Robert Wodrow, for example, the early historian of the Church of Scotland, corresponded for many years with the Mather family in New England. On 23 January 1713 he wrote to Cotton Mather:

> From a child almost I have loved the Mathers, though I never proposed to myself the happiness and honour of writing to any of them. Mr. Eliot's Life was what I read with much sweetness when at the university near twenty years ago; Mr. Nathaniel Mather's Life was most refreshing long since. My worthy father ... put your learned and worthy father's Eleutheria into my hands.[28]

Wodrow's correspondence with Cotton Mather extended over twenty years, and books were also exchanged between the two men. Wodrow also had other American correspondents: Benjamin Colman of Boston, and the Revd Edward Wigglesworth, professor of divinity at Harvard.

John Maclaurin, a minister in Glasgow, brother of Colin Maclaurin the mathematician at the university, corresponded with Jonathan Edwards over a long period, and the Revd John Erskine, whom Rush met in Edinburgh, probably through Maclaurin, developed a wide correspondence with America. From 1744 to 1753 Erskine was minister in the town of Kirkintilloch, not far from Glasgow, and during that period he began to write to numerous American divines:

> His chief correspondents on the American Continent, while he remained at Kirkintilloch, were Mr. Cooper, Dr. Colman, Mr. Foxcroft, Mr. Morehead, Messrs. Prince, senior and junior, of Boston; Mr. Parsons of Newburgh in Massachusets, (in whose house Mr. Whitefield died in 1770); Mr. Roby of Lynn, Mr. Davies and Mr. Dickinson of New Jersey; and Jonathan Edwards of Northampton.[29]

Erskine himself survived all these men and maintained his correspondence with many of their descendants.

John Erskine's interest in America was informed, wide-ranging, and life-long. His biographer goes as far as to say that, 'It appears, indeed, that to have the advantage of American books, and to furnish his friends beyond the Atlantic with whatever he could send them of the literature of Great Britain, and especially on the subjects on which his own studies were chiefly employed, was a primary object in all his correspondence with America.'[30] With Jonathan Edwards in particular Erskine carried on a considerable book-exchange. He began by sending the American a copy of *The Remains of Mr. Hall* which he had edited—Hall had been a close friend and fellow student. Edwards wrote back commiserating him on the loss of his friend and enclosing a copy of his own book, *A Treatise Concerning Religious Affections* (1746). In another letter, Edwards sketched out the plan of the treatise he was about to write on the freedom of the will: *A Strict and Careful Enquiry ... into the Freedom of the Will*, published in 1754, was to be one of the best known of his works. Most interesting of all, perhaps, is a letter dated 11 December 1755, in which Edwards acknowledges receipt of Lord Kames's *Essays* (i.e. *On the Principles of Morality and Natural Religion*, published in 1751), and tells Erskine that he has already had an opportunity of reading this book as well as Mr Hume's *Essay* (i.e. *Enquiry Concerning the Principles of Morals*, 1751) on the same subject; one of the earliest pieces of evidence of the knowledge of Scottish philosophy in America.[31] After Edwards's death, Erskine was to be responsible for the publication in Scotland of many of his theological works.

Finally, Francis Hutcheson, who provided the initial philosophical impetus behind the Scottish Enlightenment, was himself in communication with America. McCosh prints an interesting letter from Hutcheson to the Revd Thomas Drennan, Presbyterian minister in Belfast, written in Glasgow on 16 April 1746. Between the lines of this letter one may read the whole history of the struggle between the Old Lights, or advocates of rigid orthodoxy, and the New Lights, the defenders of the new spirit of moderation which Hutcheson himself embodied and for which he provided the philosophic basis, in Scotland, and of the division between the Old Side and New Light, in America:

> I had this day a letter from a presbytery of Pennsylvania, of a very good turn, regretting their want of proper ministers and books, expecting some assistance here; it was of a very old date of October last. I shall speak to some wise men here, but would as soon speak to the Roman conclave as our presbytery. The

Pennsylvanians regret the want of true literature; that Whitfield has promoted a contempt of it among his followers, and bewailing some wretched contentions among themselves. The only help to be expected from you is sending some wise men if possible. I shall send them my best advice about books and philosophy, and hope to be employed to buy them books cheaper here than they are to be got anywhere.[32]

Interesting as they are, these examples of letter and book exchanges between ministers in Scotland and America are hardly sufficient to establish the existence of any close link between Presbyterian Scotland and even some of the American colonies. Yet correspondence of the type cited may not have been at all uncommon, and there is other evidence to support the view that a shared religious life and problems did for a time at least have the effect of drawing the two countries together. From early in the eighteenth century official ties did exist between the Church of Scotland and the Presbyterian Church in America. The 'Society in Scotland for Propagating Christian Knowledge', established in 1709, had by 1730 become deeply concerned for the spiritual condition of the American Indian. Three boards of correspondents were set up, for Boston, New York (later New Jersey), and Connecticut, and missionaries were sent to the American frontier.[33] In 1747, the *Scots Magazine* was able to report the success of these endeavours:

The progress made in spreading the gospel among the infidel Indian natives, living on the borders of the provinces of New-York, New-Jersey, and Pensilvania, by means of the missionary ministers employed there by the society in Scotland for propagating Christian knowledge, has been so remarkable, as appears by their journals lately printed in Philadelphia, that it is with great pleasure the society inform the publick of the promising prospect they have of promoting the knowledge of Christianity in those dark corners of the world....[34]

A few years later, the Society would provide most of the funds for the conducting of Moor's Indian Charity School at Lebanon, Connecticut, run from 1754 by Eleazar Wheelock; out of this school developed Dartmouth College, of which Wheelock was the first president.

In more ways than this the Church of Scotland acted as a source of funds for the activities of the Presbyterian Church in America.

In 1752, for example, the General Assembly of the Church authorised a collection at church doors in all parishes, on behalf of German Protestants 'in Pensilvania and North America', 'in order to provide but tolerable subsistence for ministers and school-masters . . .'.[35] Again, in 1760, the magazine printed a long memorial from the Revd Charles Beatty, of Newshaminy, Pennsylvania, to the Assembly, on the state of Presbyterian ministers in that colony owing to the French and Indian wars. Money was needed for the support of ministers preaching to the Indians, or to congregations who were unable to pay them.[36] On this occasion too, the Assembly authorised a collection in every parish.

In addition to money, the Church of Scotland was in a position to supply the Presbyterian Church in America with badly needed trained clergymen.[37] When official relations between the Churches entered a new and interesting phase in 1770, a central point raised by the Americans was their growing requirement for more ministers. The synods of New York and Philadelphia had decided to corre-spond with the Protestant Churches in Europe:

> Having formed such a resolution, it was natural for them first to turn their eyes to the Church of Scotland, to which they are of all others most entirely conformed, and from which indeed they may be said to have derived their origin. Many or most of the first Presbyterian ministers in this country had their education in Scotland, and formed their infant societies on the model of your most excellent constitution; and now that the body is become more considerable we continue steadily attached to the same principles. . . .

The letter goes on to describe the extent of the synods' charges throughout New York, New Jersey, Pennsylvania, Maryland, Virginia, and the Carolinas, and then approaches the question of the need for more ministers:

> We return thanks to your Venerable Body for the great assistance that has been formerly given by the Church of Scotland to the Presbyterian interest in this country. What we chiefly want at present is ministers, the demand for them being much greater than the supply. We are sensible of the difficulty of proposing any particular scheme for remedying this evil, but, perhaps, the knowledge of our situation in Scotland, by means of the present letter, may induce some piously-disposed

young men, of sound principles, to visit America, or to make such inquiries as may afterwards be followed by this effect.[38]

The Assembly appointed a committee to consider this request and prepare a reply. Signed by the Moderator, Alexander Carlyle, it was subsequently printed in the *Scots Magazine*. It began by saying that the Church of Scotland would be very willing to promote a 'brotherly intercourse' between Protestant Churches in different parts of the world by means of correspondence, and proceeded to discuss the question of ministers:

> It affords us great satisfaction to hear of the prosperity and rapid population of the provinces of New York and Philadelphia; and we are deeply affected with the circumstances of such of your people as are destitute of the religious instructions which they wish to receive. We have no doubt but that there may be found in this country, several young men, regularly educated, and well qualified by their piety and literature to undertake the charge of some of your vacant congregations, and labour among them in the work of the Lord.[39]

After all these expressions of goodwill and brotherly understanding, it is salutary to read the letter which follows this one in the columns of the magazine. The date is 1770, and Great Britain has already marched far along the road which leads to 1775. 'E.R.' complains that the original communication from the Synod of New York had been printed alongside the text of John Lathrop's sermon, 'Innocent Blood crying for Vengeance', delivered at Boston after the Massacre of 1770, which he maintained did little credit to the Church of Scotland's American progeny.[40] The inaccuracies in this complaint did not go unnoticed in America; John Witherspoon read it and wrote an effective reply, pointing to E.R.'s confusion of a minister in Boston with the Presbyterian synods of New York and Philadelphia as a typical example of British ignorance of America.[41]

The growing pressure of political events is clear again in a letter which, in compliance with the ideas expressed in its original communication, the Synod of New York wrote to the General Assembly two years later in 1772. Having mentioned the flourishing state of the College of New Jersey, it then treats more delicate matters:

> We beg leave to mention our expectation, that manifesting

and maintaining our connection with the church of Scotland, may be the means of securing our constitutional privileges, especially our religious liberties: not that we apprehend any injury at present, but future contingencies are uncertain, and we esteem it an advantage, that our state and importance should fall under the Public notice, as well as that we should have the opportunity, on any emergency, of asking the advice and assistance of your respectable body.[42]

The reference to 'our constitutional privileges' and 'our religious liberties' makes it quite clear what kind of future contingencies the Synod had in mind; political domination by British Parliament and King, and the threatened establishment of Episcopacy in the Colonies. At this date, the Church of Scotland had not adopted a firm position on these questions, and Witherspoon and his colleagues were certainly aware of the great significance of any kind of support for their point of view which could be won from the representative body of the Scottish Church—the only representative body in the kingdom of Scotland. The *Scots Magazine* contains no record of an Assembly reply.

The political implications of these exchanges between the Presbyterian Churches in Scotland and America are of course particularly fascinating, but they should not be allowed to obscure the more obvious cultural implications. The American demand is primarily for Scottish-trained ministers. The introduction of Scottish ministers would mean of course the introduction of the Scottish educational and cultural tradition in which they had themselves been trained. Even if it is difficult to establish just how many Scottish ministers did cross the Atlantic in this period, the cultural impact that significant numbers must have produced was in fact reinforced by a parallel development.

As the Scottish interest in Moor's Indian School suggests, the religious tie between Scotland and America always involved a specific concern for educational matters. The Presbyterian tradition in Scotland had always placed a high value on education; that pattern was repeated in America. A year before Moor's Indian School was established in Connecticut Scottish interest had been requested in relation to a college of a more ambitious kind. The College of New Jersey had been founded by the Synod of New York in 1746.[43] From the beginning it had been plagued by lack of funds. At length the trustees decided to send representatives to

Great Britain in quest of financial support. The men chosen were Gilbert Tennent, and Samuel Davies, John Erskine's correspondent, later fourth president of the College. For eleven months during the years 1753–4, the two emissaries stayed in Britain conducting their campaign. In Scotland they achieved considerable success. The *Scots Magazine* for 1754 reports that on 27 May, two petitions were brought before the General Assembly:

> ...one from the trustees of the college of New-Jersey and the other from the Synod of New-York; both setting forth the great advantages that must arise from the erection of a college at New-Jersey, where a great many students may be educated; the great difficulties they labour under, through the want of money, to carry their design of properly endowing the said college into execution; and therefore praying for a general collection. By a committee then named, a draught of an act and recommendation for a general collection to be made at all the church-doors in Scotland, for the behoof of the said college, was presented on the 31st; and, after some amendments, approved of. The assembly, besides, recommended to ministers to apply to the nobility and gentry, as they may have opportunity to give their charitable assistance in this matter.[44]

The total sum realised in Scotland is estimated at over £3,200, money which was largely used in the building of Nassau Hall and the president's house. On 24 September 1755, the trustees of the College acknowledged their indebtedness to the Scottish Church by returning thanks to the Assembly for the collection that had been granted to their institution.[45]

The success of Tennent and Davies led in subsequent years to similar appeals on behalf of other American colleges: the College of Philadelphia, King's College, New York, the College of Rhode Island, and Newark Academy. All except that on behalf of Newark in 1773, met with success. And the experience of John Ewing, an able scholar, later Provost of the University of Pennsylvania, who led Newark's appeal, shows that even in 1773 an ardently patriotic American could be enthusiastically received in Scotland. 'Without application' Ewing received the degree of Doctor of Divinity from the University of Edinburgh, and the towns of Glasgow, Montrose, Perth, and Dundee all presented him with their freedoms. He became friendly with Blacklock, the blind poet, and other

Edinburgh intellectuals, and on Principal William Robertson he made a particularly deep impression.[46]

Scottish ties with American education in the years before the Revolution were much more varied and extensive than this discussion of Scottish financial contributions suggests; and they did not exist solely as a by-product of the links between the Presbyterian churches in Scotland and America. Scottish teachers found their way in significant numbers to the American colonies,[47] and several individual Scots made important contributions to the development of American universities. One such was James Blair, educated at Marischal College, Aberdeen, and the University of Edinburgh, who in 1693 was largely responsible for the founding of the College of William and Mary. Another was William Smith, also an Aberdonian, appointed first provost of the newly-established College of Philadelphia in 1755, and responsible for a significant liberalising of the college curriculum in America; through Smith's influence a college ceased to be thought of as a school for clergymen. Of equal or even greater significance for the future of American education was the appointment of a third Scot, John Witherspoon, as sixth president of the College of New Jersey.

Since its foundation in 1746, the College of New Jersey had enjoyed twenty years of rather precarious existence. The root of its troubles lay in the unfortunate brevity of the incumbencies of its first five presidents—Jonathan Dickinson, Aaron Burr, Jonathan Edwards, Samuel Davies and Samuel Finley—all of whom had died in office before the College under their charge had had sufficient time to achieve real stability. In 1766 the position was further complicated by the fact that the College had again become involved in the controversy which had long divided the Presbyterian Church in America. The split paralleled that in the Church of Scotland between Old Light and New Light with one important difference; whereas in Scotland it was the Old Light party which embraced the new, popular, spirit of revivalism, in America it was the New Light side which did so. The College of New Jersey had been founded by the New Light Synod of New York. However, in the difficulties confronting the College in 1766 the Old Side party in the American Church saw an opportunity for increasing their influence there.[48] The New Light answer was the nomination of John Witherspoon, of the Laigh Kirk, Paisley, Scotland, as the new president. In the Church of Scotland Witherspoon was a leader of the Popular or Old Light party, and so, in the American situation, would be inclined to support the New Light, revivalist side.[49]

Witherspoon did not accept the offer of the presidency of the College of New Jersey immediately; his wife in particular was at first determinedly opposed to the idea of going to America. For long she resisted all the pleas of Richard Stockton and Benjamin Rush, the College's representatives in Scotland, and of their Scottish friends. At one time, accepting his wife's inflexibility, Witherspoon proposed that the post should be offered to Thomas Randall, a Perthshire minister, or to another friend, the Revd Charles Nisbet of Montrose. But in the end Mrs Witherspoon underwent a change of heart, and the Witherspoons sailed for Philadelphia in May 1768.[50]

The consequences of Witherspoon's arrival at Princeton enable us to see with exceptional clarity the significance of the educational ties between Scotland and America in the pre-Revolutionary period. In so far as he headed an educational institution which under his direction quickly became one of the most influential in America, Witherspoon's position may be regarded as exceptional. Yet he was not the only Scot to occupy such a position, and more importantly, what he brought to America did not differ fundamentally from what the humblest Scottish graduate schoolteacher had to offer: a background and training in the traditions of the Scottish Enlightenment. That background and training emerge most clearly in the study of two subjects, both of which figure prominently in the educational pattern Witherspoon established at Princeton: philosophy and rhetoric or belles-lettres.

A notable characteristic of the Scottish eighteenth century philosophers is their concern with speculations on the origins of ideas of beauty and taste. The best-known product of such interests is probably Archibald Alison's *Essays on the Nature and Principles of Taste* published in 1790, but Alexander Gerard, professor of divinity at Aberdeen, published his *Essay on Taste* as early as 1759. By then John Stevenson, professor of logic at Edinburgh from 1730 to 1775, had been lecturing for almost twenty years on the precise nature of taste and elegance in literary composition. From 1748 to 1751 at Edinburgh, and afterwards at Glasgow University, Adam Smith delivered a set of lectures on the same topic. Lord Kames's *Elements of Criticism*, 1762, furthered the same kind of study; and of course Hugh Blair at Edinburgh had followed Smith's example for more than twenty years before his *Lectures on Rhetoric* was

finally published in 1783. But however much the study of rhetoric—
the discovery of the origins of beauty and taste in style—may have
had philosophical overtones, and admittedly both Smith and Kames
were chiefly renowned as philosophers, Blair's work makes it clear
that the study was at bottom a strictly practical affair. It is no
accident that rhetoric became a North British speciality. The impulse
underlying all aspects of this kind of enquiry is the same as that
which had enabled Thomas Sheridan to gain his audience of three
hundred gentlemen in Edinburgh in 1761, to hear a series of lectures
on the correct speaking of English and which had enabled the
'Select Society' of the city, whose membership included Kames,
Hume, Smith, Blair, William Robertson, Lord Monboddo and
many others, to follow up Sheridan's visit by establishing 'The
Society for promoting the Reading and Speaking of the English
Language in Scotland'. As we have seen, all the North Britons were
nervously eager to write English with elegance and ease; they
recognised that to do so was a precondition for their acceptance
and recognition by English cultural standards. It is clear why the
Scots should have been particularly interested in *learning* how to
write easily and elegantly.

As I believe Witherspoon quite clearly recognised, America's
position in relation to the dominant, standard-setting culture of
England had much in common with that of Scotland. One cannot
doubt that the desire to write correctly was shared by both
countries.[51] But the fact was that the tools to teach 'correctness' had
been developed almost exclusively in Scotland. Not surprisingly
Witherspoon introduced them to America.[52] Of course Witherspoon soon came to play a significant part in the whole educational,
intellectual, and political life of his adopted country. But his
contemporaries did not fail to see the consequences of the new
emphasis he placed upon the study of rhetoric. Benjamin Rush,
for example, wrote: 'He gave a new turn to education, and spread
taste and correctness in literature throughout the United States. It
was easy to distinguish his pupils every where when ever they spoke
or wrote for the public.'[53] A more detailed account of Witherspoon's impact upon the College is given by Samuel Miller in his
invaluable *Brief Retrospect of the Eighteenth Century*, published in
New York in 1803. Miller's description ends thus: 'And finally,
under his presidency, more attention began to be paid than before
to the principles of taste and composition, and to the study of

elegant literature.'[54] Lastly one may quote from an article on Witherspoon which appeared in the *Port Folio* in 1825: 'He caused an important revolution in the system of education, whereby literary inquiries and improvements became more liberal, more extensive, and more profound.'[55] There can be no doubt that the teaching of rhetoric at the College of New Jersey, with results that were evidently soon apparent, was itself a reflection of Witherspoon's own training in the Scottish philosophical and rhetorical tradition at the University of Edinburgh near the middle of the eighteenth century.

I have emphasised the close connection between rhetoric and philosophy in the Scottish intellectual tradition in the eighteenth century. Hence it is not surprising that in America receptiveness to the influence of the Scots rhetoricians should have been paralleled by, if not indeed dependent on, an equal receptiveness to the philosophers. Once again it is Witherspoon who has been most frequently credited with the introduction of Scottish philosophy to America. Witherspoon himself of course was not an original philosophical thinker. Indeed as a leader of the Evangelical party in the Church of Scotland, he might be thought of as hostile to the ideas of the Enlightenment which had provided the intellectual basis for the Moderates' position. But this is to misunderstand his position. As a theologian he remained faithful to strictly orthodox Calvinism, yet he was not prepared to secede from the Church of Scotland even when it came under firm Moderate domination. As a moral philosopher, far from being hostile to the rational ideals of the Enlightenment, his main concern was to show that those ideals could be reconciled with the tenets of Presbyterianism. To point the way towards such a crucial reconciliation was in fact one of his major contributions to America's intellectual life.[56] That Witherspoon was responsible at least for introducing Scottish philosophy to America was acknowledged by early commentators. In his *Brief Retrospect* Samuel Miller, for example, accords Witherspoon full responsibility:

> He produced an important revolution in the system of education adopted in this seminary. He extended the study of Mathematical science, and introduced into the course of instruction on Natural Philosophy, many improvements which had been little known in most of the American Colleges, and particularly in that institution. He placed the plan of instruction in Moral Philosophy on a new and improved basis; and was, it is believed, the first man who taught, in America, the

substance of those doctrines of the philosophy of the Human Mind, which Dr. Reid afterwards developed with so much success.[57]

Even more valuable evidence is provided by Frederick Beasley in a description of student days at Princeton in the 1790s:

> You are aware that in the College of Princeton, to which we were attached, after the fanciful theory of Bishop Berkely, as a kind of philosophical daydream, had maintained its prevalence for a season; the principles of Reid, and the Scottish metaphysicians superseded it, and during the period of our residence in the seminary, acquired and maintained undisputed sway. At that time, I, together with all those graduates who took any interest in the subject, embraced without doubt or hesitation the doctrines of the Scottish school.[58]

Inevitably, scholars have been able to show that the Scottish philosophers were not unknown in America before John Witherspoon's assumption of the presidency of the College of New Jersey. I. Woodbridge Riley, for example, writes:

> The Scotch philosophers were read in the college some time before Witherspoon set foot in the country. Thus, in 1764 Kames' *Principles of Natural Religion* was read by Jefferson, in 1760, Hutcheson *On Beauty and Virtue* was in the Princeton library; in 1756 one of the same author's works was being used as a textbook in the philosophy school of the Philadelphia Academy.... Moreover, in 1751, Stiles expressed his pleasure with Turnbull's scheme of treating moral, as Newton had treated natural, philosophy.[59]

And Jonathan Edwards's correspondence with John Erskine, the Edinburgh minister, shows, as we have seen, that he had read at least some of the works of Hume and Kames in the early 1750s. These facts do not, however, lessen the significance of Witherspoon's contribution. One may be sure that with or without the presence in America of a Witherspoon, the Scottish common-sense philosophy would eventually have made its impact upon America, but the presence of Witherspoon provided the ideal channel through which it might flow, first into the minds of his own pupils, and afterwards out from them into the large number of schools, colleges, seminaries and churches with which they were connected.

The ties between Scotland and America in the areas of medical study, education in general, and religion, which have been described, do provide evidence for the view that in the pre-Revolutionary period Scotland was already making a notable contribution to American cultural life. For that contribution to have been widely and immediately influential, however, the question of books and their availability must be regarded as fundamental. However important in the long run contributions made by individuals may have been—American students in Scotland or Scottish teachers in America —it is difficult to see how Scottish influence could have been quickly transmitted and widely disseminated unless Scottish books were readily available in America.

Evidence does exist of the availability of Scottish books in colonial America; but it remains somewhat limited. One aspect of Scottish interest in the furtherance and encouragement of American education took the form of donations of books by individuals and organisations to college libraries. If they had the money, colleges could of course obtain books from British booksellers with relative ease, but their financial positions were rarely so strong that gifts of books were not of great importance in building up their libraries. Hugh Simm, a Scot who accompanied Witherspoon to Princeton, had in the following year become a schoolteacher at Freehold, New Jersey. In June, 1769, he wrote home to his brother, stressing the importance of books: 'Be careful to give my service to all those who have sent Books this is a very grateful present in this part of the world where books are so very scarce.'[60] Simm's benefactors remain unknown, but there were others whom we can name. John Erskine, for example, was all his life an indefatigable donor of books to America. Harvard received its first gift from him as early as 1765; in the following year, he again sent books to Cambridge as did Kincaid, a printer and bookseller in Edinburgh. In 1771 Erskine is again listed among the donors of books.[61] Recording gifts to Dartmouth College, Eleazar Wheelock noted for 1764, 'a valuable Collection of Books, from the Rev. John Erskine and Mr. William Dickinson of Edinburgh, and an honourable Society in Edinburgh for promoting religious Knowledge among the Poor.'[62] The same society presented Harvard with twenty-five volumes in 1766, and three years later the Society for Propagating Christian Knowledge gave the same college thirty pounds sterling for the purchase of books.[63]

None of these records of Scottish donations list titles, but one may be confident that they included among them many works of the North Britons A letter dated 16 May 1771, announced to President Manning of Brown the donation to the college of a list of books which included a fourth edition of 'Lord Kames on Criticism', 'Reid on the Mind', and Robertson's *History of Scotland*.[64] A year earlier than this letter, Robertson's second major work, the *History of the Reign of Charles V*, had been published at Philadelphia, while 1773 saw the publication in the same city of Adam Ferguson's *Essay on Civil Society*. Much earlier, in 1756, Hutcheson, David Gregory, and the mathematicians Robert Simson and Colin Maclaurin, were among the authors recommended for private reading by William Smith to his students at the College of Philadelphia.[65] Maclaurin's *An Account of Sir Isaac Newton's Philosophy* was also among the books brought to Princeton by Witherspoon.

Theological works bulk largest among books of Scottish origin published in America before the Revolution. The *Sermons* of Ebenezer and Ralph Erskine, leaders of the 1733 secession from the Church of Scotland, were published by Franklin in Philadelphia in 1745; a work by Thomas Boston, *The Nature and Necessity of Regeneration*, was published at Boston in 1753, and a posthumous work by David Fordyce, professor of moral philosophy at Aberdeen, *The Temple of Virtue, A Dream*, appeared in New York in 1758. A more popular work than any of these, one that was republished many times after its first American appearance in 1775 at Philadelphia, was *A Father's Legacy to his Daughters*, rather worldly advice to young ladies, by John Gregory, professor in the medical school at Edinburgh. But pride of place in terms of popularity must go to another work by one of the most austere of the Scottish divines mentioned above: *The Gospel Sonnets* of Ralph Erskine, which was first published by Franklin in 1740, and afterwards constantly republished until the end of the century.[66] Apart from Robertson's *Charles V* and Ferguson's *Civil Society*, however, no major work of the Scottish Enlightenment seems to have been published in America before the Revolution.

Although theological and philosophical works, mostly of North British origin, bulk largest in the Scottish–American book exchange, it would be wrong to assume that no productions of the other side of Scotland's eighteenth century revival crossed the Atlantic. Largely no doubt because it had won English critical approval, Allan

Ramsay's pastoral comedy, *The Gentle Shepherd*, written largely in the Scottish vernacular, was published in America in 1750. It was published again at least once before the Revolution, at Philadelphia in 1771. And if Witherspoon's Old Light austerity is apparent in the pamphlet he wrote attacking the Revd John Home's play, *Douglas*,[67] the more liberal attitude which won him his American reputation as a promoter of literary taste and elegance is apparent in that among the books he brought to America was the work which provided the initial impulse for the whole native side of Scotland's eighteenth century cultural renaissance: Watson's *Choice Collection of Comic and Serious Poems Both Ancient and Modern*.[68]

The evidence offered makes it clear that books reflecting the different aspects of eighteenth century Scottish culture were far from unknown in colonial America. Yet there is little to suggest the really widespread circulation of such books. (The very limited reprinting of Scottish books is particularly telling.) Examinations of the contents of private American libraries in the colonial period, with one notable exception, seem to confirm that Scottish books remained relatively rare. The exception is the library of Thomas Jefferson which in any event is a 'colonial' library only in the most limited sense. Jefferson owned works by almost all the major figures of the Scottish Enlightenment: Francis Hutcheson, David Hume, Adam Smith, Adam Ferguson, Dugald Stewart, Lord Kames, Hugh Blair, William Robertson, David Gregory, Colin Maclaurin, William Cullen.[69] Six of these are represented by editions printed before the American Revolution, but of course this tells us nothing about when Jefferson acquired them, still less about when he read them. Jefferson is an exceptional case in other ways too. He is among those Americans directly exposed to Scottish intellectual influence in his formative educational years. The *Autobiography* tells us that a Scottish clergyman, Mr Douglas, taught him Greek, Latin, and French, while William Small, his Scottish professor at William and Mary, is in the same work accorded a glowing tribute and described as the man who 'probably fixed the destinies' of Jefferson's life.[70] Finally the size and range alone of Jefferson's library makes it untypical of private libraries of the same period in America. Even if one does not wish to go so far as those who rule out his library as evidence of the sources of Jefferson's thought, certainly the library does not provide a basis for drawing general conclusions about the circulation and availability of Scottish books in colonial America.

Such detailed studies of colonial libraries as exist reveal nothing to compare with the impressive list of Scottish books in Jefferson's possession.[71]

More decisive still is the evidence of the year 1782. In that year James Madison, Witherspoon, and John Lowell of Massachusetts were appointed by Congress to prepare a list of books to be imported for the use of 'the United States in Congress Assembled'. It was Madison who in the end prepared the committee's report though no doubt after consultation with the others. His list is made up of about 550 titles, a very large percentage being books concerned with different aspects of America. Of the 550 only a dozen or so are by Scottish authors. But however few, they are very much what we might expect to find: major, representative works of the first generation of the Scottish Enlightenment. Hutcheson's *A System of Moral Philosophy*; Adam Ferguson's *Institutes of Moral Philosophy* and his *Essay on Civil Society*; Robertson's *Charles V*, *History of Scotland*, and *History of America*; Hume's *History of England* and *Essays and Treatises on Several Subjects*; Millar's *The Origin of the Distinctions of Ranks*; Smith's *Wealth of Nations*.[72] Perhaps allowance has to be made for the fact that Madison was a graduate of the College of New Jersey, but rather than reflecting some kind of Witherspoon-inspired Scottish bias, this list almost certainly defines the precise extent of well-informed American interest in the Scottish Enlightenment as the Revolutionary period was coming to an end. These are the Scottish thinkers whose works were known and respected: but their inclusion in Madison's foundation list for a Library of Congress makes it certain that in 1782 they were not widely available in America.

What general conclusions are to be drawn from this survey of Scottish-American cultural relations in the pre-Revolutionary period? The economic link between Glasgow and the tobacco colonies in the Chesapeake Bay area, Scottish emigration to America, the high percentage of Scottish officials in the colonies, the presence of American students at the Scottish universities; all of these helped to produce an ideal *situation* for the transmission of Scottish cultural influences to America. The Scottish contributions to America's educational life, for example, which have been described, reflect the consequences of that situation. Yet there is no need to exaggerate Scotland's specifically cultural contribution to colonial America. The intellectual army, as it were, of the Scottish Enlightenment is already on the march at the outbreak of the American Revolution; America is an obvious objective; bridgeheads have been set up and outposts established; but the army of occupation is yet to arrive. Certainly in the colonial period the groundwork for Scottish cultural influence upon America is laid; but the major period of that influence still lies ahead.

The outbreak of the American Revolution severed the economic and political links between Scotland and America. It is the fact of this severance that has led to the view that the main period of Scottish influence on America occurred in the colonial period. Of course there is no necessary reason why sudden political change should have any effect at all on the pattern of cultural history. In the long term the Revolution probably had little effect upon the cultural relations between Scotland and America whose foundations only had been laid in the colonial period. But the question of Scotland did arise in the Revolutionary period in an oddly insistent way that cannot be ignored. Hence at this point a digression into Revolutionary politics is required.

NOTES AND REFERENCES

1. Examples of works of the first category are, Peter Ross, *The Scot in America* (New York, 1896), and George Fraser Black, *Scotland's Mark on America* (New York, 1921); in the second comes Albert Maisel, 'The Scots Among Us', *The Reader's Digest*, LXVII (August, 1955), 123–8, off-prints of which used commonly to be found in U.S. Consulates in Scotland.

2. For a full account of Franklin's two Scottish visits, J. Bennett Nolan's informative and entertaining book, *Benjamin Franklin in Scotland and Ireland, 1759 and 1771* (Philadelphia, 1938), should be consulted.

3. *A Historical Catalogue of the St. Andrew's Society of Philadelphia, with Biographical Sketches of Deceased Members, 1749–1907* (Philadelphia, 1907), p. 187.

4. See Henry Grey Graham, *Scottish Men of Letters in the Eighteenth Century*, p. 70.

5. Leonard W. Labaree (Ed.), *The Papers of Benjamin Franklin*, IX (New Haven and London, 1966), pp. 9–10.

6. Ibid., pp. 375–6. These two letters to Lord Kames may be compared with that which Franklin wrote to Sir Alexander Dick soon after his return to London from Scotland.

Writing on behalf of his son and himself, Franklin said: '. . . but no part of our Journey affords us, on Recollection, a more pleasing Remembrance, than that which relates to Scotland, particularly the time we so agreeably spent with you, your Friends and Family. The many Civilities, Favours and Kindnesses heap'd upon us while we were among you, have made the most lasting Impression on our Minds, and have endear'd that Country to us beyond Expression.' Ibid., p. 3.

7. Franklin Bowditch Dexter (Ed.), *The Literary Diary of Ezra Stiles* (New York, 1901), I, p. 310. Marchant's diary has never been printed; parts of it were copied into his own diary, by Stiles.

8. Quoted by Nolan, *Benjamin Franklin*, p. 100.

9. William L. Sachse, *The Colonial American in Britain* (Madison, 1956), pp. 34–5.

10. By 1776 Edinburgh had awarded 393 medical degrees. Of these 42 were received by Americans. See Alvin R. Riggs, 'The Colonial American Medical Student at Edinburgh', *University of Edinburgh Journal*, 20 (Autumn, 1961), 143.

11. Moultrie's father was a Scot who had himself

studied at Edinburgh. See 'Letters from a Colonial Student of medicine in Edinburgh to his Parents in South Carolina, 1746–49', *University of Edinburgh Journal*, 4 (Autumn, 1931), 270–4.

12. The New York medical school opened two years later in November, 1767. Of its six professors, Drs Bard, Tennent, Smith, Jones, Middleton and Clossy, all except Clossy had studied at Edinburgh. Riggs, 'The Colonial American Medical Student at Edinburgh', 147.

13. Whitfield J. Bell, Jr 'Some American Students of "That Shining Oracle of Physics", Dr. William Cullen of Edinburgh, 1755–1766', *Proceedings of the American Philosophical Society*, XCIV (June, 1950), 275.

14. Ibid.

15. Quoted by Nolan, *Benjamin Franklin*, p. 101.

16. Charles Campbell (Ed.), *The Bland Papers: Being a Selection from the Manuscripts of Colonel Theodorick Bland, Jr. of Prince George County Virginia* (Petersburg, 1840), pp. xvii–xix.

17. By 1776 more than fifty Americans had been elected to membership of the Royal Medical Society at Edinburgh. Riggs, 'The Colonial American Medical Student at Edinburgh', 147.

18. *History of the Speculative Society of Edinburgh* (Edinburgh, 1845), pp. 75, 89, 93.

19. Lyman H. Butterfield (Ed.), *Letters of Benjamin Rush* (Princeton, 1951), p. 27.

20. George W. Corner (Ed.), *The Autobiography of Benjamin Rush* (Princeton, 1948), pp. 49–51. An account of the life of Dr Blacklock in the *Port Folio* mentioned that several of the inmates of his house 'were students of physic, from England, Ireland, and America.... Among his favourite correspondents may be reckoned Dr. Tucker, author of "The Bermudian," a poem, and "The Anchoret," and Dr. Downman, author of "Infancy", a poem...'. See *Port Folio*, New Series, I (1806), 84–5. The Revd Dr Hugh Downman (1740–1809) was a minor English poet. Nathaniel Tucker, a native of Bermuda, practised medicine for a time with his brother Thomas Tucker, an Edinburgh graduate, in Charleston, South Carolina. In Edinburgh, Thomas Tucker had become friendly with Dr Blacklock, and through this tie he was able to arrange for an Edinburgh edition of his brother's poem, *The Bermudian*. The poem was published in Edinburgh early in 1774. Nathaniel Tucker himself arrived in Edinburgh to study medicine in the follow-ing year, and was warmly received by Dr Blacklock. Tucker's second work, *The Anchoret: A Poem*, was published by William Creech in 1776. See, Lewis Leary, *The Literary Career of Nathaniel Tucker 1750–1807* (Durham, N.C., 1951), pp. 31, 53.

21. George W. Corner (Ed.), *The Autobiography of Benjamin Rush*, p. 47.

22. Rush, *Letters*, pp. 31–32.

23. Rush, *Autobiography*, p. 43 and *Letters*, p. 62.

24. In his Edinburgh diary Rush mentions fourteen Americans studying medicine in the period 1766–8. See G. W. Corner, 'Benjamin Rush's Student Days in Edinburgh and What Came of Them', *University of Edinburgh Journal*, 15 (Autumn, 1950), 127.

25. Nolan, *Benjamin Franklin*, pp. 112–13.

26. See pp. 34–5.

27. Leonard J. Trinterud, *The Forming of an American Tradition, A re-examination of Colonial Presbyterianism* (Philadelphia, 1949), p. 32.

28. Thomas McCrie (Ed.), *The Correspondence of the Rev. Robert Wodrow* (Edinburgh, 1842), I, pp. 388–9. Cotton Mather wrote a biography of John Eliot, the English missionary in America, in 1691. Cotton Mather not his father Increase, was also the author of *Eleutheria*. Wodrow's reference to 'Nathaniel Mather's Life' may be a mistake for the *Life of Richard Mather*, by Increase Mather published in 1670.

29. Sir Henry Moncrieff Wellwood, *Account of the Life and Writings of John Erskine, D.D.* (Edinburgh, 1818), pp. 160–1.
Mr Cooper: Samuel Cooper (1725–83), recipient of the degree of Doctor of Divinity from the University of Edinburgh through the influence of Franklin. Minister of the Brattle Street Church in Boston.
Dr Colman: Benjamin Colman (1673–1747), first minister of the Brattle Street Church, awarded the D.D. degree by the University of Glasgow in 1731.
Mr Foxcroft: Thomas Foxcroft (1697–1769), minister of the First Church, Boston.
Messrs Prince: Thomas Prince (1687–1758), minister of the Old South Church, Boston, author of a *Chronological History of New England*. And Thomas Prince, (1722–48), his son, apparently also a clergyman.
Mr Parsons: Jonathan Parsons (1705–76), minister of Newburyport.
Mr Davies: Samuel Davies (1723–61), fourth president of the College of New Jersey.
Mr Dickinson: Jonathan Dickinson (1688–

1747), minister at Elizabeth, New Jersey, first president of the College of New Jersey. Jonathan Edwards (1703–58), the famous metaphysician, and the third president of the College of New Jersey.

30. *Life and Writings of John Erskine*, p. 160.
31. Ibid., p. 207.
32. James McCosh, *The Scottish Philosophy* (New York, 1875), p. 467. 'Whitfield' was of course George Whitefield, the famous English evangelical preacher. The whole evangelical, revivalist movement was distrusted by the Old Side in America, as it was by the New Lights in Scotland. For a fuller discussion of this question, see p. 34–5.
33. George S. Pryde, *The Scottish Universities and The Colleges of Colonial America* (Glasgow, 1957), p. 50.
34. *The Scots Magazine*, IX (1747), 145.
35. Ibid., XIV (1752), 480–2.
36. Ibid., XXII (1760), 266–8.
37. 'There are about an hundred and ten ministers in this presbytery and a hundred vacancies which cannot by suplyed they are verey urgent with the doctor to send for ministers from Scotland—.' Letter from Hugh Simm, who came to America with John Witherspoon, to his brother and sister-in-law in Scotland, dated at Princeton, 2 December 1768. MS. in Princeton University Library.
38. *The Scots Magazine*, XXXII (1770), 304.
39. Ibid., pp. 689–90.
40. Ibid., p. 690.
41. Revd John Witherspoon, *Miscellaneous Works* (Philadelphia, 1803), pp. 295–7.
42. *The Scots Magazine*, XXXIV (1772), 272.
43. The College opened in 1747 in Elizabethtown, New Jersey, the residence of Jonathan Dickinson, the first president. Dickinson died in the following year and the College moved to Newark, New Jersey, the home of Aaron Burr, the second president. In 1750 it was decided that the permanent site of the College should be either New Brunswick or Princeton. The decision in favour of Princeton was made in 1752, and in 1754 the building of Nassau Hall began.
44. *The Scots Magazine*, XVI (1754), 257–8.
45. Ibid., XVIII (1756), 248.
46. See 'Life of Dr. Ewing', *Port Folio*, 3rd Series, I (1813), 214–25. And cf. *Port Folio*, New Series, I (1809), 516–17.
47. Thomas Jefferson, James Madison, and John Marshall, for example, all had Scottish schoolteachers.
48. The Old Side proposed that the College should appoint a president and three professors; the president and one professor should be of their party, and in return they would give their full financial backing to the College. See Varnum Lansing Collins, *President Witherspoon* (Princeton, 1925), I, 76–7.
49. For consideration of the view that Witherspoon could be seen as satisfying the demands of both Old Side and New in New Jersey, see Douglas Sloan, *The Scottish Enlightenment and the American College Ideal* (New York, 1971), pp. 103–9.
50. For the details of this story Lyman H. Butterfield's *John Witherspoon Comes to America* (Princeton, 1953) should be consulted. In the complex negotiations which went on in order to bring Witherspoon to America one may see a perfect microcosm of the social and intellectual ties which bound America and Scotland in the pre-Revolutionary years.
51. In an article on language contributed to the *Pennsylvania Journal*, 9 May 1781, mindful no doubt of his own curriculum at Princeton, Witherspoon wrote: 'We may certainly infer, that the education must be very imperfect in any seminary where no care is taken to form the scholars to taste, propriety, and accuracy, in that language which they must write and speak all their lives. *To these reflections it may be added, that our situation is now, and probably will continue to be such, as to require peculiar attention upon this subject...*' (italics added). It is difficult not to conclude that it is Witherspoon's familiarity with the Scottish linguistic situation which makes him so alert to the problems of the American context.
52. 'During his first year as president, (Witherspoon) inaugurated the first formal course in rhetoric in the American colonies, and delivered sixteen lectures on eloquence.' L. T. Chapin, 'American Interest in the Chair of Rhetoric and English Literature in the University of Edinburgh', *University of Edinburgh Journal*, 20 (Autumn, 1961), 119. The suggestion that Witherspoon gave the first course in rhetoric in America does not accord, however, with the view of Thomas Jefferson. In his *Autobiography*, Jefferson, discussing William Small, his Scottish professor at William and Mary, writes, '...he was the first who ever gave, in that college, regular lectures in Ethics, Rhetoric and Belles Lettres.' (The date of Small's lectures is 1760–1.) See, *Autobiography of Thomas Jefferson, with an Introduction by Dumas*

Malone (New York, 1959), p. 20. William
Small had graduated at Marischal College,
Aberdeen, in 1755; he had been a student
under William Duncan, professor of natural
philosophy, whose *Elements of Logick* (1748)
was a work of great rhetorical significance.
The major point is that the teaching of
rhetoric at William and Mary originates
once again exclusively in the Scottish
rhetorical and philosophical tradition of the
eighteenth century.

53. G. W. Corner (Ed.), *The Autobiography of Benjamin Rush*, p. 51.

54. Samuel Miller, *A Brief Retrospect of the Eighteenth Century: Part First* (New York, 1803), II, 377.

55. *Port Folio*, 4th Series, XIX (1825), 77. The *Port Folio* comment is a lengthy extract from R. W. Pomeroy, *Biography of the Signers to the Declaration of Independence* (Philadelphia, 1824), Vol. V. The writer of this article seems to have drawn on Miller's book.

56. For a thorough discussion of these issues, see Sloan, *The Scottish Enlightenment and the American College Ideal*, pp. 104–9, 117–31.

57. Miller, *A Brief Retrospect of the Eighteenth Century*, II, 377.

58. Frederick Beasley, *A Search of Truth in the Science of the Human Mind, Part First* (Philadelphia, 1822), p. ii.

59. I. Woodbridge Riley, *American Philosophy: the Early Schools* (New York, 1907), p. 486.

60. MS. letter in the Princeton University Library.

61. Louis Shores, *Origins of the American College Library, 1638–1800* (Nashville, 1934), pp. 66–8.

62. Ibid., p. 100.

63. Ibid., pp. 66–8.

64. Ibid., p. 89.

65. Louis Franklin Snow, *The College Curriculum in the United States* (n.p., 1907), pp. 70–1.

66. For all references to the publication of books in America, in this and subsequent chapters, see Charles Evans, *American Bibliography*

(Chicago, 1904) or the continuation of that work up to 1823 by Shaw and Shoemaker, under the appropriate years.

67. *Douglas* was the first play performed in public in Scotland since the pressure of public opinion had compelled Allan Ramsay to close his theatre in 1736; this, added to the fact that the author of *Douglas* was himself a clergyman, insured that the play should quickly become the centre of a bitter controversy. Witherspoon's Old Light party in the Church of Scotland was horrified by the play's production and wished to censure Home formally. Witherspoon's pamphlet, a *Serious Enquiry into the Nature and Effects of the Stage*, was the best of the anti-theatrical writings. It is ironic that a copy of *Douglas* was among the books Witherspoon brought with him to America.

68. List of books once owned by Witherspoon, in Princeton University Library.

69. See E. Millicent Sowerby, *Catalogue of the Library of Thomas Jefferson* (Washington, 1952), items 1238, 1256, 1257 (Francis Hutcheson); 370, 1261 (David Hume); 3546 (Adam Smith); 2348 (Adam Ferguson); 1244 (Dugald Stewart); 1254, 4699 (Lord Kames); 4658 (Hugh Blair); 178, 468, 469 (William Robertson); 3708 (David Gregory); 3673, 3723 (Colin Maclaurin); 871 (William Cullen).

70. *Autobiography*, p. 20.

71. See, for example, George K. Smart, 'Private Libraries in Colonial Virginia', *American Literature*, 10 (1938–9), 24–52.

72. See William T. Hutchinson and William M. E. Rachal, *The Papers of James Madison*, VI (Chicago, 1969), pp. 62–115. Other Scottish works included in Madison's list are Robert Wallace's *A Dissertation on the Numbers of Mankind*, Sir James Steuart's *Inquiry into the Principles of Political Economy*, and William Guthrie's *A New Geographical, Historical, and Commercial Grammar*.

- III -

A Time of Discord

Arguing against the view that there was nothing revolutionary about the American Revolution, R. R. Palmer has maintained that the only sense in which there was no revolutionary conflict 'is the sense in which the loyalists are forgotten'. The American revolutionary consensus theory, which he rejects, he continues, 'rests in some degree on the elimination from the national consciousness, as well as from the country, of a once important and relatively numerous element of dissent.'[1] The example of the history of the Scots in revolutionary America supports Professor Palmer's case. On the face of it, the account given of the cultural situation involving Scotland and America in the years immediately preceding the American Revolution might suggest an enduring Scottish–American entente. The American image of Scotland that might well have developed from the cultural connections which have been discussed would be that of an hospitable and intellectually distinguished nation, well-disposed towards America and Americans. But whatever image these ties, which now appear so important in the intellectual development of America, may have created, it was never prominent enough to counter the very different political image of Scotland that grew up in the years before the Revolution and finally crystallised in the popular mind during the war itself. The nature of that image—and this is surely in a sense Professor Palmer's point—is very different from what is usually proposed at St Andrew's Nights and Burns' Suppers in America today. The Scots, indeed, far from being the original opponents of the oppressive policy of the British government, the proclaimers and the successful defenders of American liberty, the

47

framers of the Constitution, and the most powerful influence for everything good in the American way of life, were certainly the most unpopular national group in the colonies.[2] Here is a comment on the Scottish character which appeared in the *Virginia Gazette* in October, 1774:

> ... *Irish impudence* is of the downright, genuine and unadul-terated sort. *The Scotch Impudence* is of a different species. A *Scotchman,* when he first is admitted into a house, is so humble that he will sit upon the lowest step of the staircase. By degrees he gets into the kitchen, and from thence, by the most submis-sive behaviour, is advanced to the parlour. If he gets into the dining room, as ten to one but he will, the master of the house must take care of himself; for in all probability he will turn him out of doors, and, by the assistance of his *countrymen,* keep possession forever.[3]

Two central points in the American complaints against the Scots may be recognised here. First, the emphasis on the Scotsman's reliance on his countrymen is a reference to the common, and often accurate, allegation that the Scots never lost their clannish instincts, that they always sided together, supported each other, and never really trusted anyone who was not a fellow-countryman.[4] Secondly, the fact that the passage was written in Virginia perhaps makes it legitimate to read into it a version of the history of Scottish penetration of the Virginia tobacco trade. In November, 1777, Ezra Stiles met Mr Mc———, a Scotch merchant who told him 'that (as in Jamaica) the Scotch had got *Two Thirds of Virginia & Mary*ld. mortgaged or otherwise engaged to them or was *owned in Scotland*...,' and he comments himself, 'I have had it often suggested to me by Scotch Merchts. & Factors that the Scotch would in a very few years have all the Property in Virginia if not in gen. of No. America.'[5] Exaggerations of this kind were not without foundation in the facts of the great mercantile successes of the Scots. These successes were of course bitterly resented: Americans who found themselves in debt to merchants in Glasgow three thousand miles away might well have felt that they were the victims of cruel exploitation.

Specific reports of Scottish unpopularity in America began to arrive in Scotland soon after the outbreak of the war. In 1776, the *Scots Magazine* printed the following despatch:

> The provincials are said to have taken a dislike to the Scots. A letter from Virginia received about the beginning of July, says, that all the Scottish houses in that place have been destroyed by the Virginians, and all their goods and effects distributed amongst the populace. According to later advices, many Scottish families from Virginia are arrived at St. Domingo, having been driven from Virginia for their joining with the friends of government.[6]

Virginia is again the area specified, so that what has been said about resentment against Scottish control of the tobacco trade is relevant here too, but a new element is introduced into the situation by the report's concluding words: the Scots have been made to flee because of their Toryism. The idea of the Scots as loyalists may again come as something of a surprise: the Presbyterians as a group were ardent patriots, the Scots were Presbyterians, therefore all Scots must have been patriots—like John Paul Jones, James Wilson, John Witherspoon, General Hugh Mercer, and General Arthur St Clair. But once again the facts cannot be made to endorse this proposition.

All writers on the Scots in America during the Revolution have been forced to admit the existence of at least one group of loyalists among them: the Scottish Highlanders in North Carolina. That such a group should have come to the defence of a Hanoverian king is surprising in itself, and it becomes all the more so when one remembers the conditions at home which had forced these men to leave their native land. In point of fact, some contemporary observers did regard the continued Scottish emigrations as a potentially explosive factor in the colonial situation. In 1772, the *Scots Magazine* printed a letter from 'a gentleman of very considerable property in the Western isles', deploring the rate of emigration and suggesting that, 'Besides, the continual emigrations from Ireland and Scotland, will soon render our colonies independent on the mother-country.'[7] A letter of 1774 pointed to the danger more explicitly: it is the government's duty to do something to alleviate the conditions responsible for the emigrations; the emigrants will only add to the number of the discontented in America; 'every shipful of these emigrants that reaches their shores, will hasten that day when they shall throw off their dependence upon Britain altogether.'[8] The fears of such observers proved to be groundless. The Highlanders in North Carolina turned out to be ready to follow the wishes of the minor clan leaders who had brought them over the Atlantic and who had accepted commissions from the government. North's administration was optimistic about the effectiveness of this group of Scots loyalists. On 6 August 1776, Stiles transcribed in his diary a letter from London, published in New York on 1 July: '... Administr^a depend a great deal on the Assistance they are to get from Traitors in N^o Car^o and from the *Scotchmen* in Maryland, Virg. and the Carolinas.'[9] In fact New York itself was not wholly free from the threat represented by Scottish loyalists. In Tryon County, which included much of upstate New York, a second substantial group of Scottish Highlanders was ready and willing to fight for the King's cause. But in the event the assistance that the administration received from these Highland groups proved to be negligible. The uprising in North Carolina did not survive the single skirmish at Widow Moor's Creek in February, 1776, at which most of the Highland officers were captured, and after which most of the Highlanders returned to their homes. And a surprise march by several thousand militiamen under General Schuyler led to the disarming of the Scots in Tryon County.[10]

Scottish loyalism, however, was not confined to the Highlanders of North Carolina and New York. In December, 1775, for example, Richard Kidder Meade, later aide-de-camp to Washington, wrote a letter from Norfolk, Virginia, describing the defeat of the loyalists there, which confirms the impression that the Scots in Virginia were predominantly loyalist. In the course of the letter Meade comments that 'the Scotchmen are worse than I thought them'.[11] Again in 1775, the *Scots Magazine* printed a letter from Thomas Johnson, Esq., one of the Maryland delegates to the Continental Congress, to Horatio Gates, adjutant-general of the provincial army, which included these comments: 'Our association, I believe will occasion a good many, chiefly Scotch, to return again to their own country. On a late alarm, twelve, out of thirteen North Britons enrolled in one company, refused to march.... I am very unwilling to do any thing harsh; but it is surely time to know who may be depended on.'[12] There is considerable evidence that in New England too the Scots as a group tended to take the loyalist side. Governor Hutchinson, for example, wrote that the Scots in Boston 'were almost without exception good Subjects'. Another writer in Boston in 1770 considered that although opposition to the British government had become universal in the colonies the Scots had proved an exception. They have 'kept free from the general contagion' and have 'proved themselves good subjects and supporters of Government and order'.[13] The histories of the various American St Andrew's Societies provide further evidence of the divided loyalties of the Scots in revolutionary America.[14] Considerable contemporary evidence, then, supports the view, which recent historical research has also established, that the Scots as a national group tended overwhelmingly to side with the loyalist cause and prove themselves indeed 'good subjects and supporters of Government and order'.[15]

'A free exportation to Scotchmen and Tories' became a common Revolutionary toast,[16] and it is Scottish loyalism which largely explains both it and the general unpopularity of the Scots in America in the Revolutionary period. That unpopularity was soon not limited to Scots actually in America. In 1778, after Adam Ferguson, one of Franklin's friends in the inner circle of North Britons, had served as secretary to the Peace Commission on America, the Library Society of Charleston proposed that his book, *Essay on Civil Society* (1766)—by one 'of the kingdom of Scotland'—should be condemned to be burnt.[17] Again, in 1776, the *Scots Magazine* printed a letter from an officer of Frazer's Highlanders who had been captured with 170 of his regiment in a transport bound for Halifax. On the march inland they had been abused and reviled by the inhabitants of all the places they passed through. 'But what vexed me most,' he wrote, 'was their continual slandering of our country (Scotland), on which they threw the most infamous invectives....'[18]

A striking symptom of Scottish unpopularity in America during the Revolution is to be found in the passage in Jefferson's first draft of the Declaration of Independence where he asserted that the British were permitting their chief magistrate, 'to send over not only soldiers of our common blood, but Scotch and foreign mercenaries to invade and destroy us.'[19] The reference to the Scotch, with its implied disclaimer of any American propinquity of blood with the Scottish people, was deleted from the final version, but the fact that Jefferson could make it in the first place, is significant in itself.[20]

Popular anti-Scottish feeling did not pass unnoted in the literary compositions of the Revolutionary period. John Trumbull's satire

M'Fingal opens with an account of the ancestry of its mock hero:

> His fathers flourished in the Highlands
> Of Scotia's fog-benighted islands;
> Whence gain'd our 'Squire two gifts by right,
> Rebellion, and the Second-sight.

But a king has risen,

> Whose gracious speech with aid of pensions,
> Hush'd down all murmurs of dissensions...
> Rebellion, from the northern regions,
> With Bute and Mansfield swore allegiance;
> All hands combin'd to raze, as nuisance,
> Of Church and state the Constitutions,
> Pull down the empire, on whose ruins
> They meant to edify their new ones;
> Enslave th's Amer'can wildernesses,
> And rend the provinces in pieces.[21]

The satiric references to Scottish Jacobitism, and to the Scottish politicians, Bute and Mansfield as George III's chief accomplices in the oppressive policy towards America are, as we shall see, typical of attacks on the Scots.

A much more detailed account of anti-Scots feeling is contained in *The Patriots,* a play by Robert Munford, a Virginian, written in the period 1775–6. Much of the action is concerned with the persecution of three Scottish merchants, M'Flint, M'Squeeze, and M'Gripe, by a local, patriotic, Committee of Safety. The committee is presented throughout as stupid, prejudiced, and unthinking, while Munford's own attitude towards the popular anti-Scottish feeling is represented by the voice of a character called Trueman, a well-educated, intelligent, conservative. Trueman's attitude is expressed in this speech:

> The ungracious treatment that some Scotchmen have met with, the illiberal reflections cast out against them all, give little hope of their attachment, to a country, or to a people, where and with whom they have already tasted the bitter herb of persecution: some there are, who have behaved well, conform'd to the public will, nor given any cause of offence; yet even those have not met with the common offices of civility among us. (Act II, Sc. i.)[22]

But to the members of the Committee of Safety, Strut, Brazen, and Colonel Simple, a speech such as this sounds suspiciously close to treason. Trueman, and his friend Meanwell, are accused of taking the part of the Scots.

> STRUT. Wou'd you protect our enemies, gentlemen? Would you ruin your country for the sake of Scotchmen?
>
> TRUEMAN. Prove them to be enemies, shew that they plot the downfall of my country, and courtesy itself shall revolt against them.
>
> BRAZEN. There is sufficient proof that nine hundred and ninety-nine out of a thousand of them are our enemies.
>
> TRUEMAN. Some may be enemies, others guiltless. 'Tis ungenerous to arraign this man for the offence of his neighbour; illiberal to traduce all for the transgressions of a few. (Act II, Sc. i.)

But the committee remains unshaken. The three Scots are brought before it.

> M'FLINT. What is our offence pray?
>
> STRUT. The nature of their offence, gentlemen, is, that they are Scotchmen; every Scotchman being an enemy, and these men being Scotchmen, they come under the ordinance which directs an oath to be tendered to all those against whom there is just cause to suspect they are enemies.
>
> BRAZEN. As these men are Scotchmen, I think there is just cause to suspect that they are our enemies. Let it be put to the committee, Mr. President, whether all Scotchmen are not enemies.

The question is finally put:

> COL. SIMPLE. Is All Scotchmen enemies, gentlemen?
>
> ALL. Ay, ay. (Act II, Sc. i.)

Munford's rejection of illiberal prejudice of this kind probably reflected the attitude of many independently-minded, intelligent Americans. Nonetheless, *The Patriots* remains excellent evidence of the current of anti-Scots feeling through the Revolutionary years.[23]

Several explanations have already been offered for this upsurge of Scottish unpopularity in America during the Revolution; the loyalism of large numbers of Scots, feelings of envy and animosity roused by Scottish business success in the American trade, resent ment against Scottish clannishness which was interpreted as hostility towards all outsiders. But there were other, perhaps deeper reasons, for the situation which finally came to light during the Revolution.

If, before the outbreak of the controversy over the Stamp Act of 1763, there had ever been a genuinely popular American image of Scotland it was that which emerged during the Jacobite rebellion of 1745–6. And if eighteenth century England had never been capable of understanding that that uprising had been supported by only a section of the Scottish people, and that it had failed partly because the wealthiest and most powerful part of the country had either actively opposed it, or at least had remained aloof, then it is hardly possible that the affair could have been viewed with any greater accuracy in the American colonies, over three thousand miles away. But there is ample proof that Protestant America was seriously alarmed by the Stuart attempt to recover the Crown and proportionately relieved when news of Cumberland's victory at Culloden came through. If the number of sermons on the situation, which were afterwards printed, is any indication, then it is certain that churches up and down the colonies must have rung with denunciations of this Scotch rebellion. Even from the titles of many of these, an identification of Scotland and the Scots with the cause of the rising may easily be deduced.[24]

Now the '45 made an idelible mark on the pattern of Anglo-Scottish relations in the eighteenth century: the ideas of Scottish Jacobitism and Scottish rebelliousness ensured that relations between the countries would remain, for several decades more, as unfriendly as they had been on the occasion of the Union in 1707. Latent English distrust and dislike of the Scots broke out afresh with the accession to power of the Earl of Bute, a Scot whose family name was Stuart, in May, 1762. Under the guidance of Bute, his former tutor and 'dearest friend', George III, soon after his succession to the throne in 1760, 'had begun to edge out the trusted counsellors of the old régime'.[25] Bute remained as head of the government for only eleven months, but his influence was popularly held to be powerful throughout the bitter political struggles of the succeeding years. It is doubtful, however, whether any kind of factual basis was needed to provoke the torrent of abuse which poured upon him and all his countrymen. Attacks of an identical nature to those we have already seen in America occurred repeatedly in England: the unprincipled Scots were supposed to be growing fat at the expense of their English neighbours, the suspicious clannishness of the Scots was constantly referred to, and the partiality of Scot for Scot was now to be seen at work in the highest levels of the country's political life. The leader of the attacks on Scotland and the Scots was of course John Wilkes.

Wilkes's outlet for his views was the ironically titled *North Briton*, set up in opposition to a government paper, *The Briton*, run, typically enough, by another Scot, Tobias Smollett. The future was established in the first number, published on Saturday, 5 June 1762. 'I thank my stars,' wrote Wilkes, 'I am a *North Briton*; with this almost singular circumstance belonging to me, that I am *unplaced and unpensioned*: but I hope this reproach will soon be wiped away, and that I shall no longer be pointed at by my sneering countrymen.'[26] The second number, published a week later, continued the attack; this time the charge was the old one of Scottish Jacobitism. With a Scottish lord (Bute) in control of the Treasury, 'Our *ancient kingdom* therefore cannot but be satisfied, and by every tie of gratitude, as well as duty, must *now* be sincerely attached to the government. The most suspicious can have no doubts concerning us for the future, in case of a rebellion's springing up in any other country; which, to me, seems *highly improbable*.'[27] Yet one can never be sure of what the Scots will do. The clan chiefs had received large sums of money and had sworn allegiance to the House of Hanover; but within months they had been out in open rebellion. They had, of course, been fighting on the side of tyranny and reaction:

> ...for while the *English* were so gallantly fighting for the liberties of Europe, and indeed of mankind, they were called back to deal out halters and gibbets to their fellow subjects of *Scotland,* who were forging chains for both nations; and, worse than the infamous Cappadocians of old, not only refused the liberty they might enjoy themselves, but endeavoured to entail *their* vassalage and slavery on the whole island.[28]

Wilkes ends with an ironical aside on the growing taste in England for Scottish literary productions:

I am happy to find, that the *English* are not so sparing and penurious to us, both of money and praise, as they used to be. We are certainly growing into fashion. The most rude of our bards are admired; and I know some choice wits here, who have thrown aside *Shakespeare* and taken up *Fingal,* charmed with the variety of character, and richness of imagery.[29]

Outpourings of this kind did not pass unnoticed in Scotland; rather they produced immediate and bitter reactions. Throughout 1763, for example, the *Scots Magazine* is full of letters commenting on the situation, answering Wilkes, or attacking him in turn. One of the most effective rebuttals of the Wilkesite charges was an address to the people of England, reprinted from the *Caledonian Mercury* of 24 August 1763:

> England, I'll readily admit, is more powerful; is larger, richer, and more populous, than Scotland: but should it from thence be inferred, that every ray of royal favour ought to centre solely upon her?—Does it from thence follow, that every Scotsman, or Irishman, every Welshman or American, however qualified by services or merit, ought, with all humility, to give immediate way to an English competitor, because, may-hap, his country is more fertile, more populous or extensive?[30]

The appeal here to a kind of regional solidarity involving Scot, Irishman, Welshman, and American, in face of English supremacy, is interesting; but in the case of the American at least, it must have gone entirely in vain. American memories of the Scots and the '45 seem to have been no shorter than those of the English, and it is much more than a coincidence that Scottish unpopularity in America was growing exactly in the period that the Scots were the subject of mounting abuse in England.

The Wilkesite attacks on Scotland made effective play with the notion that the Jacobite rebellions were a threat to the principles of liberty enshrined in the English constitution. Scottish support for the Stuarts therefore identified the Scots with tyranny and reaction. In the American situation, where many Americans believed that their traditional constitutional liberties were being threatened, such an identification was of particular significance. On 29 April 1776, Ezra Stiles discussed in his diary the possibility of an end to the conflict between England and her American colonies which had begun the year before. His conclusion is: 'The Ministry & Parl^t

have no Intention of Accomodation—The Scotch Influence blinds
the Parlᵗ & Nation.'³¹ A few months later, after receiving a copy
of the Declaration of Independence, Stiles makes this entry:

> And have I lived to see such an important & astonishing
> Revolution? Scotch Policy transfused thro' the collective Body
> of the Ruling Powers in Great Britain; and their violent,
> oppressive & haughty Measures have weaned & alienated the
> affections of three Millions of people, & dismembered them
> from a once beloved Parent State. Cursed be that arbitrary
> Policy! Let it never poison the United States of America!³²

Stiles was not alone in his understanding of 'Scotch Policy' and its
ultimate responsibility for the disaffection of the American colonies.
Writing once again during the early months of the war, Thomas
Johnson of Maryland expressed the view that a major aim of the
conflict should be to 'preserve the empire entire, and the constitutional liberty, founded in Whiggish principles, handed down to us
by our ancestors....' There should be no question of a final break
with the mother-country; constitutional innovation should be
avoided so that in the end the colonies would gain the support of
'every honest Englishman' and help the 'English Whigs' to over-
throw the 'cunning Scotchmen' in the Ministry.³³ For Johnson as
for Stiles the oppressive policies of the government of George III
towards the American colonies have specifically Scottish origins.

To understand fully these condemnatory references to 'Scotch
Influence', 'Scotch Policy' and 'cunning Scotchmen', it is necessary
to glance back again to Britain's chief minister in 1763, the
Earl of Bute. Bute's successor in office was George Grenville, and
it was Grenville's administration which passed the Stamp Act and
initiated the prosecution of Wilkes for alleged libel on the King in
the *North Briton*, Number 45. The Rockingham ministry, which
followed in 1765, repealed the Stamp Act and other unpopular
measures; but eventually undermined by the actions of the King, and
faced by disruptive opposition, it could not survive beyond a single
year. Chatham, who effectively succeeded Rockingham, was before
long too ill to carry through policies opposed by George III and
a majority in Parliament, and his colleagues in the government
soon reversed his intentions by renewing the strong line with the
American colonies and taking up again the quarrel with the popular
Wilkes, who had just been elected to Parliament by the county of

Middlesex. Finally 1770 saw the establishment as chief minister of Lord North, whose policy of firmness towards the American colonies helped to gain him George III's support.

From the period of the Stamp Act, George III's opponents believed that they saw, behind all these manoeuvrings, the guiding hands of the Earl of Bute—widely reputed to be intimate with the King's mother, the Princess Dowager of Wales—and, his chief associate, the Lord Chief Justice of the King's Bench, Lord Mansfield, another Scot. Hence the repressive policies with which these men were popularly identified—those anti-America, and anti-Wilkes—were viewed as the consequence of undue Scottish influence, and as proof of united Scottish support for tyranny and oppression.[34]

The clearest American statement of the belief that the whole repressive American policy owed its origins to the machinations of Bute occurred in a letter from the American congress to the people of Great Britain, dated at Philadelphia on 5 September 1774:

> At the conclusion of the late war,—a war rendered glorious by the abilities and integrity of a minister [Lord Chatham], to whose efforts the British empire owes its safety and its fame; at the conclusion of this war, which was succeeded by an inglorious peace, formed under the auspices of a minister [Lord Bute],—of principles, and of a family, unfriendly to the Protestant cause, and inimical to Liberty:—We say, at this period and under the influence of that man, a plan for enslaving your fellow-subjects in America was concerted, and has ever since been pertinaciously carrying into execution....[35]

But the American attitude towards the Scottish share in the repressive policy towards the colonies is once again exhibited in more detail by a satirical literary production of the Revolution: *The Fall of British Tyranny*, a play probably by John Leacock, published at Philadelphia in 1776.[36] Its pervasive anti-Scottish tone is set by the opening words of the mock dedication:

> To Lord Boston, and the Remnant of the Actors, Merry Andrews, and strolling players, in Boston, Lord Kidnapper, and the rest of the Pirates and Buccaneers, and the innumerable and never-ending clan of Macs and Donalds upon Donalds, in America.

The theme re-appears near the end of the dedication:

And ye Macs, and ye Donalds upon Donalds, go on, and
may our gallows-hills and liberty poles be honour'd and
adorn'd with some of your heads; Why should Tyburn and
Temple-bar make a monopoly of so valuable a commodity?

The *dramatis personae* are then carefully identified for us: Lord
Paramount is Bute; Lord Mocklaw, Mansfield; Lord Catspaw,
North; Lord Patriot, Wilkes; Lord Kidnapper, Dunmore, governor
of Virginia; Lord Boston, Gage, the governor and captain-general
of Massachusetts, etc. Paramount opens the play in soliloquy:

Many long years have rolled delightfully on, whilst I have
been basking in the sunshine of grandeur and power, whilst
I have imperceptibly (tho' not unsuspected) guided the chariot
of state, and greased with the nation's gold the imperial
wheels! 'Tis I that move the mighty engine of royalty, and
with the tincture of my somniferous opiate (or, in the language
of a courtier) by the virtue of my secret influence, I have
lulled the axletree to sleep, and brought on a pleasing insensi-
bility....

Oh! ambition, thou darling of my soul! stop not 'till I rise
superior to all superlative, 'till I mount triumphantly the
pinnacle of glory, or at least open the way for one of my
own family and name to enter without opposition. (p. 1)

Bute's family name was Stuart, and his darker purpose is about to be
rehearsed in great detail. Paramount learns from Mocklaw that there
is a precedent for making the King's proclamation the law of the
land:

PARAMOUNT. I see it plain! this, this alone is worth a ton of
gold—Now, by St. Andrew! I'll strike a stroke that shall
surprise all Europe, and make the boldest of the adverse
party turn pale and tremble—Scotch politics, Scotch
intrigues, Scotch influence, and Scotch impudence (as they
have termed it) they shall see ere long shine with unheard
of splendour, and the name of Lord Paramount the mighty,
shall blaze in the annals of the world with far greater
lustre (as a consummate politician) than the name of
Alexander the Great, as an hero! (p. 3)

In the next scene, his plan is revealed through a dialogue with
Mocklaw.

PARAMOUNT. I shall at this time but just give you a hint of

the plan I've drawn up in my own mind. You must have perceived in me a secret hankering for majesty for some time past, notwithstanding my age;—but as I have considered the great dislike the nation in general have, as to my person, I'll waive my own pretensions, and bend my power and assiduity to it in favour of one, the nearest a kin to me, you know who I mean, and a particular friend of yours, provided I continue to be dictator, as at present.... (p. 4)

War with America will be fostered; Britain will be left defenceless by the removal of her troops to America; the French and Spanish fleets will appear in the Channel; and 'my kinsman' will land in Scotland with thirty thousand men and march on London. Later, thinking about the outcome of his design, Paramount soliloquises on his native land:

I'll draw in treasure from every quarter, and, Solomon-like, wallow in riches; and Scotland, my dear Scotland, shall be the paradise of the world. Rejoice in the name of Paramount, and the sound of a bawbee shall be no more heard in the land of my nativity. (p. 8)

The rest of the play is mainly concerned with the American victories in the early stages of the War.

The satire here is far from skilful, but the attitudes it reveals confirm in detail the general picture offered of American feeling towards the Scots and their alleged responsibility for Britain's war-like policy towards the colonies. Even such a fantastic idea as that Bute had been plotting all along to bring back the Stuart Pretender apparently was widely circulated. In a sermon on American affairs, preached at the opening of the Provincial Congress of Georgia, in 1775, afterwards published at Philadelphia, the Revd John J. Zubly said that, 'It may be owing to nothing but the firm attachment to the reigning family that so many Americans look upon the present measures as a deep laid plan to bring in the Pretender. Perhaps this jealousy may be very groundless, but so much is certain, that none but Great-Britain's enemies can be gainers in this unnatural contest.'[37]

Not surprisingly, all the Scots in America were hardly prepared to acquiesce weakly in sweeping denunciations of their native land. Such attacks must have been particularly galling to those Scots who did play a leading part in the Revolution. But for one who hated and despised the Scots with uncompromising thoroughness, no record was sufficient to excuse a Scot his nationality. In his diary in July 1777, Stiles set down what was probably the most vivid of all the denunciations of the Scots and Scotland. Witherspoon had tried to defend the Scots in Congress, but Stiles refuses to be silenced by him on the subject of 'Scots Perfidy & Tyranny & Enmity to America.' 'Let us boldly say,' wrote Stiles, 'for History will say it, that the whole of this War is so far chargeable to the Scotch Councils, & to the Scotch as a Nation (for they have nationally come into it) as that had it not been for them, this Quarrel had never happened. Or at least they have gloried in the Honor of exciting & conduct^g these Measures avowedly by their Earl of Bute behind the Curtain.'[38]

Witherspoon was in fact one of the Scots who reacted vigorously against the calumnies to which all his countrymen were subjected. On 17 May 1776, on the occasion of a general fast throughout the colonies, he preached a sermon at Princeton to which he appended 'An Address to the natives of Scotland residing in America'. The *Address* was published in Glasgow in 1777, in London in 1778, and printed in the *Scots Magazine,* also in 1777.[39] Witherspoon began by denying the validity of sweeping accusations against the Scots as a national group:

> It has given me no little uneasiness, to hear the word *Scotch* used as a term of reproach in the American controversy; which could only be upon the supposition, that strangers of that country are more universally opposed to the liberties of America, than those who were born in South-Britain or Ireland. I am sensible that this has been done, in some newspapers and contemptible anonymous publications, in a manner that was neither warranted by truth, nor directed by prudence. There are many natives of Scotland in this country, whose opposition to the unjust claims of Great Britain has been as early and uniform, founded upon as rational and liberal principles, and therefore, likely to be as lasting, as that of any set of men whatever.[40]

But even Witherspoon is willing to suppose that, 'in some provinces especially, the natives of Scotland have been too much inclined to support the usurpations of the parent state....' If this is the case, then the main reason, Witherspoon declares, is the frequency with which American writers and newspapers have seen in John Wilkes a real ally—Wilkes who is known to the Scots only for his 'contempt and hatred of the Scots nation'. The rest of the address is taken up with a straightforward rehearsal of the advantages that will follow from American independence. No one has taken Witherspoon's 'excuse' for the Scots very seriously, but since he was, after all, in an ideal position to know the truth concerning the Scots his comment is not to be dismissed too quickly as no more than a piece of special pleading.

The part that Wilkes played in exacerbating Anglo-Scottish relations has already been established, and the coincidence of the period of his fulminations with that in which anti-Scots feeling was growing in America also noted. In addition, it is true that Wilkes's campaigns inevitably brought him into sympathy with the American side in the dispute between the colonies and the mother-country. Hence Witherspoon is right in asserting that the American patriots regarded Wilkes as an important ally. The Boston Sons of Liberty indeed carried on an extensive correspondence with him asking for information and guidance; and in 1769 the South Carolina Assembly voted Wilkes £1,500 to help to pay his debts.[41] In London, some Americans formed close ties with him; Arthur Lee, who had studied medicine in Edinburgh, was a particularly ardent Wilkesite, and it was probably through Lee that Benjamin Rush dined with Wilkes in the King's Bench Prison in January, 1769.[42] Describing this meeting, Rush wrote, 'He spoke with as much virulence as ever against Scotland, for, you must know, all the Scotch members of Parliament, in both Houses, are against America.'[43]

More important, however, than any of these American connections of Wilkes is the fact that at least the first two numbers of the *North Briton* were reprinted at New York. Significantly, the date of republication was 1769, or seven years after their first appearance in London. This may indicate no more than the perennial interest of any anti-Scots writing—the *North Briton* was reprinted in full in London in the same year—but it is more probable that the two numbers, the anti-Scottish character of which has already been indicated, were reprinted then to take advantage of, or perhaps to encourage, the growing resentment in America towards everything Scottish. Unfortunately, it is not possible to date with certainty another piece of Wilkesite material which was reprinted in Boston—a pamphlet called *Britannia's Intercession for the Deliver-*

ance of John Wilkes, Esq.; from Persecution and Banishment. To which is added, a Political and Constitutional Sermon, and a Dedication to L——— B———. The Boston pamphlet is a reprint of the seventh London edition. Internal evidence indicates that the pamphlet could not have been written before 1766. If we remember the close ties between Wilkes and the Boston Sons of Liberty in 1769, it is very probable that *Britannia's Intercession* was printed there about that time.

The pamphlet is written in the form of a parody of a religious service, with Wilkes in the role of the godhead. Although the following extract may suggest that the whole is a piece of ironic anti-Wilkesite writing, this is not so:

> *Then shall be said the Wilkonian creed, by the orator, and the People repeating it after him.*
> I believe in Wilkes, the firm patriot, maker of number 45, Who was born for our good, Suffered under arbitrary power Was banished and imprisoned. He ascended into purgatory, and returned some time after. He ascended here with honour, and sitteth amidst the great assembly of the people, where he shall judge both the favourite and his creatures. I believe in the spirit of his abilities, that they will prove to the good of our country. In the resurrection of liberty, and the life of universal freedom for ever. (pp. 10–11)

The American Wilkesites were not allowed to have things all their own way. In 1769 once again, one of the major Scottish rejoinders to Wilkes's attacks was reprinted at Philadelphia, a pamphlet probably by Boswell, called *A North Briton Extraordinary*. A quotation from its early pages shows again the continuity between anti-Scottish sentiment in England and America. 'America' could easily be substituted for 'South Britain' here:

> ...the epithet *Scottish* is now hardly ever to be met with in South Britain, except as conveying an idea of the highest reproach; and the vulgar of that country, both high and low, affect to regard every native of North Britain as constitutionally a villain, either utterly devoid of every generous independent sentiment, and of our country in general as the disgrace and ruin of their own.[44]

Boswell's chief aim is to rebut the charge that the Scots are by nature reactionaries and supporters of tyranny: the charge which,

as has been suggested, had a special relevance in the Revolutionary
context. He argues that quite the reverse is true: the Scots have
always been true defenders of popular liberties. (Witherspoon
probably was drawing on this pamphlet in the defence of the Scots
he offered in Congress.)

The evidence offered above is probably sufficient to bear out the
contention that American anti-Scottish sentiment was closely related
to identical English feelings, and that Witherspoon's view of the
importance of Wilkes in explaining the failure of many Scots to
support the Revolution is at least worthy of serious consideration.[45]
Nonetheless the main significance of Witherspoon's *Address* is its
confirmation of the fact of Scottish loyalism. Nor can his argument
about the role of Wilkes rebut the more obvious economic and
political explanations of the behaviour of the majority of his
countrymen.

If some Scots in America were influenced in their conduct by
anti-Wilkesite feelings, it is probably also true that many more
were encouraged to side with the loyalists because of the
absence of any kind of pressure from their homeland to take any
other point of view. Wilkes's comment on the Scotch Members
of Parliament, for example, quoted by Rush in his letter, is strictly
true: no group of members could be relied upon to support the
royal government and its party line more confidently than the
Scots. This was no doubt a consequence of the fact that the
Scottish returning procedures were even more undemocratic, and
open to corruption, than those of England. In Edinburgh, twenty-
five persons, thirteen of whom formed a quorum, elected the
member for the city.[46]

The question of a general 'Scottish attitude' towards the American
war is a complex one.[47] North's cabinet contained two Scots who
were both powerful advocates of active prosecution of the war:
Alexander Wedderburn, the Solicitor-General, and Robert Dundas,
the Lord Advocate. Another Scot, Lord Mansfield, was the chief
spokesman for the government in the House of Lords. It has been
suggested that, 'It is doubtful whether Scotsmen took much interest
in the American question, and whether the attitude of their representatives at Westminster coincided with that of any but the upper
class.'[48] Although the second half of this suggestion may well be
true, there is ample evidence for denying the first part. Scottish
newspapers and magazines, in their treatment of the war, suggest

the existence of a keenly interested public, very well informed on the whole situation. Five times between 1768 and 1775, the Speculative Society at Edinburgh debated the American controversy. And as we have seen, Glasgow and the south-west had particular reason to be concerned about what was happening.

Merchants in the Glasgow area were at first opposed to the war, and addresses to the King in support of governmental policy could be obtained neither from Glasgow nor Edinburgh. It was only in the autumn of 1777, when hope of an early end to hostilities had gone, that the cities each offered to raise a regiment to send to America. On the other hand, a large part of the recruitment necessary for the prosecution of the war took place in the Scottish Highlands; in 1777–8, no fewer than six new Highland regiments were added to the regular army. All in all, there was little on the surface in Scotland which could have suggested to any Scot beyond the Atlantic that there was any effective opposition in his home country to the war policy of the North administration.

We have already seen that some Americans did look for possible support from one important Scottish body: the Church of Scotland. Such expectations of support were by no means unreasonable. The American War of Independence has sometimes been called the Presbyterian Revolution, and that description is not an illogical one at least in terms of one aspect of the pre-Revolutionary situation: the widespread belief, which existed from the early 1760s on, that the British government was about to establish Episcopacy in the American colonies.[49] In 1765, the *Scots Magazine* published a London report on the subject: 'We hear,' it ran, 'that the great uneasiness which universally prevails throughout the northern American colonies, has been considerably increased by their fears, that Episcopacy would shortly be imposed on them from hence; to get rid of which their ancestors fled to the wilds of America.'[50] Three years later, the magazine printed a much more colourful extract from a letter from North America which shows that the concern over such a move had in no way abated:

> The bare mention of establishing Episcopacy in this country, has raised an universal discontent among the people. I most sincerely wish, for the peace of my neighbours and the whole British colonies, that an end was put to their fears on this subject by authority, as I firmly believe the sight of lawn sleeves in this country would be more terrible to us than

10,000 Mohawks, or the most savage Indians in this quarter of the globe.[51]

Three years later the magazine reported a protest drawn up against a convention at Williamsburg in Virginia on 4 June 1771, which had addressed the King in favour of an American Episcopate. The protest noted that only twelve ministers had been present at the convention, out of at least a hundred in the colony, and another objection ran as follows:

> Because the establishment of an American Episcopate, at this time, would tend greatly to weaken the connection between the mother-country and her colonies, to continue their present unhappy disputes, to infuse jealousies and fears into the minds of Protestant, dissenters, and to give ill-disposed persons occasion to raise such disturbances as may endanger the very existence of the British empire in America.[52]

On the eve of the outbreak of the war, accounts of continuing anti-Episcopal feeling and the identification of Episcopalianism with Toryism were very common. For example, the magazine printed a letter from Boston, brought to London about the middle of November 1774:

> The people in Connecticut province have espoused the cause with more warmth than in this, and are determined to purge their colony of all Tories. To that end they have, after committing other outrageous acts, attacked the Episcopal clergy, and treated them with great indecency.... It will next come to the turn of the Episcopal clergy in this province, if the troops should be withdrawn. In that case it is expected the church of England would be wholly extirpated, and her clergy banished.[53]

Evidence on the other side, of the identification of the Presbyterians with the open advocates of independence is provided in a pamphlet by Myles Cooper, the Anglican president of King's College, New York, advocating submission to the authority of the King. In discussing the American Congress, Cooper complains that, '... the mystery was, that the gentlemen of the congress in whom we confided as the faithful guardians of the safety, as well as rights of America, were disposed to enter into a league, offensive and defensive, with its worst enemies, the New-England and other Presbyterian republicans.'[54] A letter from London, dated 30 June 1775, repeats the charge that Presbyterian doctrine lies behind the whole revolutionary movement: 'We are informed,' it runs, 'that there are at present in the different provinces of America upwards of one thousand six hundred Presbyterian parsons and teachers, who, by the doctrine they preach, inspire the Americans to take the field; assuring them, if they fall, they fall in the service of God.'[55]

Clearly there is much in the American situation just described that must have drawn the sympathy of many members of the Church of Scotland, especially when we recall the ample evidence of Scottish awareness and concern for the Church in America in the years before the Revolution. And at the General Assembly of the Church in the critical year of 1776 there certainly existed, among the members of the Popular or Evangelical party, considerable opposition to the American policies of the government of George III. Principal Robertson and his dominant Moderate party, however, were able to smooth over these differences, and the traditional Address to the King, 'Breathed a spirit of mildness becoming the Church of Scotland, and at the same time shewed their loyalty to his Majesty.' It asked for 'submission to legal authority', and was unanimously approved.[56]

The mildness of this Address must have come as a considerable disappointment to many people both in America and Scotland. But despite the Address, many ministers of the Popular party maintained their opposition to the war. John Erskine, for example, with his many American connections, consistently opposed the government's warlike policy. In 1776 he republished in Edinburgh, under his own name, a pamphlet entitled *'Shall I go to war with my American brethren?'* which had appeared anonymously in London as early as 1769. In October, 1776, he published anonymously, *Reflections on the Rise, Progress, and probable Consequences, of the present Contentions with the Colonies, by a Freeholder*, in which he recommended a middle way in the disputes between the countries. And again in 1776, he published another anti-government pamphlet, *The Equity and Wisdom of Administration, in the measures that have unhappily occasioned the American Revolt, tried by the Sacred Oracles*.[57]

Another staunch defender of the Americans was the Revd Charles Nisbet, Witherspoon's friend, whom he had at one stage recommended for the presidency of the College of New Jersey.

Nisbet's biographer describes him as one who.

> in principle and feeling sided with the colonies. His friend,
> Dr. Witherspoon, had in 1768, removed to America, and was
> known there as the active, uncompromising patron of the
> Colonial claims and feelings. Mr. Nisbet, it is believed,
> substantially agreed with him in his general sentiments.... In
> short, Mr. Nisbet was a decided and warm friend of America,
> in the contest in which she was engaged; and manifested his
> friendship as far as he was allowed by his situation.[58]

One of his friendly manifestations was a sermon he preached in
his church in Montrose, on the occasion of a public fast appointed
by the government, from the text of the writing on the wall. On a
similar occasion the tenor of Nisbet's preaching was so distasteful
to the opinions of Montrose Town Council that its members rose
in a body and walked out of his church.[59] James Lyndsay of Kirk-
liston, whom Henry Marchant heard preach in 1771, was another
'High son of Liberty and great Advocate for America'.[60] And the
Revd Dr Thom, of Govan Parish Church in Glasgow, was still
another Scots clergyman whose sympathy for the colonists' cause
was frequently expressed and widely known.
  Several of Franklin's friends among the North Britons were also
sympathetic towards America or at least opposed to the policy of
North's administration. Hume, though a stalwart Tory, attacked the
government's policy towards the colonies with great vehemence.[61]
Adam Smith advocated colonial representation in Parliament.[62]
Lord Kames defended the theory of Parliament's right to tax
America; but as the situation developed, he proposed 'a con-
solidating union with America' which would have provided for
full representation in Parliament: he had written to Franklin on this
subject both in 1765 and in 1767.[63] John Millar was a powerful
advocate of the rights of the colonists. William Robertson's position
is not easy to determine. Marchant's diary records a meeting with
him on 31 October 1771: 'Dr. Robertson', wrote Marchant, 'from
his Conversation I take to be a friend to civil and religious Liberty,
and fully imagines America must in some future period be the seat
of a mighty Empire.'[64] But Robertson was apparently unable to
accept the idea of American independence, and as we have seen,
he led the Moderate support for the government in the Church of
Scotland.

All these individual friends of America, and there must have been many others, could do nothing at all, however, to change the popular impression that the Scots as a whole were the most ardent supporters of North's war policy. That they existed is proof enough of the inaccuracy of the popular opposition claim that the Scots were docile supporters of a reactionary government. But these individuals, however numerous they may have been, spoke only for themselves; significantly no organised opposition developed which could have been regarded as the voice of at least a section of Scotland. That this was the case must have played an important part in determining the attitude of Americans towards Scotland, and of the Scots in America towards the Revolutionary situation.

That the American revulsion against the Scots lasted at least as long as the war is shown by a statute of the Georgia Assembly of August, 1782, which declared that 'the People of Scotland have in General Manifested a decided inimicality to the Civil Liberties of America and have contributed Principally to promote and Continue a Ruinous War, for the Purpose of Subjugating this and the other Confederated States.'[65] As a result, no Scot was to be allowed to settle, or carry on any kind of trade, in Georgia, unless he had supported the patriotic side. In such an atmosphere as this, it is evident that the cultural ties between Scotland and America must have suffered severely.

The war disrupted many connections. The link between the Chesapeake and the Clyde based upon the tobacco trade, was broken.[66] Scottish emigration to America was temporarily halted. As representatives of the British government, Scots no longer held important and influential positions in the civil administration of the colonies. The ties between the Presbyterian Churches in the countries were never again so close as they had been in the pre-Revolutionary years.[67] Colleges no longer found in Scotland financial support.

In other ways, little change took place. The flow of American medical students to Scotland slackened during the Revolution, but did not stop, and increased again as soon as the war ended.[68] Scottish books continued to be published in America: Lord Kames's *Six Sketches of the History of Man* at Philadelphia, in 1776; Thomson's *Seasons*, and a play by John Home, *Alonso and Ormisinda*, in Philadelphia in 1777; *The Life of David Hume, Esq.: the Philosopher and Historian written by himself*, in Philadelphia in 1778;

and two novels by Henry Mackenzie, *The Man of Feeling*, and *Julia de Rouhigné*, at Philadelphia, in 1782. And the personal ties between individuals in Scotland and America remained unbroken.

After the Revolution, Scottish intellectual and literary influences upon America were certainly destined to increase. A considerable period of time, however, had to elapse before these became sufficiently strong and distinctive to create a new *popular* image of Scotland in America. But the possibility of such a development was present even in the darkest days of American anti-Scottish prejudice. On 15 August 1776, Ezra Stiles commented in his diary on Dr Witherspoon's *Address* to the Scots in America: 'Too much Scoticism!' wrote the irate Stiles, 'He wants to save his Countrymen, who have behaved most cruelly in this American conflict.'[69] For 23 August, eight days later, Stiles makes a much briefer entry: 'Reading Robertson's Charles V'.[70]

NOTES AND REFERENCES

1. R. R. Palmer. *The Age of the Democratic Revolution*, I (Princeton, 1959), p. 190.
2. Reference to claims as grandiose as these may be found in John H. Finley's, *The Coming of the Scot* (London and New York, 1940), p. 67.
3. 'Reflections on the Scottish Character', *William and Mary College Quarterly*, 3rd Series, XI (April, 1954), 291.
4. The sentiments expressed in this letter to his brother, by Hugh Simm, written on 8 June 1769, while he was schoolteacher at Freehold, New Jersey, may well have been typical of those of the Scottish immigrant:

   I often take much satisfaction in traversing the silent and lonely woods which are all now in their bloom and verdure but am very sencibly disconsolate in not having any acquaintance with whom I might converse there being none here who have any relation to Scotland except a millar who came from Killburney about 16 years ago and two families the decendents of one Kerr who was bannished here for being concerned at the affair of Badal Bridge—(Original in Princeton University Library). The reference here is to the battle of Bothwell Bridge, 1679, at which the Scottish Covenanters were defeated, and after which many of their number were transported to the American colonies.
5. Stiles, *Literary Diary*, II, 227–8.
6. *The Scots Magazine*, XXXVIII (1776), 366.

7. Ibid., XXXIV (1772), 516.
8. Ibid., XXXVI (1774), 64.
9. Stiles, *Literary Diary*, II, 38.
10. See William H. Nelson, *The American Tory* (Oxford, 1961), pp. 102–3.
11. Campbell (Ed.), *The Bland Papers*, I, 39. In his *The King's Friends* (Providence, 1965), p. 181, Wallace Brown writes: 'All the evidence confirms that the Scots made up the backbone of Virginia Loyalism.'
12. *The Scots Magazine*, XXXVII (1775), 587.
13. See Brown, *The King's Friends*, pp. 21, 261.
14. See J. H. Easterby, *History of the St. Andrew's Society of Charleston, South Carolina, 1729–1929* (Charleston, 1929), pp. 50–2.
15. Wallace Brown's study, *The King's Friends*, is based on an analysis of all those loyalists who at the conclusion of the war laid claims before the British Government Commissioners. Mr Brown distinguishes between native-born American claimants and foreign-born claimants in each state. In states where the percentage of foreign-born claimants is substantial, the Scottish share of that percentage is significantly high. In Delaware 10 per cent of the foreign-born claimants are Scots; in Maryland, 17 per cent; in South Carolina, 19·6 per cent; in New York, 21·5 per cent; in Georgia, 32 per cent; in Virginia, 42 per cent; in North Carolina, 54·3 per cent. Such figures put the fact of Scottish loyalism almost beyond dispute.

16. Brown, *The King's Friends*, p. 260.

17. *Port Folio*, 4th Series, XVIII (1824), 396.

18. *The Scots Magazine*, XXXVIII (1776), 427.

19. Quoted by Graham, *Colonists*, p. 152.

20. John Witherspoon was responsible for the deletion of the unfriendly reference to his fellow-countrymen. See Richard H. Lee, *Memoir of the Life of Richard Henry Lee* (Philadelphia, 1825), I, 176. Jefferson's indictment of the Scots is peculiarly ironic in the light of Professor Howell's argument that Jefferson's framing of the Declaration owes a major debt to the *Elements of Logick* of William Duncan, the Scottish philosopher, and teacher of William Small at Aberdeen University. See W. S. Howell, 'The Declaration of Independence and Eighteenth-Century Logic', *William and Mary College Quarterly*, 3rd Series, XVIII (October, 1961), 463–84.

21. John Trumbull, *M'Fingal, A Modern Epic Poem* (Hartford, 1856), pp. 22–3.

22. The play is reprinted in full in the *William and Mary College Quarterly*, 3rd Series, VI (July, 1949), 448–503.

23. A letter written by a Scottish loyalist from Norfolk, Virginia, on 27 November 1774, to Charles Steuart, the Receiver-General, American Board of Customs, makes it clear that Munford's play arose directly out of his own experience: it explains that Munford was one of those who defended a group of local merchants, probably Scottish, who had been accused of breaking the tea embargo. See the Steuart papers, National Library of Scotland, MSS 5025–46.

24. For example, a sermon by Hull Abbot, *The Duty of God's People to Pray for the Peace of Jerusalem: and especially for the Preservation and Continuance of their own Privileges, both Civil and Religious, when in danger at Home or from Abroad. A Sermon on occasion of the Rebellion in Scotland rais'd in favour of a Popish Pretender* (Boston, 1746).

25. See George Rudé, *Wilkes and Liberty* (Oxford, 1962), p. 20.

26. *The North Briton from No. I to No. XLVI inclusive* (London, 1769), I, 3.

27. Ibid., II, 4.

28. Ibid., II, 4.

29. Ibid., II, 5.

30. *The Scots Magazine*, XXV (1763), 419.

31. Stiles, *Literary Diary*, II, 10.

32. Ibid., pp. 21–2.

33. Quoted by Nelson, *The American Tory*, p. 119.

34. Rudé summarises popular feeling in England in the 1760s thus: 'It was widely believed— and it needed no invention by Burke and the Rockingham Whigs—that corruption was more rampant than ever it had been, and that the influence of the Crown was being used to staff the administration with new Favourites and "King's Friends", who formed a secret Closet party, beyond the control of Parliament and guided behind the scenes by the sinister combination of the Earl of Bute ... and the Princess Dowager of Wales.' *Wilkes and Liberty*, p. 186. Equally relevant to my argument is Rudé's comment in a footnote on the same page. 'The point here argued is not so much that these views were justified as that they were widely believed to be true and aroused widespread "discontents".' The 'discontents' in question clearly came to be felt in the American colonies just as keenly as in England.

35. *The Scots Magazine*, XXXVI (1774), 692.

36. Sabin's *Dictionary of Books Relating to America* attributes the play to Leacock. In a footnote on p. 48 of his *History of the American Drama, from the beginning to the Civil War* (New York, 1943), Arthur Hobson Quinn refers to a statement that 'Joseph Lacock, Coroner, wrote a play with good humor, called British Tyranny'.

37. John J. Zubly, D.D., *The Law of Liberty. A Sermon on American Affairs, Preached at the Opening of the Provincial Congress of Georgia. Addressed to the Right Honourable the Earl of Dartmouth* (Philadelphia, 1775), p. 24.

38. Stiles, *Literary Diary*, II, 184–5. A political cartoon, *The Scotch Butchery, Boston. 1775*, shows Boston being bombarded by 'English Ships with Scotch Commanders' to the satisfaction of Bute and Mansfield. Scottish soldiers are attacking unarmed fugitives with bayonets, but English ones are 'Struck with horror and are dropping their arms.' See M. Dorothy George, *English Political Caricature to 1792* (Oxford, 1959), p. 152.

39. *The Scots Magazine*, XXXIX (1777), 113–20.

40. John Witherspoon, *An Address to the Natives of Scotland residing in America* (London, 1778), pp. 2–3.

41. See Raymond Postgate, *That Devil Wilkes* (London, 1956), pp. 162–72.

42. Wilkes was finally sentenced in June, 1768, for a libel against the King which had appeared in the *North Briton*, No. 45.

43. Rush, *Letters*, p. 72.

44. (James Boswell), *A North Briton Extraordinary ...* (Philadelphia, 1769), p. 9.

45. Cf. Courtlandt Canby, 'Robert Munford's *The Patriots*', *William and Mary College*

Quarterly, 3rd Series, VI (July, 1949), 439. In a footnote on this page Canby suggests that a connection existed between English and American anti-Scottish sentiment.

46. Henry W. Meikle, *Scotland and the French Revolution* (Glasgow, 1912), p. 16.

47. See Dalphy I. Fagerstrom, 'Scottish Opinion and the American Revolution', *William and Mary College Quarterly*, 3rd Series, XI (April, 1954), 252–75.

48. William Law Mathieson, *The Awakening of Scotland* (Glasgow, 1910), pp. 73–4.

49. For discussions of the Presbyterian contribution to the Revolution, see Gaius Jackson Slosser (Ed.), *They Seek a Country* (New York, 1955), pp. 150–62, and Trinterud, *The Forming of an American Tradition*, pp. 242–57. Trinterud's account is more conservative.

50. *The Scots Magazine*, XXVII (1765), 550.

51. Ibid., XXX (1768), 373.

52. Ibid., XXXIII (1771), 490.

53. Ibid., XXXVI (1774), 582.

54. Ibid., XXXVII (1775), 33.

55. Ibid., XXXVII (1775), 307. John Witherspoon and his students at the College of New Jersey are certainly to be included in this number. Charles Steuart's Scottish correspondent in Norfolk, Virginia, wrote to him on 5 November 1774 describing a journey made by a fellow-Scot to the northern states: 'He is much disgusted with the proceedings to the North; Yr. Old Acquaintance Dr. Witherspoon has lost his esteem greatly. Mr. A. tells me he heard forty boys repeat orations at the Princetown Commencement, every one of them full of the Old Cameronian resisting sentiments.' (Richard Cameron, killed in 1680, was an extreme Presbyterian who rebelled against the government of Charles II. See the Steuart papers, National Library of Scotland, MSS 5025–46. This contemporary view offers useful confirmation of Carl Becker's opinion of Witherspoon's influence in America: 'During twenty years previous to the Revolution, many men went out from Princeton to become powerful moulders of public opinion. Few were counted as theologians of note; few were set down as British Loyalists. But they were proud to be known as Americans and patriots: ministers who from obscure pulpits proclaimed the blessings of political liberty; laymen who professed politics with the fervor of religious conviction.' See Carl L. Becker, *Beginnings of the American People* (Ithaca, 1960), p. 194.

56. *The Scots Magazine*, XXXVIII (1776), 272–3.

57. Wellwood, *Life and Writings of John Erskine*, pp. 265, 89.

58. Samuel Miller, *Memoir of the Rev. Charles Nisbet, D.D.* (New York, 1840), pp. 74–5.

59. Ibid., pp. 75, 77.

60. Stiles, *Literary Diary*, I, 308.

61. See Mathieson, *The Awakening of Scotland*, p. 75.

62. Ibid., pp. 75–6.

63. Alexander Fraser Tytler of Woodhouselee, *Memoirs of Henry Home of Kames* (Edinburgh, 1814), II, 96–100.

64. Stiles, *Literary Diary*, I, 307.

65. Quoted by Graham, *Colonists from Scotland*, p. 153.

66. For a consideration of the consequences of this breakdown, see T. M. Devine, 'Glasgow Merchants and the Collapse of the Tobacco Trade 1775–1783'. *Scottish Historical Review*, 52 (April, 1973), 50–74.

67. Somewhat ironically the conclusion of the war brought about a temporary alliance between the Episcopal Churches of Scotland and America. In 1783 Samuel Seabury was appointed first Bishop of the Episcopal Church in America. He travelled to London expecting to be consecrated there by the Anglican bishops. Meeting only a series of difficulties, in 1784 he finally travelled to Aberdeen where he was duly consecrated by the non-juring Scottish bishops.

68. Nathaniel Tucker arrived in Edinburgh to study medicine in 1775. George Logan, a Pennsylvanian Quaker followed him to Edinburgh in 1776; three years later Logan became the first American to be made president of the Royal Medical Society in the university. Other American medical students at Edinburgh in the war years included three Virginians named Stuart, Harris and Buchner, a D'Arcy from Maryland and a Gibbons from Georgia. See Riggs, 'The Colonial American Medical Student at Edinburgh', p. 147. William Charles Wells from Carolina was admitted to the Speculative Society in February, 1777. Yet another American who studied at Edinburgh during the war was Nicholas Romayne: 'At the commencement of the war of the Revolution, he repaired to Edinburgh, where he pre-eminently distinguished himself by his wide range of studies, his latinity, and his medical knowledge.' See John W. Francis, *Old New York, or, Reminiscences of the Past Sixty Years* (New York, 1858), pp. 102–3.

69. Stiles, *Literary Diary*, II, 41.

70. Ibid., p. 43.

-IV-

Land of Learning

Emblematic of the continuity of Scottish intellectual influence upon America before and after the Revolution was the arrival in Philadelphia on 9 June 1785, of the Revd Charles Nisbet of Montrose, on his way to take up office as first president of Dickinson College in Carlisle, Pennsylvania. The founder of Dickinson was Benjamin Rush through whose efforts Nisbet was first elected president, and then, like Witherspoon, persuaded .o cross the Atlantic. Rush had known Nisbet in Scotland, and of course also knew that Dr Witherspoon had thought highly enough of his scholarly abilities—he was popularly known in Scotland as 'the walking library'[1]—to recommend him in his own place for the presidency of the College of New Jersey. Another consideration must have helped Rush to persuade his fellow-trustees to appoint Nisbet: the Montrose minister's consistently liberal attitude towards America during the Revolutionary war. This aspect of his career was always remembered in America. In 1824 the *Port Folio* published a brief notice of his life, mentioning his political views and implying that he was the leader of the members of the Popular party in the Church of Scotland who, in the General Assembly of 1776, wished to debate the Address to the King.[2] It was his abhorrence of precisely these views which caused William Creech to write a bitter letter to the Edinburgh press when news of Nisbet's American appointment was first made public:

Sir,
   You have informed us that a Reverend clergyman has lately received an appointment in America. Pray, Sir, is this the same

person whose letter addressed to Dr. Wotherspoon [*sic*] I lately read?—If it is, I congratulate Scotland on his departure, and I shall pity America on his arrival. Is this the man who encourages our youth to emigration, and advises the Rev. Dr. Wotherspoon to banish the poor Loyalists, 'these *vipers* in your bosom,' as he calls them.[3]

There is no question but that Nisbet is the subject of Creech's attack; if nothing else, the remark on the clergyman's interest in American emigration would confirm the identification. In Aberdeenshire, Nisbet was well known among the poorer people for his close ties with America, and he was continually applied to by prospective emigrants. A letter he wrote to Witherspoon in 1784 confirms this: 'people of fashion,' he wrote, 'and such as would be thought courtiers' still say that America might easily have been conquered. 'The case is otherwise with the common people, who rejoice in that liberty which they are sensible they want, and which they hope to share.'[4]

Nisbet had unquestionably idealised America as the land of freedom and democracy but even so, it was not easy to persuade him to make the decisive break with his native land. Rush appealed to him in terms even more extravagant than those in which he had earlier appealed to Witherspoon: under Nisbet's direction, Rush wrote, Dickinson could not help becoming the first college in America; God's favour was apparent on every side; America was all and more than the British liberal could imagine.[5] Nisbet did receive some more realistic accounts of what he was being asked to undertake; and many of his friends at home, including Lady Leven, Rush's old friend, who, as she said herself, had the best of reasons not to act in any way ungenerously towards him, advised caution in risking so much on what was clearly an uncertain venture.[6] But Rush's rhetoric once again prevailed and Nisbet left Montrose for Pennsylvania. On his arrival at Carlisle, he was bitterly disappointed. The realities of his situation were utterly out of keeping with the glowing picture Rush had painted. The buildings which housed the college were quite inadequate; the faculty was too small to accomplish the necessary work; the funds of the college were much less secure than he had been led to believe; and the state of the country in general proved to be quite unlike his expectations. Within a short time he and his family were ill with malaria. All these vexations, added to a natural homesickness, caused him to resign his position early in the fall of 1785 and determined him to return to Scotland. But no ship was then available; in the winter Nisbet's health improved and finally, in May 1786, he was re-elected president. Dr Nisbet was never really happy at Carlisle; but after these early uncertainties, he never again looked back. Having finally settled down to the task, he did not allow his personal dissatisfactions to come between himself and the duties he had undertaken, and for the rest of his life he laboured, admired and loved by his students, to raise Dickinson College to the position of eminence it attained in the years before his death.

Nisbet himself delivered four sets of lectures in the College curriculum. Even the names of these suggest their Scottish origins: Logic, Philosophy of the Mind, Moral Philosophy, and Belles-Lettres.[7] Particularly interesting is the presence, at Dickinson as at Princeton, of a course in Belles-Lettres. Moral philosophy, and the philosophy of the mind, were of course the central concerns of the school of Scottish common-sense philosophers. No record of text-books used at Dickinson has survived, but one may confidently suggest that the course in Belles-Lettres involved the study of Blair and probably Kames; that in Philosophy of the Mind, of Reid; in Moral Philosophy, of Hutcheson and probably Beattie and Balfour; in Logic, of William Duncan.

Princeton and Dickinson, actually headed by Scotsmen, may have been the first American colleges to reveal the decisive influence of the Scottish Enlightenment in their pattern of education, but that pattern in its various aspects soon began to appear elsewhere. Princeton, with its many politically and intellectually distinguished alumni, was in itself a potent influence. In Virginia, for example, both Washington College and Hampden-Sydney College owed much in their educational pattern to Princeton.[8] But no such immediate link was needed for the basic elements of the Scottish curriculum to begin to appear. A course in Rhetoric and Belles-Lettres or in Criticism, for example, became an inevitable part of any college curriculum, and invariably the texts were Blair and Kames. At Yale, Blair's *Rhetoric* was introduced as a text-book in 1785 and remained in use until 1824 at least.[9] John Duncan, a Scottish traveller in America in 1818–19, states that Blair's first volume was studied in the third term of the sophomore year and the second volume in the first term of the senior year.[10] Blair was introduced at Harvard in 1788;[11] Samuel Miller, in his *Brief Retrospect of the*

Eighteenth Century, a survey of the intellectual history of Europe, states that his *Lectures on Rhetoric* was studied there during the second year,[12] while an article in the *North American Review* confirms that this was still the case in 1818.[13] Rhode Island College introduced the study of Kames's *Elements of Criticism* in 1783, and in 1803 both Blair and Kames were being studied.[14] The curriculum announced for Union College in 1804 included the reading of Blair's *Lectures* in the junior year and Kames's *Elements of Criticism* in the senior.[15] Miller mentions a course on Rhetoric and Belles-Lettres, based on Blair, at William and Mary.[16] In addition to those colleges mentioned, it is known that Blair was adopted as a text, between 1800 and 1835, at Columbia, Pennsylvania, North Carolina, Middlebury, Williams, Amherst, Hamilton, and Wesleyan.[17]

In his *History of American Philosophy*, Herbert Schneider refers to the development of American interest in Scottish philosophy:

> About 1820 ... there occurred a significant revolution in the very idea of what constitutes philosophy, as well as in its instruction. The Scottish philosophy invaded the country and rapidly crowded out the older eighteenth-century texts. Thomas Reid's *Intellectual and Active Powers* (as his two works were usually called for short) and Dugald Stewart's *Elements of the Philosophy of the Human Mind* (often referred to as *Intellectual Philosophy*) and *The Active and Moral Powers* set the pattern for the new division of philosophy into mental and moral.[18]

Schneider is clearly right in seeing the Scottish influence marked by the division of philosophy into its moral and mental compartments, but he is over-conservative in setting the date of the revolution at 1820: its origins go back to the immediate post-Revolutionary period, and by the turn of the century it was well advanced. The chapter in Miller's *Brief Retrospect* which discusses the development of philosophy in the eighteenth century is entitled 'Philosophy of the Human Mind'; among the philosophers discussed at some length are Hume, Reid, Stewart, and Monboddo. Reference is also made to Kames, Ferguson, Smith, Campbell, and Oswald. As we have already seen, Hutcheson was being studied in Moral Philosophy courses even before the Revolution, and this continued to be true for many years thereafter. Miller's survey of college curricula, in an appendix to the second volume of his *Brief Retrospect*, indicates that by about 1800, courses in Moral Philosophy usually given in the junior or senior years, had become standard at most colleges.

Courses in the Philosophy of the Human Mind became common soon after the publication of the first volume of Dugald Stewart's *Elements of the Philosophy of the Human Mind* in 1792. Miller records that the 'Moral School' at William and Mary studied Duncan, Reid, and Professor Stewart.[19] (Stewart's immediate acceptance as a standard authority must have been largely due to his being recognised as a follower of Reid, whose position was already well established.) The *North American Review* note on the Harvard curriculum in 1818 specifies the study of Stewart's *Elements* by both juniors and seniors.[20] By 1825, Stewart's successor at Edinburgh, Brown, was also being taught there.[21] At Yale, Stewart's *Philosophy of the Mind*, according to John Duncan, was being studied in the senior year by 1818, and this was still the case in 1824.[22] At Brown, Stewart was being studied in 1827, along with Campbell's *Philosophy of Rhetoric*.[23] The moral philosophy taught at the University of Virginia, instituted in 1825, had a strongly Scottish emphasis. Examination papers set around 1828 demanded considerable knowledge of the Scottish common-sense school. Answers included extended and thoughtful discussion of Brown, Blair, Stewart, and Adam Smith.[24]

From this account it is clear that the 'revolution' Schneider talks of as occurring about 1820 had been in preparation for half a century at least. Indeed by 1820 the revolution was over, the new orthodoxy well established. The common-sense philosophy of the Scottish Enlightenment had been largely assimilated into the whole range of America's cultural and intellectual life. The pattern of American education had clearly been radically influenced by it. America's literary culture had largely adopted its principles of criticism and taste. Even America's political thought had been affected by it. James Wilson, that other distinguished Scottish signatory of the Declaration of Independence, a major contributor to American political philosophy and debate during and after the Revolutionary period, owed much to his background in the Scottish common-sense school. In fact it is probably true that the ready acceptance of the Scottish philosophy in America had something to do with the way in which its metaphysical assumptions underwrote central aspects of the natural law democratic tradition. Again the Scottish philosophy of common-sense represented a reaction against Humean scepticism; as such it must have appealed strongly to those conservative upholders of religious orthodoxy who continued to exercise a powerful

78 SCOTLAND AND AMERICA

influence on America's educational and cultural establishment. Whatever the reason, there can be no doubt that by 1820 the philosophy of the Scottish Enlightenment in its post-Humean phase, had already made a decisive impact upon America.[25]

The widespread use in college curricula of the works of the North British circle in Scotland obviously entailed the publication and circulation of their books in America. Thus, after the Revolution, the extent of the publication of Scottish books in America increased enormously. Of course it is true that after the Revolution American publishers were in a particularly favourable position over the republication of British authors. In the absence of any kind of international copyright arrangement it cost them nothing to publish a British work. But copyright in eighteenth century Britain itself, not to mention the colonies, was so vexed a question that it is hard to believe it could have had any material effect on the republication of Scottish books in colonial America. Had the interest and demand existed the books would have been made available—as indeed to a limited extent they were. Hence the great expansion in the republication of Scottish books in post-Revolutionary America clearly reflects developments of a more substantial kind than simply the creation of the new, no copyright situation.

At Philadelphia, Hutcheson's *Introduction to Moral Philosophy* was published in 1788; Reid's *Intellectual and Active Powers of Man* in 1792, and again in 1818. *The Works of Thomas Reid* appeared at Charlestown, Mass., in 1813-15, and in 1818, and at New York in 1822. The first volume of Stewart's *Elements of the Philosophy of the Human Mind* appeared at Philadelphia in 1793—one year after its publication in Britain; the second and third volumes were printed at Boston and Philadelphia respectively, in 1814 and 1827, the years in which they appeared in Britain. Meantime editions of the *Elements* also appeared at Brattleborough, Vermont, in 1808 and 1813; at Boston in 1818, 1821, and 1822; at New York in 1818; and at Albany in 1821 and 1822. Stewart's *Philosophical Essays* was published at Philadelphia in 1811, while his *General View of the Progress of metaphysical, ethical, and political philosophy, since the revival of letters in Europe* appeared at Boston in 1817 and 1822. On the other hand, the alleged anti-religious tendency of Hume's philosophy probably prevented the widespread American circulation of his works. Campbell's *Dissertation on Miracles*, which was an attempt to refute Hume, appeared in Philadelphia in 1790, but nothing by Hume, except his *Life*, appeared in America until the first two volumes of his *History of England* were published at Philadelphia in 1795. The first American publication of his *Philosophical Essays* did not occur until 1817, when it appeared (with Campbell's *Dissertation*) at both Georgetown and Philadelphia. Hume's *History of England* was a much more popular work. A new seven volume edition was published, probably simultaneously, in Baltimore, Philadelphia, New York, and Boston in 1810. It was also published at Albany in 1816, and Philadelphia in 1821–2. Campbell's own major work, *The Philosophy of Rhetoric*, while never quite as popular as the rhetorical studies of Blair and Kames, nevertheless had a considerable American vogue. It was published at Boston, probably in 1808, and again in 1811 and 1817; at Newburyport, probably in 1809; and at Philadelphia in 1818. Dugald Stewart's successor as professor of moral philosophy at Edinburgh, Thomas Brown, was for a time neglected in America, but the publication of his lectures, as we shall see, brought about an immediate change. Brown's *Inquiry into the relation of cause and effect* appeared in Andover in 1822, and his *Lectures on the philosophy of the human mind* in the same town in the same year.

William Duncan's *Logic*, 'Designed particularly for young gentlemen at the university, and to prepare the way of the study of philosophy and the mathematics', was first published at Philadelphia in 1792; later publishings occurred at New York in 1802, 1816 and 1818, and at Albany in 1804, 1811, 1814, and 1815. Adam Smith's *Wealth of Nations* was published at Philadelphia in 1789; it was published again in the same city in 1796 and 1816, and again at Hartford in 1804, 1811, and 1818. Smith's *Theory of Moral Sentiments* was published at Philadelphia and Boston in 1817, and at New York in 1822. James Beattie's *Evidences of the Christian Religion* appeared at Philadelphia in 1787 and 1809, and at Annapolis in 1812; his *Elements of Moral Science* at Philadelphia in 1782, 1794, 1806, and 1809, and at Baltimore in 1813. *The Works of James Beattie* was published at Philadelphia in 1809.

William Robertson's *History of the Reign of Charles the Fifth* had been published in Philadelphia in 1770; his *Historical Disquisition concerning the Knowledge which the Ancients had of India* appeared there in 1792, and his *History of America* in New York in 1798. The last two books of that work—those concerned with Virginia and New England—were published at Philadelphia in 1799, and at

Walpole, New Hampshire, in 1800. *Charles V* was published again at New York in 1804. In 1812 in Philadelphia two publishers produced what may have been rival editions of the *History of America*, the *Historical Disquisition*, and *Charles V*. The *History of America* was published again at Philadelphia in 1821 and 1822. The first American edition of Robertson's *History of Scotland* occurred in the same city in 1811, while all four of his major works were published at Albany in 1822. An interesting footnote to Robertson's reputation as a model of English style[26] is the appearance at New York in 1810 of a work entitled *Beauties of Dr. Robertson*. Adam Ferguson's *Essay on Civil Society*, which the Charleston Library had once wanted to burn, originally published in America at Philadelphia in 1773, was republished there in 1804 and 1819, and at Boston in 1809; his *History of the Progress and Termination of the Roman republic* was published at Philadelphia in 1805 and 1811. Joseph Black's *Lectures on the Elements of Chemistry* was published at Philadelphia in 1806–7.

This record of American interest in works of Scotland's eighteenth century intellectual renaissance is impressive but it does not set forth the whole story. Even comparatively minor productions of that movement were welcomed in America. Alexander Gerard's *Essay on Taste*, originally published in 1759, was published at Philadelphia in 1804, while Archibald Alison's *Essays on the nature and principles of Taste* appeared at Boston in 1812. William Smellie's *Philosophy of Natural History* was published at Philadelphia in 1791, at Dover, New Hampshire, in 1808, and at Boston in 1820—it was read by seniors at Harvard in 1825,[27] while *The Elements of General History*, by Alexander Tytler, Kames's biographer, seems to have enjoyed a surprising American vogue. This work was published at Concord in 1801, 1820, and 1823; at Philadelphia in 1809, 1813, and 1817; at New York in 1817 and 1819; at Hartford in 1818, 1820, 1821, and 1823; and at Boston in 1820. Another Scottish historian whose work excited some interest in America was John Gillies, Robertson's successor as royal historiographer for Scotland. His *History of Ancient Greece*, 'a work with a strong Whig bias especially welcome to the Jeffersonian Republicans',[28] was published at New York in 1814, and at Philadelphia in 1822; another work, the *History of the world from the reign of Alexander to that of Augustus*, was published at Philadelphia in 1804 and 1809. It is to Kames himself, however, along with Hugh Blair, that we must look, to find the most widely published and circulated of all the North Britons. The titles listed above will have already suggested that, in comparison with the years before the Revolution, American interest in Scottish books is now less purely theological and philosophical; this truth will become even clearer when the publishing of Scottish literary works is considered. But perhaps the change is also indicated by the fact that Kames and Blair, the chief representatives of the Scottish concern for taste and style, easily excel in popularity any of their fellow-authors already mentioned. Lord Kames's *Elements of Criticism* was first published in America at Boston, in 1796, but before 1835, the work had appeared in nine other editions.[29] Blair's record is even more astonishing. His *Lectures on Rhetoric and Belles Lettres* was first published at Philadelphia in 1784, a year after its appearance in Scotland. In 1788, there appeared at Albany the first of many abridged editions of the work. But in the period 1805–23 alone, adding together complete and abridged versions produces the extraordinary total of fifty-six editions of the work. Editions of course appeared in Boston, Philadelphia, Baltimore, and New York, but many others were the work of printing presses in small towns which rarely produced literary works of any kind. For example, between 1798 and 1820 the press at Morristown, New Jersey, published in all seventy-four titles: religious material easily bulked largest, followed by annual almanacs, and works of a political nature. In the twenty-three years surveyed, history, biography, education, medicine, and belles-lettres each provided a single title, the final category being represented by *Lectures on Rhetoric and Belles Lettres. By Hugh Blair, D.D. and F.R.S.Edin. One of the ministers of the High Church, and Professor of Rhetoric and Belles Lettres in the University of Edinburgh. Sixth American, From the last Edinburgh Edition. Morristown, (N.J.) 1814.* In the same period, five other titles were published in Morristown though printed elsewhere: one of these was another, abridged, edition of Blair.[30] The issues of the Brooklyn Press in New York between 1799 and 1820 were similar to those of the Morristown press: religious material predominated along with almanacs and orations. But here, too, Blair's *Rhetoric* appears: in 1807 and again in 1812.[31] Editions of the work, usually abridged, also appeared in Albany, Brookfield, Wilmington, Exeter, Haverhill, Portland, Concord, Brattleboro, Windsor, Troy, New Brunswick, Poughkeepsie, Northampton, Salem, Worcester, Hartford, and Wendell.

Reasons for this exceptional popularity of Blair's work are not difficult to find. The careful, logical arrangement of the lectures made them an ideal textbook; as a result English composition was taught from Blair both at school and college.[32] Blair's reputation as a minister and preacher was also for long extremely high—his *Sermons* was reprinted many times in America. But it is to the strictly practical nature of much of Blair's work that one must return: his chapters on the different kinds of public speaking, in popular assemblies, at the Bar, and from the pulpit; his disquisition on the ideal organisation of a discourse among its several parts; his comments on pronunciation, and the means of improving in eloquence; all these must have been earnestly studied by innumerable rising American politicians, lawyers, and preachers. It is easy to understand that no minister's library could have been complete without a copy of Blair.

On the long-term effects of this widespread study of Blair and his fellow Scottish rhetoricians one may only speculate. The tradition of political oratory in America must owe much to it; and it is probably true that the general level of American writing was improved by it. But it is difficult not to believe that about this study of English composition, in terms of taste and correctness, there was something severely limiting. In America, as in Scotland, its effects, at least from the point of view of potential, native, linguistic vitality, were probably slightly debilitating. It is not, after all, without significance that in 1781, in his article in the *Pennsylvania Journal*, Witherspoon denounced the American language and coined the term 'Americanism', by analogy with 'Scotticism'. The study of the Scottish rhetoricians seems to me to lie behind a great deal of the genteel tradition in American writing and criticism: its emphasis upon smoothness, elegance, and correctness in style, and its aversion to anything with a vernacular flavour. One might go so far as to say that the study of rhetoric in schools and colleges impeded the development of a native American literary idiom.[33] In any event, the popularity of Blair represents the penetration into all levels of educated society of the special North British pre-occupation with taste and style, present in the first instance in the courses taught by men such as Nisbet and Witherspoon.[34]

Republication in America, although the most important, was not the only means through which the works of the North Britons were made available to American readers. After the Revolution American colleges continued to receive gifts of books from Scottish donors, sometimes from the same individuals who had sent over books in the pre-Revolutionary period. Immediately after the war, the Revd John Erskine, for example, resumed his gift-giving habit. On 6 September 1785, Ezra Stiles noted in his diary: 'This Aft. I rec^d a letter from that aged & learned Divine the Revd Jno Erskine, D.D. one of the Ministers of Edinburgh dated 29th Jany last with a Present of 20 Volumes of Books for our Coll. Library, & others for myself. The Books came safe.'[35] Soon afterwards, on 26 November, he wrote: 'Yesterday I rec^d a Letter dated 19 June past with a Packet of Books from Rev. Dr. Jno Erskine of Edinburg.'[36] Entries of a similar kind occur on 5 January 1786, 11 August 1786, 8 November 1787, 21 February 1788, 23 March 1789, 8 January 1791, and 8 November 1791.[37] Harvard received books from Erskine in 1765, 1776, 1771, 1784, and 1791, and Ebenezer Baldwin's *Annals of Yale College to 1831* states that between 1788 and 1795, Dr Erskine contributed 120 volumes to the college library.[38] Unfortunately none of these volumes are specified, but it is reasonable to suppose that included among them were some of the distinguished works of Scotland's own eighteenth century thinkers.

The Princeton library had suffered severely during the Revolution, especially during the period in which Nassau Hall had been occupied by the British and American forces in turn. From a letter which Dr Witherspoon wrote to the Earl of Buchan on 24 May 1788, we learn that Scottish books had been among those lost. Witherspoon describes his satisfaction at the appointment of Walter Minto, a product of the University of Edinburgh, and another protégé of Buchan, to the professorship of mathematics in the College (Minto had been another Scottish supporter of American Independence)[39] and then takes up the topic of the library:

> I mentioned to Dr. Erskine my Intention of applying to the many Scot Authors now in Life with the greatest part of whom I was personaly acquainted in early Life begging that they would present our College Library with their Works this would be a great addition to our Stock and is the more needed that Several of them which we had bought before the War were carried off so that except what is in my own Library I do not recollect that we have any of them at all.... By a Letter just received from Dr. Erskine I find he has communicated this Decision [to obtain the books through friends and agents] to

Your Lordship and that you have been so kind as to offer to apply to some that I have not named I will therefore take the Liberty of regarding your Lordship's good Offices in this Matter in Concurrence with Dr. Erskine not only in Edin but elsewhere.[40]

The success which this appeal met with is uncertain, but it is unlikely that it could have been promoted by Erskine, Buchan, and their friends, without considerable effect. Certainly, in 1802, when the interior of Nassau Hall was destroyed by fire, Scottish interest and concern were again demonstrated by donations of books often precisely of the kind suggested in Witherspoon's letter. Dr Erskine sent twenty works of theology and history; the Revd Dr Jamieson of Edinburgh and the Revd Dr Dick of Glasgow sent copies of their own works; William Creech, who had been so bitter in 1783, sent eleven volumes, mainly theological in character; Professor Dalzel sent a copy of his standard Greek textbook, *Collectania Majora*; the Revd Mr Alison donated a copy of his well-known *Essays on the Nature and Principles of Taste*; and Professor Dugald Stewart gave his *Elements of the Philosophy of the Human Mind*, his *Life of Dr Reid*, and Reid's own *Inquiry into the Human Mind*. With these are listed only five works from English donors. Significantly, two Bostonians donated copies of Kames's *Elements of Criticism*.[41]

The widespread study and circulation of the works of the North Britons undoubtedly had some effect on the American view of Scotland.[42] Although it is difficult to determine what exactly constitutes evidence in this connection, it seems reasonably clear that by the opening of the nineteenth century constant attention to Scottish authors and texts had produced general recognition of Scotland's intellectual achievements in the previous century. If the literary periodicals of the day are looked upon as useful indices of what educated opinion was thinking and saying then the reputations of leading members of the Scottish intellectual world were by then firmly established in America. No doubt as a result, Scotland itself was commonly associated with a notion of intellectual distinction.

American critics confidently identified Hume and Robertson as the great historians of the eighteenth century. In the *Brief Retrospect*, having mentioned the historical writings of Smollett, Miller goes on:

Dr. Smollett was followed by his countryman Mr. Hume, who made trial of his distinguished powers in the same field, and with splendid success. He far excelled all his predecessors in beauty and excellence of historical style, and at once raised the character of his country, in this branch of literature, to a very high rank.[43]

The manner in which Miller automatically equates individual success with national prestige is noteworthy. Hume, Miller continues, was almost immediately followed by William Robertson:

> Soon after Mr. Hume's publication, his countryman and con-temporary, Dr. Robertson, gave to the public his *History of Scotland*, which was followed by the *History of Charles V* and the *History of America*. This gentleman unquestionably deserves a place among the greatest historians of the age, if he does not occupy the very first station. Though his narrative is not equal to Mr. Hume's in ease and spirit, yet he exceeds him in uniform purity, dignity, and elegance of diction. In these respects Dr. Robertson may be pronounced to stand at the head of all modern historians, and perhaps to have no superior of any age.[44]

Hume and Robertson were frequently linked in discussions of historians, and a recurring feature, as here, is the emphasis on their styles. In 1806, such a discussion appeared in the *Port Folio*, for long the leading American literary journal: Hume, despite his excel-lencies, 'is surpassed by Robertson, who in his *History of Scotland*, his first, and, in our opinion, his happiest production, has exhibited a model of English composition superior to the style of any of his countrymen'.[45] Again, in 1809, another article in the same magazine praised Hume at considerable length, quoted Gibbon on the debt he owed to both Hume and Robertson, and defended Smollett from French criticisms.[46] In 1804, Brockden Brown's *Literary Magazine* had published a lengthy biographical article on Robertson.[47]

As early as 1801 the *Port Folio* observed that 'it is very fashionable, among young students, to read the histories of Dr. Robertson', and recommended that the *History of Scotland* should not be neglected in favour of those of *Charles V* and *America*.[48] But the best evidence of the American popularity of Hume and Robertson is supplied by an article which appeared in the *North American Review*, the most authoritative of all such American journals, in the year 1832. The subject under discussion is the controversial one of the character of Mary Queen of Scots. The writer refers to the widespread influence of the histories of both Hume and Robertson:

No historian has been more read than Robertson in this country, though now the world begins to acquiesce in Johnson's opinion, that 'he would be crushed by his own weight.' Hume, too, another great enemy of Mary, has exercised an unbounded influence over American readers, insomuch, that several years ago, the youth of our country, though sworn friends of freedom, were almost unanimous in favor of the unfortunate but usurping Charles, and were ready to justify transactions in the English history, which were most decidedly opposed to their own feelings and opinions.[49]

Of the Scottish philosophers, it was Dugald Stewart who received most attention, though his debt to the whole 'Scottish School' was generally recognised. Stewart was not in fact an original philosophical thinker: he may fairly be seen as a more elegant and polished Thomas Reid. American familiarity with these and other Scottish thinkers often seems to be taken for granted and in the case of writers who had almost certainly themselves been trained in the Scottish philosophic school, this is easy to understand. Certainly, even if other evidence were lacking, American interest in, and study of Reid, Hume, Stewart, and Brown could be confidently asserted from the familiarity and readiness with which, from early in the nineteenth century, these philosophers are referred to and discussed in magazines and reviews.

Much of the praise that Stewart received rested on the beauty of his language and style, a beauty which characterised both his public lectures and his writings. In 1811, the *American Review*, edited by Robert Walsh, published some 'Letters on France and England', written by a young American who had resided for some years in both countries. Among these occurs a comparison between the professor of history and moral philosophy of the college of France and Professor Dugald Stewart, 'whose lectures I attended in Scotland'. 'I cannot recollect, or mention,' wrote the young American, 'the official exhibitions of Dugald Stewart to whom I allude, without feelings of the most enthusiastic respect, and of the liveliest gratitude. I have never found any public speaker, in any situation, more eloquent in manner and in language, and never have been made to feel more sensibly, by any orator, the dignity of human knowledge,—the beauty of human genius—or the elevation of human virtue.'[50] A few months later, the same magazine discussed Stewart's *Philosophical Essays* at length. The *Edinburgh Review*'s praise of the book, 'this new and illustrious proof, of the unrivalled genius and learning of their countryman', is cited, and a long extract on the subject of taste printed.[51] A long essay on the sublime in the *Port Folio* in 1812 is concerned mainly with Stewart, though Blair and Kames are also brought into the discussion.[52] In 1815, an article in the *Analectic Magazine* discussed at length the criticisms of Stewart which had recently appeared in the London *Quarterly Review*. The American writer opens his article thus: 'In common with many of our countrymen we had adopted the metaphysical doctrines of Dugald Stewart', and goes on to defend the Scottish philosopher from the *Quarterly*'s attack.[53] Notices of Stewart's publications, either original, or reprinted from the British reviews, became standard features in the American magazines.[54] Evidence of his enduring popularity is provided by two comments from the *North American Review*. An article in 1824, declared that 'There have been eight editions, comprising 7500 copies of Stewart's Philosophy published here since its first appearance in Europe thirty years ago.'[55] An essay written in 1830 discussing Stewart and the rest of the Scottish school offered an explanation of this popularity:

> Hume was perhaps superior in taste as well as natural acuteness and sagacity to Stewart; but such were the strange aberrations of his intellect, when applied to the study of metaphysics and morals, that his works on these subjects have little or no value, excepting as curious indications of the progress of learning, and of its state at a particular period. Reid, the founder of the Edinburgh school, was deficient in the graces of manner, which belonged to his pupil, who is, therefore, on the whole, at present and will probably long remain, among English authors, the most popular professor of moral science.[56]

Stewart's successor as professor of moral philosophy at Edinburgh was Thomas Brown. During his lifetime, Brown's fame outside Edinburgh did not compare with that of his distinguished predecessor; after the posthumous publication of his lectures, however, his reputation suddenly increased. According to McCosh the publication of his lectures 'excited an interest wherever the English language is spoken, quite equal to that awakened by the living lecturer among the students of Edinburgh. They continued for twenty years to have a popularity in the British dominions and in the United States greater than any philosophical works ever enjoyed before.'[57] In 1821, a *North American Review* article on a book by Brown opened with the comment that, 'The philosophy of the late lamented Dr. Brown is scarcely known in this country'. 'It was presumed,' the article goes on, 'that considerable interest would attach among us to the speculations of the successor of Dugald Stewart, whose own work on the Mind has passed, we believe, through as many editions in the United States as in Great Britain, and who is well known, on becoming *emeritus*, to have warmly recommended Dr. Brown to the chair of moral philosophy in the university of Edinburgh.'[58]

Three years later, however, in a discussion in the *Review* of Brown's *Philosophy of the Mind*, the introduction of 'the metaphysical, or rather physiological portion of Dr. Brown's *Lectures…* as a classical manual at Harvard University' is noted.[59] In the next year, 1825, another article on Brown's character and writings was described as the work of 'an American correspondent' who 'has obligingly furnished us with the following interesting particulars, which the numerous admirers of Dr. Brown in this country will receive much pleasure in perusing.'[60] Finally, an article in the same journal in 1829, discussing the 'History of Intellectual Philosophy', referred at length to Hume and the Scotch school: Reid, Stewart, Adam Smith, and Brown, 'whose "Lectures" have attracted a good deal of attention in this country.'[61]

References to, and discussions of, Kames and Blair in the reviews and journals are perhaps not quite as frequent as one might expect; but it is not impossible that this is, in fact, a reflection of their great popularity. A late review of a new edition of Kames suggests that this is so: 'The current value which a continued use, during a long series of years, has stamped upon Lord Kaimes' [*sic*] *Elements of Criticism*, renders any commendation on our part, altogether superfluous.'[62] But evidence of Blair's fame and popularity from an early date is not entirely lacking. He is quoted in the *American Museum* in 1787 in an attack on Johnson's language: twelve years later, an article on style in the *Monthly Magazine* refers to his work as 'in many respects superficial and inaccurate', but 'greatly and deservedly popular'.[63] Brockden Brown's *Literary Magazine* published a sketch of Blair's life in 1806, and in 1815 there appeared in the *Analectic Magazine* a long review of the *Life of Blair* by John Hill.[64] Having discussed the decline of Blair's reputation as a sermon-writer, the article turned to his criticism suggesting that 'As a critical writer, Dr. Blair has suffered much less from the lapse of years. His lectures have found their place, and established their character, among a highly respectable rank of books, and will always be esteemed valuable as an exercise of correct taste, and an accumulation of good sense, on the various branches of the art of speaking and writing.'[65] An article in the *American Quarterly Observer* in 1833, on the 'Qualifications of a Critic', shows that Blair and Kames are still the authorities to agree or disagree with,[66] while Blair's enduring reputation is confirmed by an article in the *Knickerbocker Magazine* in the same year:

> Dr. Blair is by far the best of modern writers on Rhetoric and Belles Lettres. No latent beauty, or striking thought in the countless productions of ancient and modern orators, has escaped his profound research, or been unperceived by his cultivated taste. And the peculiarities of every style, he has elucidated with a happiness of diction, and propriety of remark, which has long placed his great work decidedly at the head of every similar production.[67]

Apart from this growth of individual reputation, there is no doubt that the widespread circulation of the works of the North Britons had produced in America, by about 1800, a deep respect for Scotland's general intellectual eminence. Probably the earliest expression of this respect occurred in 1791, when the *American Museum* reprinted from an English source, an article surveying English literature in the eighteenth century. A section of this article was devoted to a lengthy summary of the contributions of the North Britons:

> This survey of things, brief as it was intended to be, would be imperfect, if some notice were not taken of the distinguished figure made by the writers of Scotland during this period, and especially in the latter part of it, when a wonderful ardour for literary eminence, and elegant composition, animated the gentlemen who inhabited that division of the united kingdoms. In philosophy Maclaurin has been already mentioned; and Simpson [*sic*] might be added in mathematics. Blackwell might justly have been celebrated for his depth in ancient literature, if he had not disgraced it by pedantry and affectation. The Scottish authors have particularly applied themselves to metaphysical disquisitions, and the cultivation of sentimental ethics. The turn begun by Hutcheson was greatly improved, and appeared in

many ingenious productions, by which the knowledge of the principles and affections of the human mind, has been highly promoted. In specifying Hume, Lord Kaims [*sic*], Reid, and Adam Smith, they are only mentioned historically, without any enquiry how far their respective systems are founded in truth.... The progress of society and manners has, likewise, been deeply investigated by the writers of North Britain. To North Britain, also, we are indebted for Hume and Robertson, our two classic historians.... In short, Scotland had its full share in contributing to the literary glory of the age.[68]

Similar laudatory references to the achievements of the North Britons became increasingly common, often with the implication that much of what has been said here was soon taken for granted. In 1799, an article on style in the *Monthly Magazine* remarked that 'the most popular British writers are natives of Scotland';[69] in 1803, a biographical notice of Henry Mackenzie in the *Port Folio* alluded to the achievements of the North Britons and to the successes of *Douglas* and *Ossian*;[70] a similar notice of William Wilkie, author of the forgotten epic the *Epigoniad*, later in the same year, referred again to the distinguished names in the North British circle;[71] in 1806, the *Port Folio*, mentioned 'the eminent Scotch literati, Robertson, Hume, Millar, Adam Smith, Ferguson, Reid, Blair and Stewart....'[72] And in a biographical sketch of Alexander Carlyle in the same year, reference was once again made to the literary circles of Edinburgh and to 'that illustrious class of cotemporaries [of Carlyle] who adorned the last age of Scottish literature.'[73]

Such allusion, comment and criticism make it clear that by the end of the eighteenth century Scotland had come to be recognised in America as a centre of learning. This reputation in turn led to the use of Scotland as a standard by which to measure the achievements of other countries—particularly in the field of education.[74] The coupling of respect for the Scottish educational system with the apparent contrast between the barrenness of Scotland's natural resources and her intellectual distinction, became an American commonplace. It occurred as early as 1805 in Brown's *Literary Magazine*:

> It is somewhat remarkable, that in those civilized countries whose climate is most cheerless, and soil most rude, knowledge and genuine refinement should be more thoroughly established, and more extensively diffused than elsewhere. Thus, in Europe,

if we would seek for the greatest and most general intellectual cultivation we must not turn our eyes to Italy, or Portugal, or Spain, and not even to Hungary, Provence, or South Britain, but to the frosty regions of Denmark and Sweden, and especially to the bleak hills of Scotland. The establishments for public education in Scotland, seem to excel those of all other nations, not only in their methods of instruction, but in their number and diffusion.[75]

The article goes on to draw an unfavourable comparison between the state of education in Pennsylvania and in Scotland. But the Scottish educational system had been offered as a model for Americans at an even earlier date. In 1786, Benjamin Rush had published a pamphlet on the educational policy to be followed in Pennsylvania which was afterwards reprinted in the *Scots Magazine*.[76] Rush, whose pamphlet demonstrates the kind of enduring influence that might result from a period of study in Scotland, having compared Oxford and Cambridge most unfavourably with the Scottish universities, advocated the establishment of 'free schools' throughout the state after the Scottish example. Rush also noticed the similarity between the systems adopted in Scotland and New England which was to be commented on by many later writers. A writer on American education in the *Analectic Magazine*, in 1813, declared that it was:

> the just pride of our countrymen that an opportunity of acquiring a good education is in no other part of the world so common, or so easy of access. The disciples of Calvin introduced into Scotland, Switzerland and Connecticut, nearly at the same time, a system of education, accessible to persons in every situation of life, which is still the pride and boast of these countries.[77]

Similar comparisons, often linked with remarks on the likeness in character and bearing between the New Englanders and the Scots, became common in the books of Scottish travellers in America.[78]

These evidences of American awareness of Scotland's intellectual distinction, beginning before the end of the eighteenth century, and increasing through the early decades of the nineteenth, reflect the depth of the penetration by the North Britons, and their successors in the second generation of the Scottish intellectual movement, into America's intellectual life. Few of the references quoted above suggest only a formal, detached admiration; the suggestion of a familiarity, shared by the writer and his readers, is much stronger. It is as though Robertson, Hume, Kames, Blair, and Stewart have become domesticated upon the American scene. When this situation is viewed in relation to that which was largely responsible for producing it—the widespread study of these and other Scottish authors in college and university, already begun in 1783, and steadily increasing in the following decades—then it is clear that the years before the Revolution only prepared the way for this development. Certainly the pre-Revolutionary situation ensured that Scottish influences should be brought to bear on America; but it is in the post-Revolutionary period that the impact of the Scottish Enlightenment upon America is consolidated and expanded. Even so it is only after 1800 that American recognition of Scottish intellectual distinction becomes fully evident, and that recognition itself may in part have been due to the new wave of Scottish influence, literary, intellectual, and in a sense political, which began to make itself felt in America in the first decade of the nineteenth century.

The period between 1800 and 1830 was not a good one in relations between Great Britain and America; in a way, the War of 1812 can be seen as no more than a symptom of the ill-feeling between the two countries, which existed on all levels. The part that the *Edinburgh Review*, and later, *Blackwood's Magazine*, played in the extremely bitter intellectual and cultural debate carried on in this period between the countries, though its nature remains somewhat controversial, has always been recognised. (This debate has sometimes been referred to as the 'literary quarrel', and from this point I shall so describe it.) But whether American readers felt that the Scottish periodicals were friendly or hostile to their country is in the end scarcely relevant. The major point is that in America, just as in Great Britain, the reviews represented a new and dominant influence on the intellectual and literary world in the early decades of the nineteenth century. Admired or despised, everywhere they were read. No eighteenth century journal ever rivalled the prestige and authority so quickly accorded to the *Edinburgh Review* and perhaps no similar periodical of a later period so dominated the intellectual life of its time. American readers were no doubt particularly interested in certain topics to which the reviews frequently returned.

And it is of course around these topics that the literary quarrel raged:
the state of American literature and culture; the reports of British
travellers in America; and political relations between Great Britain
and America. But concentration on these lively topics should not
make us forget that for the reader in America, as elsewhere, they
represented only a fraction of the general intellectual sustenance that
the great reviews provided.

After the appearance of the first number of the *Edinburgh Review*,
on 10 October 1802, in its blue and buff covers—the colours of the
uniform of George Washington, as well as of the followers of Fox
—Francis Jeffrey became permanent editor of the magazine. Jeffrey
and his co-founders, Henry Brougham, and the Revd Sydney Smith,
were astonished by the immediate, overwhelming success of their
venture. Jeffrey in particular had been very pessimistic about the
prospects of any kind of favourable reception. 'The success,'
Brougham wrote, 'was far beyond any of our expectations. It was
so great Jeffrey was utterly dumbfounded.'[79] Contemporaries have
recorded their impressions of the impact of the first number.
Cockburn asserted that the effect was 'electrical'. 'And instead of
expiring as many wished, in their first effort, the force of the shock
was increased on each subsequent discharge. It is impossible for
those who did not live at the time, and in the heart of the scene, to
feel, or almost to understand the impression made by the new
luminary, or the anxieties with which its motions were observed'.[80]
Mrs Fletcher concurs: 'I, who knew Edinburgh both before and
after the appearance of the Edinburgh Review, can bear witness to
the electrical effects of its publication on the public mind, and to the
large and good results in a political sense that followed its
circulation'.[81] Jeffrey's doubts must have been entirely allayed by
this instantaneous success; by the middle of 1803, he was already
interested in the possibility of an American circulation for his
journal. On 2 July of that year, he wrote to his brother, John Jeffrey,
who was in business in Boston: 'I am glad you have got our Review,
and that you like it ... I wish you would try if you can *répandre* us
upon your continent, and use what interest you can with the literati,
or rather with the booksellers of New York and Philadelphia.'[82]

What may one deduce from these few lines? The phrasing of 'I
am glad you have got our Review', perhaps suggests that John Jeffrey
had acquired his copy independently rather than that he had received
a copy specially sent to him by his brother. It is interesting that

Jeffrey does not mention the Boston booksellers. Could it be that some arrangement had already been made with them? In any event there is ample evidence of the speed with which the *Edinburgh Review* began to be read in America. Native literary magazines began to reprint sections of articles from the *Review* within a year or two of its initial publication.[83] Such reprinting, as it developed, would in itself have ensured that the *Review*'s influence would soon have made itself felt. But American interest in the Scottish review was not to be satisfied by the reprinting of selected articles by local periodicals. Within a few years the *Edinburgh Review* was being reprinted entire in New York and Boston. The exact date at which such reprinting began is difficult to establish, but Ezra Sargeant of New York probably began publication in 1810.[84] A year or two later the work of publication was taken over by the firm of Eastburn, Kirk and Company. John Duncan, who was in New York in 1817, records that both the *Edinburgh* and *Quarterly Reviews* were regularly reprinted there, while another British traveller, Henry Fearon, confirms this. 'The "Edinburgh" and "Quarterly Reviews",' wrote Fearon, 'are reprinted by Messrs. Kirk and Mercein of this city.'[85] In 1816 the firm of Kirk and Mercein published a *General Index* to the *Edinburgh Review* for the period from 1802 onwards—which certainly suggest that complete runs of the periodical were fairly generally available in America.[86] From a speech of C. J. Ingersoll, delivered in 1823, we know that the American circulation of the review was then as high as four thousand copies—equalling that of the *North American Review*, the best of the native journals.[87] Such a figure strengthens one's impression that the *Edinburgh Review* was available to, and was probably read by, the majority of those who composed America's intellectual and literary world.

One consequence of its American circulation was deep and lasting American respect for the *Edinburgh Review*.[88] The clearest evidence of that respect, however, is to be found not in expressions of opinions by individuals or eulogies in contemporary periodicals—significant of course as these are—but in a sequence of events both highly romantic and dramatic. In the summer of 1810, Mrs Archibald Fletcher took a country house near Lasswade, on the River Esk, not far from Edinburgh.[89] It was here, through Mrs Craig Millar, that she met Monsieur and Madame Simond and their niece, Charlotte Wilkes. Madame Simond was an American from New York; Charlotte was the daughter of Charles Wilkes, brother of Madame

Simond. It was probably through Mrs Fletcher or her friend Mrs Millar, that Francis Jeffrey met Charlotte in the same summer. Jeffrey's first wife had died in 1805 and an attachment soon developed between Miss Wilkes of New York and the famous editor of the Scottish journal. At the end of the summer, Miss Wilkes returned to New York, but on 29 August 1813, Jeffrey sailed for America, and in January, 1814, returned home with Charlotte as his bride. Though his trip took place, of course, while Britain and the United States were at war, the romantic visit of the editor of the *Edinburgh Review* did not pass unnoticed.

Henry Brevoort, friend and correspondent of Washington Irving, in London at this time, wrote to Irving on the subject of Jeffrey's impending American visit. Brevoort had not been much impressed by Jeffrey at the beginning of their acquaintance. Writing to Irving from Edinburgh on 9 December 1812, he suggested that 'this little inky Hector', was entirely ignorant of the true condition of America:

> His opinion of the Society in NY & Philad: is singularly ludicrous; I marvel that the polished Town of Wapping was not coupled with Glasgow & Manchester, as rivalling us in elegance.—The chief source of his American intelligence is a brother, who resided a number of years in Boston, moving in a sphere which I should judge authorises his humble opinions of American civilization.[90]

Brevoort hardly writes here in the best tradition of American democracy, but further contact was to change at least his general estimate of Jeffrey's character. On 24 June 1813, he wrote to Irving from London, mentioning Jeffrey's impending departure for America, and proceeding:

> I am deeply indebted to him, both for his hospitality to me in Edinb: as well as for the letters he gave me to persons in London; I have endeavoured to repay him by giving him a letter to you, one to Mr Hoffman, one to our friend Mrs. Renwick (who is his namesake) besides many others to different parts of America—.... You will find him full of the most precise as well universal knowledge of men & things on this side the Water, which he will delight to communicate as copiously as you please.... It is essential that Jeffrey may imbibe a just estimate of the U States & its inhabitants, he goes out strongly biassed in our favor, and the influence of his good opinion

upon his return to this Country would go far to efface the calumnies & the absurdities that have been laid to our charge by ignorant travellers.[91]

An account of Jeffrey's impending visit duly appeared in the *Analectic Magazine*, of which Irving was then editor. The version made public also emphasised the need to impress such a visitor as favourably as possible:

> We understand that Mr. Jeffrey, the celebrated editor of the *Edinburgh Review*, is about to visit this country, on business relative to the estate of a brother lately deceased at Boston. He was to sail in the ship Hercules, for Boston, whose arrival is daily expected. It is his intention also to visit our principal cities, and we trust that every facility will be given, both by government and individuals, to make his tour satisfactory and agreeable. To the representations of a man of Mr. Jeffrey's talents, information and literary influence, we may look with confidence for having this country vindicated from many of the gross aspersions that have been cast upon it, by narrow-minded or hireling travel writers. It is the interest of both nations to have a proper knowledge and estimation of each other, and we think that Mr. J. has hitherto in his writings shown a more candid and liberal disposition towards us, than most of his cotemporaries.[92]

Jeffrey was in fact welcomed to America as a very important person indeed. If Henry Tuckerman's account, written at mid-century, is to be relied on, Jeffrey was met on his arrival in New York by representatives of the city's intellectual life. 'One cool morning,' writes Tuckerman, 'during our last war with England, a group of Knickerbocker *savans* might have been seen on the Battery, eagerly watching the approach of a vessel.' If there is an element of the fanciful in Tuckerman's description of the event, his account of the motives which had occasioned it is convincing. 'The learned coterie,' he writes, who eagerly greeted Francis Jeffrey, 'beheld in him the incarnation of mental vigour, wit, knowledge, and pleasantry, which, under the name of the Edinburgh Review, had been their chief intellectual repast for several preceding years.'[93] Jeffrey's treatment during his stay in America was to bear out the implications of such a welcome. In Washington he met both President Madison and James Monroe, then Secretary of State; with them he discussed the war, and in particular, the controversial subject of the right of search of ships. Rather than the case of the British opposition, which he had argued in the *Review*, Jeffrey apparently presented that of the British government in these disputes. Lord Cockburn suggests that '... he seems to have thought that it would be paltry not to stand by his country, before an enemy who had him in his power'.[94] That the editor of a British literary magazine should be treated in such a way, should be admitted to the highest levels of what was, at the time, an enemy's executive power, is an ideal indication of the stature and prestige by then achieved by the magazine of which he was head. It is perhaps equally significant that Brevoort, and the *Analectic*, could see producing a good impression on Jeffrey as somehow capable of changing the whole course of British–American cultural relations.

The respect for the *Edinburgh Review* reflected by this attitude towards its editor had of course existed in America for many years before Jeffrey's visit and it continued to be present for many years after that journey. In 1809, in reprinting a review from the Edinburgh journal, the *Port Folio* observed that it was 'written with the usual spirit and sagacity by which that publication is remarkably distinguished'.[95] Next year it referred to 'a recent number of that far famed journal the Edinburgh Review, *which acquires new vigour as it proceeds*'.[96] In the same year, 1810, in discussing *English Bards and Scotch Reviewers*, it mentioned 'the Caledonian champion Jeffreys' who 'has long been known as the leading editor of the far famed and far dreaded Edinburgh Review.'[97] An article of a more critical kind, entitled 'Strictures on the Edinburgh Review', appeared in the *Port Folio* in 1812, but there is still no question of the status of the Edinburgh reviewers: they 'confessedly stand at the very head of the British critics'.[98]

By the 1820s, American writers were in a position to look back and see the importance and influence of the *Edinburgh Review* in literary history. An article in the *Port Folio*, in 1820, asserted that 'It may truly be said, that this publication, which commenced its career in 1803, forms an epoch in literary history, of no ordinary magnitude, since, if we mistake not, periodical criticism in general, has been much altered since that time; most of the old journals having been more or less remoulded according to the plan of the *Edinburgh Review*.'[99] A year earlier, an article in the *Analectic Magazine*, on both the *Edinburgh* and *Quarterly Reviews*, had referred to Henry Brougham's political activities on behalf of America, and had described the *Edinburgh* in terms that were much more than respectful. 'The Edinburgh Review,' it noted, 'now extends to the sixtieth number; perhaps this voluminous work contains more original views in every department of human knowledge—a greater display of genius and learning—a more complete history of the progress of literature in the 19th century, than has ever been given to the world, in any age or country.'[100] Again, in 1823, in his book *Randolph*, the Baltimore novelist and editor John Neal, author too of a series of articles on American culture published in *Blackwood's Magazine* between 1824 and 1825, wrote of the influence and prestige of the *Review* in America: 'It is a work of great influence here; and, though I defy you to point out a page of English, in the last two volumes,—unpolluted with jargon, barbarism, or provincialism, yet it is one of our standards.'[101]

Probably the clearest indication of the *Edinburgh Review*'s influence in America is referred to by the article in the *Port Folio* in 1820: the remoulding of periodicals according to its pattern. The *North American Review*, founded in Boston in 1815, was from the outset clearly modelled after the *Edinburgh*. In a footnote to an article on Irving's *Sketch Book*, in 1820, the Scottish journal recognised its off-spring:

> ...we have lately received two numbers...of *The North American Review, or Miscellaneous Journal*, published quarterly at Boston, which appears to us to be by far the best and most promising production of the press of that country that has ever come to our hands. It is written with great spirit, learning and ability, on a great variety of subjects; and abounds with profound and original discussions on the most interesting topics. Though abundantly patriotic, or rather national, there is nothing offensive or absolutely unreasonable in the tone of its politics; and no very reprehensible marks either of national partialities or antipathies.... It is a proud thing for *us* to see Quarterly Reviews propagating both truths and original speculations in all quarters of the world; and, when we grow old and stupid ourselves, we hope still to be honoured in the talents and merits of those heirs of our principles, and children of our example.[102]

The *American Review*, eight numbers of which were published in Philadelphia between 1811 and 1812, under the editorship of Robert

Walsh, was the first 'Scottish' quarterly to appear in America.[103] Like the *Analectic Magazine*, founded in 1813, both in format and manner, it was closely akin to its Scottish original. More significant, however, than the format of these American periodicals is the nature of the literary discussion that they reveal. Here again the influence of the *Edinburgh Review* is apparent. But caution has to be exercised in this connection. As Professor Charvat has noted, as a result of the assimilation into American education and intellectual life of so much of Scottish thought, most of the leading American critics had themselves been trained in the Scottish philosophical and aesthetic tradition and so, like the Scottish critics, tended to treat literature from the point of view of that tradition.

Apart from its effect in specific areas, there can be no doubt that the influence of the *Edinburgh Review* in general helped to sharpen American awareness of the intellectual eminence of both the city and the country of its origin. What should be recalled at this point are the arguments and evidence adduced earlier on the spirit of nationalism present in both the *Edinburgh Review*, and later, *Blackwood's Magazine*. The Scottish magazines were identified as exactly that by most Americans. Such was their prestige, in fact, that the concept of the 'Scotch Critics' or 'Scotch Reviewers' became firmly engraved on the American mind. Commenting on *Paul Clifford*, the novel by Bulwer Lytton, in 1830, the *American Monthly Magazine* said: 'Mr. Bulwer seems to think Scotchmen and critics are the same thing, using the two words alternately; and we believe it is true that every periodical of consequence in great Britain is edited by one of that nation. They are the right material for it.'[104] So too when Robert Walsh, in his *Appeal from the Judgements of Great Britain* (1819), assailed the contributors to the *Edinburgh Review*, he distinguished them throughout as the 'Scottish critics'.

It is their criticisms of America that bring upon the Edinburgh reviewers the full fury of Walsh's attack. No other subject of course could possibly have aroused an equally passionate interest in America. An extraordinary self-consciousness has always charac-terised American culture. In the early decades of the republic's existence it took the form of an intense preoccupation with any European expression of opinion or comment on the American experiment. That the *Edinburgh* and *Blackwood's* both frequently returned to the question of America ensured that they would be read and re-read in America. Such attentiveness to foreign opinion perhaps suggests a sensitivity to criticism, and in fact American readers were often very sensitive indeed. It is true that the *Edinburgh Review* did not always show much consideration for the delicacies of American feeling; hence it is unsurprising that the passions it excited in its American readers were sometimes those of anger and outraged resentment. But the furore aroused by some caustic and sarcastic remarks should not now be allowed to mislead us. The truth of the matter is that 'America is appreciated, understood, and treated fairly by the Edinburgh Review'.[105]

This conclusion may well come as something of a surprise; but a conclusion of any other kind would have created a much greater problem.[106] Traditional Scottish interest in America was still strong enough in 1802 to guarantee that no new magazine could afford to ignore American affairs; and that an organ of liberal opinion, such as the *Edinburgh Review*, should have demonstrated real hostility towards the United States was as inconceivable in 1802 or later, as it would have been for *The Bee* in the 1790s or any other journal of similar principles published in Scotland since 1783.[107] Of course the *Review*'s political opponents, such as the writers in *Blackwood's*, were always ready to suggest that it was their Whig principles alone which made the Edinburgh reviewers adopt a friendly attitude towards America. But if this was hypocrisy, then it was hypocrisy with a history stretching back to the days of the American War. The Edinburgh reviewers had no need, as their opponents claimed, to 'take up' America, for whatever purpose; respect for America had always been an integral part of the Scottish liberal tradition to which they belonged.

Respect for America is quite clear in the stand that the *Edinburgh Review* takes on the major issues of the literary quarrel: American culture, British travellers in America, and the political situation. As far as politics is concerned, the *Review* is certainly prepared to draw relevant contemporary conclusions from the errors of British policy in the Revolutionary period. In a discussion of biographies of Washington in 1808 reference is made to the American War:

> The sanguine people of this country would do well, though the retrospect cannot be pleasing, sometimes to turn back their thoughts upon this unhappy contest,—to recollect, that measures, triumphantly voted wise and just and vigorous, proved only wasteful folly,—that a spirit of arrogant domin- ation, and heedless indifference to the rights of others, lost the

wing of an empire,—that there may be abounding loyalty, with very deficient prudence,—and that counsels called factious, because opposed to the wishes of the court, may, when misfortune shall have silenced both sycophancy and prejudice, come to be acknowledged as the oracles of wisdom.[108]

But the definitive articles for the *Review*'s own political attitude towards the United States are those published in 1812 and 1814, on the subject of 'War with America'. The first article suggests that the war had arisen, not out of any genuine sense of grievance, but out of widespread, disreputable, anti-American sentiment. It is widely supported because the Americans are less esteemed and more un-popular 'than the base and bigotted Portugueze, or the ferocious and ignorant Russians'; the only basis for such adverse feelings is that arising out of assertions of the superiority of British culture over American: 'Their manners, it seems, are not agreeable:—society with them is not on a good footing:—and, upon the whole, they are far from being so polite and well-bred as might be desired'.[109] Nothing can equal 'the unexampled and unnatural folly of this war between men of the same kindred and tongue—the only two free nations that are now left in the world....'[110] In repeating these sentiments, the 1814 article returns to the question of American unpopularity:

> Why the Americans are disliked in this country, we have never been able to understand.... They are brave, and boastful, and national, and factious like ourselves;—about as polished as 99 in 100 of our own countrymen in the upper rank—and at least as moral and well educated in the lower.... We see nothing then from which we can suppose this prevailing dislike of them to originate, but a secret grudge at them for having asserted, and manfully vindicated, their independence. This, however, is too unworthy a feeling to be avowed; and the very imputation of it should stimulate us to overcome the prejudices by which it is suggested.[111]

The *Review* was well aware that ironies of this kind were unlikely to have much effect on stalwart representatives of Tory prejudice against America. For the defenders of the status quo in England, the success of republican America was a bitter pill indeed; hence their excesses of pleasure at any kind of adverse criticism made by no matter whom upon America. In a review of Birkbeck's *Notes on America*, in 1818, direct reference is made to this group and their eccentricities:

> They who hate America, as it were, personally; who meanly regard with jealousy every step she advances in renown, or foolishly view with apprehension each accession to her power, or ridiculously consider all that she gains of wealth as taken from England—this class of reasoners (if the term may be so applied) can with difficulty conceal their dismay at the testimony borne by Mr. Birkbeck, to the prodigious rapidity with which that marvellous community is advancing in every direction.[112]

The generally favourable attitude towards America revealed in passages such as these is maintained in the *Edinburgh Review*'s contributions to the many bitter controversies which developed out of the published accounts of British travellers in America. In the travel literature were brought together all aspects of the cultural and social dispute between the two countries, with the result that it became the focal point of the entire literary quarrel. After its first review of a travel book about America, the *Edinburgh*'s comment was that 'an accurate, unprejudiced, and philosophical account of the United States' was 'still a *desideratum* in Literature'.[113] Many years, and numerous travel books, were to pass by, before it was going to find any such account.

The books of British travellers were of course almost always deeply coloured by their authors' political persuasions. If the writer was a liberal, like Birkbeck mentioned above, then the chances were excellent that his account of America would be favourable and optimistic; if a Tory, then it would almost certainly be an essay in detraction and abuse. The *Review*'s position on works of the latter category is unmistakable: Ashe's *Travels in America* formed 'the most comprehensive piece of national abuse we ever recollect to have perused'.[114] Mrs Trollope's famous *Domestic Manners of the Americans* (1832) was 'a spiteful ill-considered, and mischief-making book'.[115] The *Review* sums up its objections to the books of both Mrs Trollope and Captain Basil Hall—Hall's *Travels in North America* (1827) also had been hostile towards America—thus: 'Captain Hall and Mrs. Trollope have one and the same specific for the maladies of the Americans. It is the Tory toast, in the Tory sense of it—

Church and King.'[116] But here again there is a single article which
effectively defines the *Edinburgh*'s views on the travel controversy:
'America' which appeared in 1824. The article is a defence of
America from most of the common charges of travellers, written in
a vein of ironic deprecation. The roads, coaches, inns of America are
as we would expect them in any new country. What inconveniences
the English traveller in an American inn is that he cannot be alone:

> There is nothing which an Englishman enjoys more than the
> pleasure of sulkiness,—of not being forced to hear a word
> from any body which may occasion to him the necessity of
> replying. It is not so much that Mr. Bull disdains to talk, as that
> Mr. Bull has nothing to say. His forefathers have been out of
> spirits for six or seven hundred years, and seeing nothing but
> fog and vapour, he is out of spirits too; and when there is no
> selling or buying, or no business to settle, he prefers being alone
> and looking at the fire.... In short, with many excellent
> qualities, it must be acknowledged that the English are the most
> disagreeable of all the nations of Europe,—more surly and
> morose, with less disposition to please, to exert themselves for
> the good of society, to make small sacrifices, and to put them-
> selves out of their way.[117]

Another notorious charge against the Americans was their habit of
spitting: 'We are terribly afraid that some Americans spit upon the
floor, even when that floor is covered by good carpets. Now, all
claims to civilization are suspended till this secretion is otherwise
disposed of. No English gentleman has spit upon the floor since the
Heptarchy.'[118] The article goes on to consider other complaints in a
similar manner. Only with the appearance of James Stuart's *Three
Years in North America*, in 1833, did the *Review* find a travel book
which approached its ideal of such a work about America. Its
comment was suitably enthusiastic:

> We have long wished to see such a book, was the gratulatory
> notice with which the appearance of Mrs. Trollope's work was
> hailed by those who seem to imagine, that to speak favourably
> of America is to speak disparagingly and factiously of Britain.
> The publication of the volumes before us, affords us the
> opportunity of saying in our turn, that we have long wished to
> see such a book—a book of Travels in Federal America, written
> by an honest, dispassionate, and competent observer ... we,
> therefore, strongly recommend it to all who wish to obtain

sound and correct information as to the actual conditions of the vast and interesting countries of which it treats.[119]

Of course the *Edinburgh Review* was in no sense committed to a campaign of 'white-washing' America. In the article on the travellers' complaints about America, from which quotation is made above, reference is made to the uncalled for American prickliness towards criticism of any kind:

> We really thought at one time they would have fitted out an armament against the Edinburgh and Quarterly Reviews, and burnt down Mr. Murray's and Mr. Constable's shops, as we did the American Capitol. We, however, remember no other anti-American crime of which we were guilty, than a preference of Shakespeare and Milton over Joel Barlow and Timothy Dwight.

Such feelings of antagonism on the part of Americans are unjustified:

> It is very natural that we Scotch, who live in a little shabby scraggy corner of a remote island, with a climate which cannot ripen an apple, should be jealous of the aggressive pleasantry of more favoured people; but that Americans, who have done so much for themselves, and received so much from nature, should be flung into such convulsions by English Reviews and Magazines, is really a sad specimen of Columbian juvenility.[120]

The reference, in the earlier part of this passage, to American literature, is in fact the key to American complaints against the *Edinburgh Review*; it was the *Review*'s slighting references to American literary culture which gave real offence.[121] But even here it appears that American complaints were more validly directed against the *Review*'s failure to discuss more American literature, rather than the severity it displayed towards those items it did review. It made no errors of judgment in discussing American writing, and even where its comments were unfavourable, they were never prejudiced. Quite the reverse. Barlow's *Columbiad* had 'enormous' and 'intolerable' faults; but Barlow himself, nonetheless, was 'a giant, in comparison with many of the puling and paltry rhymsters, who disgrace our English literature by their occasional success'.[122] Irving and Brockden Brown both received much more praise than blame,[123] and in view of the long tradition of Scottish-American ties in theology, it was perhaps fitting that in the *Edinburgh Review*, as in its rival *Blackwood's*, the American writer who received the highest praise should have been Jonathan Edwards: 'We do not scruple to say, that he is one of the acutest, most powerful, and, of all reasoners, the most conscientious and sincere'.[124]

Destined to play a part in Scottish–American relations of almost equal importance to that of the *Edinburgh Review*, the *Edinburgh Monthly Magazine* was inauspiciously launched by William Blackwood early in 1817. It was only with the seventh number, after the services of J. G. Lockhart and John Wilson ('Christopher North') had been secured, and after its title had been changed to *Blackwood's Edinburgh Magazine*, that it burst upon the Edinburgh literary scene with an effect that equalled or surpassed that of the first number of the *Edinburgh Review* in 1802. A specific political purpose lay behind the production of *Blackwood's*: the discomfiture of the Whigs, who through the *Edinburgh* had long dominated both the political and literary circles of Edinburgh. The Whigs were now attacked and reviled with a virulence which was quite unparalleled. High Tory in tone and principle, then, it was inconceivable that *Blackwood's* should not play its part in the American controversy.

Like the *Edinburgh Review*, *Blackwood's* was soon being widely read in America. In 1822, a few lines of an American poem published in the magazine indicated that *Blackwood's* had become part of the normal reading of the American *littérateur* who,

> ... took
> The Edinburgh and Quarterly Reviews
> and also Blackwood's Mag ...[125]

Again, the New York editor of Wilson's *Noctes Ambrosianae*, writing in 1854, remarked that only in New York itself had he been able to find a set of the magazine which included, in the first number, the 'Chaldee Manuscript' article which had caused such a sensation in Edinburgh on its first appearance. The same editor also maintained, despite the popularity in Britain of the *Noctes Ambrosianae* series, which ran in *Blackwood's* from 1822 until 1835, that 'it was peculiarly in America that their high merit and undoubted originality received the heartiest recognition and appreciation.'[126]

John Neal's articles in 1824 and 1825 highlighted *Blackwood's* interest in America. But, given its political principles, it was inevitable that the magazine's typical attitude should differ sharply from that of the *Edinburgh Review*. In 1824, *Maga*, as it was popularly

called, contained an article on relations between Britain and America
which offered an explanation of its views on America. If it has
often appeared unduly critical, then that is because of the political use
to which both Whigs and Radicals have put America:

> Now it is these people who put any writers among us on the
> *qui vive* to find out holes in the coat of America. A party, or
> two parties exist among us—they are one in baseness, though
> two in proposed plans of operation for doing mischief—who
> are determined to overthrow the constitution established
> among us, *per fas et nefas,* and one of the engines which they
> consider as the most conducive to the furtherance of their design
> is the constitution of the United States. . . . From these we hear
> nothing but eternal praise of the institutions of America, mixed
> with all kinds of insulting slanders on our own.[127]

Blackwood's then, 'must continue to question the exact fitness of
things under these so bepraised institutions'.[128] *Maga* chose to adopt
an honest, down-to-earth, no-nonsense, attitude: 'We butter no
man'.[129] Such an attitude, supported by an effective irony, had
already appeared in their views on America. *Maga* despises the 'cant
of liberality', which makes editors and essayists 'fawn upon
America';[130] no nation has ever been great that did not 'hold the rest
of the world in contempt'.[131] A true spirit of rivalry between
nations is admirable: 'We love independence in others, as well as in
ourselves; a generous rivalry, nay, even a generous enmity, are things
that we love, knowing, that between people so opposed, there is a
mutual respect and admiration. . . .' America will think better of us,
'who tell him plainly the mingled way in which we regard him',
than of, 'the complacent, milk-and-water, how-d'ye-do sort of a
fellow, that humbly canvasses a bow from him, and solicits the
honour of his friendship and acquaintance'.[132]

However, as the domestic political situation continues, from
Maga's point of view, to deteriorate; as the forces which are moving
the country towards the crisis of 1832 grow steadily stronger, a
shrillness, amounting to hysteria, becomes apparent in the magazine
spreading out to its attitude towards America. America, that
'immense Free-and-Easy Club',[133] becomes England's greatest
enemy:

> From no other country has England so much to fear, as from
> America. No other country is so much our rival in general

interest—entertains towards us so much jealousy and antipathy —is so anxious to make common cause against us at all opportunities—is so much above the control of other powers in her hostility to us—is so desirous of stripping us of territory—and is so advantageously situated for injuring us. In addition to this, she has been hitherto distinguished as a nation almost above all others, by her capacious [sic] spirit, and her utter contempt of principle.[134]

Finally, in 1832, we reach what is perhaps the high-point of a tradition which began with Scottish upper-class enthusiasm for the American policies of George III:

We therefore hope that all true Britons hate American manners, and, to the full extent of their influence, the American people. They must either do that, or hate their own manners and themselves; for manners are not matters of indifference, but of mighty importance to the whole moral and intellectual character. 'Manners maketh man,' is a wise old adage; and it is painful to see what they have made of the Americans. But in a century or less there will be a fine smash among their democratic institutions. . . .[135]

Earlier *Blackwood's* had shown a greater sense of responsibility in discussing the main issues of the literary quarrel. Its editors saw themselves as avoiding the 'everlasting contradictions of the Edinburgh' and the 'open rancour of the Quarterly'.[136] Their contributions were concentrated mainly in the articles written by the American, Neal. Neal later declared that his writings were part of a pre-conceived plan to turn the fire of *Blackwood's* upon the calumniators of his country, but this seems little more than a *post factum* judgment.[137] Much of his writing is strictly in key with the no-nonsense *Blackwood's* approach, and he is ready even to advocate the 'healthy rivalry' attitude which *Maga* became so attached to. Neal did suggest that the British travellers in America were 'a set of chaps who have done more mischief, and sowed more evil, rancorous thought, between two great proud nations—forty times over, than all the war, in which they have encountered each other'.[138] And his survey of the leading figures in American literature and the other arts, though not always accurate, was certainly very full indeed.

One consequence of the publication of these articles was *Blackwood's* readiness to pose as the disseminator of truth about

America; 'a truer notion', it was asserted, 'a much better knowledge of the American people, of their habits, views, and real temper, has begun to prevail in this country, as well as in Europe', principally due to 'the papers which have appeared, month after month, for the last year and a half, in the pages of this very Magazine'.[139] But *Maga*'s later record on the subject of the British travellers in America hardly shows its contributors as subscribing to the views Neal had expressed. They are offended by American boasting: 'They are all loud in their praises of themselves, and their institutions....'[140] Hence, while they cannot accept the excesses of Mrs Trollope's work, they can write of her 'two very entertaining volumes', and view her exaggerations as only adding to the fun.[141] Stuart's book, of course they cannot accept:

> 'The best book about us and our country'—said an American gentleman in our hearing—'is Stuart's Three Years.' 'Do you say so,' asked we, 'because it eulogizes you and your country— or because it libels us and ours?'[142]

Their palm is reserved for *Men and Manners in America* (1833), by Thomas Hamilton, author of the much admired novel, *Cyril Thornton*. But it is significant that their praise of Hamilton tends to become an attack on the British reform movement:

> There was the greatest need ... of a cool and dispassionate survey of America, by a traveller who united the power of genius and the talent of description, with a practical acquaintance with men in all the varieties of political condition; who had seen enough of tyranny to hate its oppression, and enough of democracy to dread its excesses.... Such a traveller is Mr. Hamilton; and we cannot but congratulate our countrymen on the appearance of his valuable work at the present crisis, when all the ancient institutions of our country are successively melting away under the powerful solvent of democratic fervour.[143]

And the article goes on to use Hamilton's right-wing criticism of the American government and universal suffrage as means of attacking the Reform Bill.

On American literature, *Blackwood's* was often surprisingly favourable. Irving and Brockden Brown were both highly praised,[144] and here again *Maga* liked to claim that it had recognised the merits of these American authors, before anyone else in Britain.[145] Such recognition, which expanded greatly in the period of Neal's contributions, set a pattern which the magazine never completely abandoned.

American reactions to the part played in the literary quarrel by the Scottish magazines and writers were often quite explicit. As we have seen, the *Edinburgh Review* from an early stage was accepted as a literary authority, but the stand it took on political questions involving America was also frequently noted. In 1815, describing it as 'able and well-written', 'sound in principle, forcible in argument, correct in inference', and declaring that it 'must be viewed as virtually one of the ablest and most satisfactory of replies to that nefarious tissue of calumnies on the American character, which appeared in a late number of the London Quarterly Review', the *Port Folio* reprinted the second of the *Edinburgh*'s articles on 'War with America'.[146]

In 1818, referring to a recent review of Franklin's correspondence, the *Analectic Magazine* commented that, 'The Edinburgh lately has looked pleasantly enough on American productions'.[147] In the same year, the *North American Review* defended the 'Scotch Reviewers' from an attack made on them in Solyman Brown's *An Essay on American Poetry*:

> The principal poem in the collection is the Essay on American Poetry, in which, after beginning, as in his preface, with something about Greece and Rome, he takes up the gauntlet against the Reviewers of Great Britain—the Scotch Reviewers in particular, against whom he inveighs with peculiar bitterness. Why all this gall towards the Scotch Reviewers, we cannot imagine, especially if he alludes, as is probable to the writers of the Edinburgh Review, whose opinions concerning our nation we have ever considered as more liberal than those of most of their brethren, and who must be allowed, by all who have read the article in that work on the subject of Peace with America, written not long before the close of the late war—a composition, which we might defy any American to read, without a glow of national exultation—to have done ample justice to all the honourable and generous traits of our character.[148]

In 1819, however, appeared the work which contained the bitterest of all American attacks on the *Edinburgh Review*: Walsh's *Appeal from the Judgments of Great Britain*. The substance of Walsh's

attack on the 'Scottish critics' is the failure of the *Review* to be fair
to American literature and culture. Against the *Review*'s treatment
of these, he sets its frequent expressions of interest in, and concern
for, America, and rather like *Blackwood's*, chooses to see in this
juxtaposition evidence of a deep-dyed hypocrisy. Walsh made some
serious and damaging criticisms, but his views did not go un-
challenged in America, particularly after the appearance in 1820, of
the *Edinburgh*'s restrained but effective reply to his charges.[149] The
Analectic reprinted this article in full, with the editorial comment
that 'Much praise has been given in some late American publications,
to the candour and liberality said to be discoverable in the following
critique. We confess ourselves unable to perceive any foundation for
such compliments.'[150] The *North American Review* tended to support
Walsh,[151] and again in 1820, the *Port Folio* assailed the *Edinburgh* on
account of the publication of Smith's comment 'Who reads an
American book?'[152]

Blackwood's Magazine at first derived some credit from its praise of
American authors, but Neal's reputation in his own country was
such that the publication of his articles was greeted only with
contempt.[153] The articles were published anonymously, but despite
this and Neal's attempt to pose as an Englishman, their authorship
was quickly identified in America: the *Port Folio* did not hesitate to
ascribe 'these foolish and wicked lucubrations' to the renegade
Neal.[154]

There can be no question of the striking impact made by both
the *Edinburgh Review* and *Blackwood's Magazine* in America. The
Edinburgh Review in particular is an influence to be reckoned with in
early nineteenth century America. Its comprehensiveness; its
encyclopaedic concern for everything from politics to poetry; the
detailed thoroughness of its reviews; most of all perhaps the tone
of intellectual and critical self-confidence so characteristic of its
judgments; all of these contributed to its lofty reputation. Seconded
by the appearance of *Blackwood's Magazine*, that reputation did
much to confirm and maintain the position of intellectual eminence
gained initially for Scotland by the North Britons of the previous
century.

NOTES AND REFERENCES

1. James Henry Morgan, *Dickinson College, The History of One Hundred and Fifty Years, 1783–1933* (Carlisle, 1933), p. 54.
2. *Port Folio*, 4th Series, XVII (1824), 2.
3. Creech, *Edinburgh Fugitive Pieces*, pp. 227–8. Creech's concern for 'the poor Loyalists'

was probably shared by many of his contemporaries. Scottish Loyalists forced to
return to their native land, many of them
in straitened financial circumstances, and
Scottish merchants and investors whose
business ventures had suffered badly as a
result of the war, must have done much to
ensure that bitterness towards America
should endure for a decade or more after
the conclusion of the war. John Witherspoon arrived in Great Britain in 1784 once
again seeking financial aid for the College
of New Jersey. His old friends Nisbet and
John Erskine soon made it clear to him that
this time no Scottish money would be
forthcoming for Nassau Hall. (See Collins,
President Witherspoon, II, 140–1.) Again, on
25 August 1790, the semi-official *Gazette of
the United States* printed part of a letter
'from a respectable citizen of Edinburgh,
to a gentleman [in Philadelphia]', dated
28 April 1790. The extract included these
sentences: 'I am sorry to say, the people of
this country, (Scotland), seem still unfriendly to the Americans, and that the
news printers cannot be prevailed on to
copy any thing from your papers. The
insertion of General Washington's speech
to the second meeting of Congress, cost
the friends of America here, 25 £. sterling.'

4. Whitfield J. Bell. Jr., 'Scottish Emigration
to America: a Letter of Dr. Charles Nisbet
to Dr. John Witherspoon, 1784', *William
and Mary College Quarterly*, 3rd Series, XI
(April, 1954), 286.

5. See Morgan, *Dickinson College, The History
of One Hundred and Fifty Years, 1783–1933*,
pp. 31–2.

6. Letter from the Countess of Leven and
Melville to Charles Nisbet, 26 July 1784,
printed in Samuel Miller's *Memoir of
Charles Nisbet*, p. 105. '...it would give me
pain to think of counteracting a design and
earnest wish of my kind friend, Dr. Rush,
whose name, upon *one* particular account,
especially, will ever be dear to me and all
this family.' The reference is to Rush's
service in the burial of Lady Leven's son,
Captain William Leslie, killed at the Battle
of Princeton in 1776.

7. Miller, *Memoir of Charles Nisbet*, p. 155.

8. Princeton graduates filled many of the
teaching posts in these colleges, while their
curricula were much influenced by the
Princeton example. See Richard Beale
Davis, *Intellectual Life in Jefferson's Virginia,
1790–1830* (Chapel Hill, 1964), p. 48.

9. Snow, *The College Curriculum in the United
States*, pp. 90, 129.

10. John Morison Duncan, *Travels through part
of the United States and Canada in 1818 and
1819* (New York, 1823), I, 134–5.

11. Snow, p. 83.

12. Miller, *Brief Retrospect of the Eighteenth
Century*, II, 494.

13. *North American Review*, VI (1817–18) 422–3.

14. Snow, pp. 109, 113. Both Blair and Kames
were part of the Brown curriculum in
1827. See Snow, p. 122.

15. *Port Folio*, New Series, V (1808), 212–14.

16. Miller, II, 503.

17. William Charvat, *The Origins of American
Critical Thought, 1810–1835* (Philadelphia,
1936), p. 31.

18. Herbert W. Schneider, *A History of
American Philosophy* (New York, 1946), p.
238.

19. Miller, II, 503.

20. *North American Review*, VI (1817–18),
422–3.

21. Snow, p. 126. Scottish philosophic texts
had been almost certainly introduced at
Harvard much before this—by David
Tappan, Hollis Professor of Divinity, 1792–
1803. See Sydney E. Ahlstrom, 'The
Scottish Philosophy and American Theology', *Church History*, XXIV (Sept., 1955),
262.

22. Duncan, *Travels*, I, 135. Snow, p. 129.

23. Ibid., p. 122.

24. See Davis, *Intellectual Life in Jefferson's
Virginia*, p. 66. Davis's detailed account of
the intellectual life of Virginia in the period
1790–1830 provides useful confirmation of
the view that the North British thinkers
were a potent and pervasive influence in
post-Revolutionary America. Having
agreed that there were still evidences of
neo-classicism in the literary life of Virginia
in the immediate post-Revolutionary
period, he goes on: 'But in the first thirty
years of the nineteenth century the writers
of Jeffersonian Virginia were as much
influenced as other Americans by the
Scottish school of rhetoricians, aesthe-
ticians, and common-sense philosophers...
by 1800 Blair's *Lectures on Rhetoric*, Lord
Kames's *Elements of Criticism*, and Reid's
works were widely used in schools and
especially in colleges, along with Hartley,
Adam Smith, and Hume. A little later
Dugald Stewart's and Archibald Alison's
philosophical writings were generally read.'
Ibid., p. 257.

25. See Arnaud B. Leavelle, 'James Wilson and the Relation of the Scottish Metaphysics to American Political Thought', *Political Science Quarterly*, 57 (1942), 394–410.
26. See p. 85.
27. Snow, p. 126.
28. Davis, *Intellectual Life in Jefferson's Virginia*, p. 83.
29. Charvat, *Origins of American Critical Thought*, p. 30.
30. See Douglas C. McMurtrie, 'A Bibliography of Morristown Imprints, 1789–1820', *Proceedings of the New Jersey Historical Society*, LIV (April, 1936), 129–55.
31. Oscar Wegelin, 'The Brooklyn, New York, Press. 1799–1820', *The Bulletin of the Bibliographical Society of America*, IV (July–October, 1912), 38. Douglas C. McMurtrie, *Issues of the Brooklyn Press. A List of books and pamphlets printed in Brooklyn, New York, from 1799 through 1820, in supplement to Wegelin's Bibliography* (New York, 1936), p. 14.
32. This is confirmed by the appearance of editions of Blair 'reduced to question and answer', or 'with appropriate questions'.
33. Cf. Richard Beale Davis's judgment on Blair's *Lectures on Rhetoric*: 'An elementary, down-to-earth textbook, on its bad side it encouraged artificial, impersonal, and un-idiomatic precision in expression, encouraged Latinity of diction and neglected emotion and sensibility.' *Intellectual Life in Jefferson's Virginia*, p. 260.
34. 'The number of sizes and editions of Hugh Blair's famous *Lectures on Rhetoric* (1783) attest what we know from other sources, that every fairly well-read Virginian used this as a sort of textbook for English composition, oratory, and aesthetic theory while he was in school and long after he had completed his formal education.' Davis, *Intellectual Life in Jefferson's Virginia*, p. 79. What was true of Virginia was clearly equally true of the rest of America.
35. Stiles, *Literary Diary*, III, 183.
36. Ibid., 198.
37. Ibid., pp. 205–6, 235, 287, 306, 349, 408–9, 434.
38. Shores, *Origins of the American College Library 1638–1800*, pp. 66, 67, 68, 84.
39. Minto published a book on the new planet, Uranus, in 1783; a copy was sent 'To his Excellency Benjamin Franklin LL.D. in Testimony of Esteem & Veneration. From the Author.' In 1787, Minto, then teaching at Erasmus Hall, sent a copy to Washington whom he described as 'the man who has done so much for the rights & happiness of humankind'. Luther P. Eisenhart, 'Walter Minto and the Earl of Buchan', *Proceedings of the American Philosophical Society*, XCIV (June, 1950), 284. Erasmus Hall Academy was established in Flatbush, New York, in 1787. Originally a small, private school, it was the first secondary school to be chartered by the Regents of the University of the State of New York and hence is regarded as the nucleus of the New York secondary school system.
40. Eisenhart, 'Walter Minto and the Earl of Buchan', p. 290.
41. See 'Donations in Books and Apparatus Received for the use of the College of New Jersey since it was consumed by fire March 6th, 1802'. Unpublished MS in Princeton University Library.
42. The circulation of Scottish books in colonial America was not great. (See pp. 41–2). Studies of the holdings of private libraries in Virginia in the pre-Revolutionary period reveal few Scottish titles. In the same state however, in the period 1790–1830, private libraries which do not contain some examples of the work of Scottish philosophers, rhetoricians or historians are exceptional. Richard Beale Davis does not suggest that the list of Scottish books owned by John Holt Rice, a Presbyterian professor at the theological seminary established at Hampden-Sydney —i.e. Alison's *Essay on Taste*, Blair's *Lectures*, Brown's *Inquiry into Cause and Effect* and *Philosophy of the Human Mind*, Campbell's *Philosophy of Rhetoric*, Ferguson's *Essay on the History of Civil Society*, Kames's *Elements of Criticism*, Reid's *Works*, three philosophical works by Stewart, and Hume's *Essays*—was in any way typical, but most libraries seem to have included at least some of these titles. See, *Intellectual Life in Jefferson's Virginia*, pp. 107–8.
43. Miller, *Brief Retrospect of the Eighteenth Century*, II, 135.
44. Ibid., p. 136.
45. *Port Folio*, New Series, I (1806), 44–5.
46. Ibid., New Series, I (1809), 97–100.
47. *Literary Magazine and American Register*, II (1804), 541–6.
48. *Port Folio*, I (1801), 338.
49. *North American Review*, XXXIV (1832), 148. The view of Hume's unfortunate influence expressed here echoes very closely Jefferson's opinion on the same subject. In

1807 Jefferson opined that Hume's *History of England* 'is so plausible and pleasing in its style and manner, as to instil its errors and heresies insensibly into the minds of unwary readers'. In 1810, he was even more explicit: 'Every one knows that judicious matter and charms of style have rendered Hume's history the manual of every student. I remember well the enthusiasm with which I devoured it when young, and the length of time, the research and reflection which were necessary to eradicate the poison it had instilled into my mind.' Nevertheless Hume 'still continues to be put into the hands of all our young people, and to infect them with the poison of his own principles of government'. See Sowerby, *The Library of Thomas Jefferson*, I, 157.

50. *The American Review of History and Politics*, I (1811), 157–8.
51. Ibid., pp. 355–66.
52. *Port Folio*, New Series, VII (1812), 265–81.
53. *Analectic Magazine*, VI (1815), 302–17. In the next year another article appeared on the same subject, again concluding that the objections of the *Quarterly* were ill-founded. See *Analectic Magazine*, VII (1816), 401–13.
54. See, for example, *The Literary Gazette, or, Journal of Criticism, Science, and the Arts*, I (1821), 817–19; *The United States Review and Literary Gazette*, II (1827), 428–39; *American Quarterly Review*, VI (1829), 360–78.
55. *North American Review*, XVIII (1824), 162. The figure is quoted from C. J. Ingersoll's *Discourse concerning the Influence of America on the Mind*.
56. Ibid., XXXI (1830), 213–14. An interesting sidelight on Stewart's own American connections is provided by a reference in a work by James Stuart, a Scottish traveller in America. In Washington, Stuart visited the Library of Congress:

In the library was pointed out to me a copy of Dugald Stewart's Philosophy of the Human Mind, on the first page of which is pasted the following original letter of its illustrious and amiable author to Mr. Jefferson:—'Dear Sir,—The book which accompanies this letter is the only performance which I have yet ventured to publish. I hope you will do me the honour to give it a place in your library, and that you will accept of it as a mark of my grateful recollection of the attentions

which I have received from you at Paris. —I am, Dear Sir, your most obedient and faithful servant, Dugald Stewart. College of Edinburgh, 1st October, 1792.'

James Stuart, *Three Years in North America* (Edinburgh, 1833), II, 51. Stuart was a grandson of the Revd John Erskine. Jefferson's friendship with Dugald Stewart over a period of months in 1789 in Paris was of an exceedingly close nature.

57. McCosh, *The Scottish Philosophy*, p. 324.
58. *North American Review*, XII (1821), 395.
59. Ibid., XIX (1824), 11n.
60. Ibid., XXI (1825), 38.
61. Ibid., XXIX (1829), 100. Other discussions of Brown's philosophy occur in *The United States Review and Literary Gazette*, II (1827), 161–84, and in the *Southern Review*, III (1829), 125–56.
62. *Knickerbocker Magazine*, II (1833), 64.
63. *Monthly Magazine and American Review*, I (1799), 167; *American Museum*, II (1787), 197–8.
64. *The Literary Magazine and American Register*, VI (1806), 74–6.
65. *Analectic Magazine*, V (1815), 189.
66. *American Quarterly Observer*, I (1833), 287–99.
67. *Knickerbocker Magazine*, I (1833), 321.
68. *The American Museum, or Universal Magazine*, X (1791), 275.
69. *Monthly Magazine and American Review*, I (1799), 168.
70. *Port Folio*, III (1803), 188–9.
71. Ibid., pp. 369–70.
72. Ibid., New Series, I (1806), 358.
73. Ibid., II (1806), 197.
74. See, for example, *The Literary Magazine*, VIII (1807–8), 240; *Port Folio*, New Series, II (1809), 282–3.
75. *Literary Magazine*, IV (1805), 266.
76. *A Plan for the Establishment of public Schools and the Diffusion of Knowledge in Pennsylvania. To which are added, Thoughts upon the Mode of Education proper in a Republic.* See *The Scots Magazine*, XLVIII (1786), 437–42.
77. *Analectic Magazine*, II (1813), 305.
78. See, for example, John Melish, *Travels through the United States of America in 1806, 1807, and 1809, 1810, 1811* (Belfast, 1813), p. 101. And Duncan, *Travels*, I, 106.
79. Quoted by J. A. Greig, *Francis Jeffrey of the Edinburgh Review* (Edinburgh and London, 1948), p. 60.
80. Cockburn, *Life of Jeffrey*, I, 106.

81. Mrs (Eliza) Fletcher, *Autobiography* (Boston, 1876), p. 82.

82. Cockburn, *Life of Jeffrey*, II, 84–5.

83. A comment on *Ossian* in C. B. Brown's *Literary Magazine*, IV (1805), 364, is taken almost verbatim from the *Edinburgh Review*, VI (1805), 462. Reprintings of *Edinburgh Review* criticisms begin to appear in the *Port Folio* also in 1805. For example, see Port Folio, V (1805), 36–7, or 306–8, 313–15: the *Review*'s notice of the *Lay of the Last Minstrel*.

84. In a letter of 17 May 1814, Jefferson wrote to a Philadelphia bookseller who had offered to supply him with the *Review*: 'I have long been a subscriber to the edition of the Edinburgh Review first published by Mr. Sargeant, and latterly by Eastburn Kirk and Co. and already possess from No. 30 to 42 inclusive ...'. See, *The Library of Thomas Jefferson*, V, 57. No. 30 is the issue for January, 1810.

85. Duncan, *Travels*, I, 202; Henry Bradshaw Fearon, *Sketches of America* (London, 1818), p. 36.

86. The *Index* announces itself as 'Reprinted for Thos. Kirk and Thos. R. Mercein, at the office of the Edinburgh and Quarter Review'. Complete sets of early numbers of the *Edinburgh Review* were frequently advertised for sale in Virginia newspapers. See Davis, *Intellectual Life in Jefferson's Virginia*, p. 76.

87. See Charvat, *The Origins of American Critical Thought*, p. 29.

88. Jefferson's opinion, expressed in 1814, was probably quite typical: 'This work is certainly unrivalled in merit, and if continued by the same talents, information and principles which distinguish it in every department of science which it reviews, it will become a real Encyclopaedia, justly taking its station in our libraries with the most valuable depositories of human knowledge.' See *The Library of Thomas Jefferson*, V, 57.

89. Mrs Fletcher, *Autobiography*, p. 98.

90. George S. Hellman (Ed.), *Letters of Henry Brevoort to Washington Irving, together with other unpublished Brevoort Papers* (New York, 1916), I, 66.

91. Ibid., pp. 95–7.

92. *Analectic Magazine*, II (1813), 350.

93. Henry F. Tuckerman, *Mental Portraits; or, Studies of Character* (London, 1835), pp. 198–9.

94. Cockburn, *Life of Jeffrey*, I, 179.

95. *Port Folio*, New Series, II (1809), 154.

96. Ibid., IV (1810), 294.

97. Ibid., V (1811), 440.

98. Ibid., VII (1812), 323–4.

99. Ibid., 4th Series, X (1820), 486.

100. *Analectic Magazine*, XIII (1819), 124.

101. Fred Lewis Pattee (Ed.), *American Writers, A series of Papers Contributed to Blackwood's Magazine (1824–1825)* (Durham, 1937), p. 234.

102. *Edinburgh Review*, XXXIV (1820), 161.

103. Charvat, p. 170.

104. *American Monthly Magazine*, II (1830–1), 273.

105. Paul Wheeler Mowbray, *America Through British Eyes: A Study of the Attitude of the Edinburgh Review toward the United States of America from 1802 until 1861* (Rock Hill, S.C., 1935), p. 40. Mr Mowbray's conclusion is arrived at after an exhaustive examination of all the material referring to America published in the review. The use of the adjective 'British' seems to me somewhat question-begging; otherwise I am in complete agreement with the findings of Mr Mowbray's study.

106. A more conventional conclusion is that drawn by William B. Cairns, in his *British Criticisms of American Writing, 1815–1833* (Madison, 1922), p. 12: the Edinburgh Reviewers 'were willing to draw Whig political morals from America, praising religious toleration, and admitting that America was well and cheaply governed. But their fairness in these matters only heightened the complacency with which, when domestic diversions failed, they amused themselves by baiting the new nation.'

107. For an account of *The Bee*, see the Appendix, pp. 237–9.

108. *Edinburgh Review*, XIII (1808–9), 153.

109. Ibid., XX (1812), 460.

110. Ibid., p. 457.

111. Ibid., XXIV (1814–15), 264–5.

112. Ibid., XXX (1818), 120–1. And cf. XL (1824), 427.

113. Ibid., II (1803), 453.

114. Ibid., XV (1809–10), 442.

115. Ibid., LV (1832), 487.

116. Ibid., p. 503.

117. Ibid., XL (1824), 434–5.

118. Ibid., p. 435.

119. Ibid., LVI (1832–3), 460–1.

120. Ibid., XL (1824), 432–3.

121. In particular Sydney Smith's notorious 'who reads an American Book?' passage.

See *Edinburgh Review*, XXXIII (1820), 79. And cf. XV (1809–10), 445–6, and XXXI (1818–19), 144.

122. *Edinburgh Review*, XV (1809–10), 39.

123. Ibid., XXXIV (1820), 160–1; XXXVII (1822), 337; L (1829–30), 126–7.

124. Ibid., L (1829–30), 131.

125. *Blackwood's Magazine*, XI (1822), 686.

126. R. Shelton Mackenzie (Ed.), *Noctes Ambrosianae, by the late John Wilson* (New York, 1854), I, xiv. *Blackwood's* was probably being reprinted in New York at an early date.

127. *Blackwood's Magazine* XVI (1824), 477–8.

128. Ibid., p. 481.

129. Ibid., XI (1822), 685.

130. Ibid., p. 691.

131. Ibid., p. 692.

132. Ibid., p. 684.

133. Ibid., XXXII (1832), 93.

134. Ibid., XXIV (1828), 638.

135. Ibid., XXXII (1832), 93.

136. Ibid., XVI (1824), 619.

137. See, Pattee, *American Writers*, p. 16.

138. *Blackwood's Magazine*, XVIII (1825), 328.

139. Ibid., p. 356.

140. Ibid., XXXI (1832), 832.

141. Ibid., p. 831.

142. Ibid., XXXV (1834), 405.

143. Ibid., XXXIV (1833), 288.

144. Ibid., VI (1819–20), 554–61, and VII (1820), 360–9.

145. Ibid., XI (1822), 684.

146. *Port Folio*, 3rd Series, VI (1815), 533.

147. *Analectic Magazine*, XI (1818), 111.

148. *North American Review*, VII (1818), 207–8. The article mentioned must in fact be the 1814 'War with America'.

149. The *Edinburgh's* reply constitutes probably the best summing-up of its position on America. See *Edinburgh Review*, XXXIII (1820), 395–431.

150. *Analectic Magazine*, New Series, II (1820), 303.

151. *North American Review*, X (1820), 334–71.

152. *Port Folio*, 4th Series, IX (1820), 502.

153. *Analectic Magazine*, II (1820), 411–17.

154. *Port Folio*, 4th Series, XVIII (1824), 492. Neal left Baltimore soon after attacking the Baltimore statesman, William Pinckney, who had just died, in *Randolph*, an epistolary novel (1823).

-V-

Land of Romance

The nature of the objections to be raised against a description of the Scottish impact upon America, in the period after the Revolution, which took account only of the North Britons, and their successors, has already been suggested. Hume, Robertson, Smith, Blair and the rest, however important, represented no more than one current within the cultural renaissance which developed in Scotland throughout the eighteenth century. The second current, originating in a revived interest in the native Scottish cultural tradition, in Scottish antiquities, and in national traditions generally, became in the end an equally important part of that renaissance. There is no reason why both courses should have had an equal importance outside Scotland, in America or anywhere else, but failing to see that to talk of the North Britons alone is not good enough, could lead one to conclusions whose limitations might go unrecognised. In America's case certainly, this would be so.

Superficially, there is at least one reason which might suggest that the position of the North Britons was the more important. The North Britons' concern was with the standard English, or European, critical and intellectual values. The contributions which they made, so successfully, in so many different fields, may readily be seen within the general context of eighteenth century thought. Though this did not mean that they were in any way entirely divorced from their Scottish background, it did ensure for them an ease of exchange in the intellectual currency of their day. An American might easily have been a student of, say, Blair's *Lectures on Rhetoric*, without his in any way identifying Blair with a distinctively Scottish intellectual movement. It is this that makes one hesitate to assert that the

North Britons and their successors, despite the fact that with the emergence of the great reviews national identification became on the whole clearer and more positive, could ever have created an American image of Scotland which was both popular, and based solely on that country's intellectual distinction.

The course parallel to that of the North Britons, on the other hand, was by definition, local, regional, native, national, and to that extent, at first glance at least, less 'exportable'. In fact, it does seem to have been slower in winning recognition both inside and outside Scotland. But it grew in importance as the movement of which it was itself a part—European romanticism—gained impetus, until, by the early decades of the nineteenth century, the bearers of its tradition, pure or impure, dominated the Scottish literary and cultural scene. It is here that the obverse side of the coin of its nativism becomes apparent. In the sense that the movement only existed in and through its Scottishness, any impact that it had was bound to be distinctively, unmistakably, Scottish; awareness of Scotland was the necessary consequence of awareness of this side of her cultural life. Here again, language provides the simplest kind of evidence: a work written, throughout or in part in the vernacular, if accepted at all, could only be accepted on its own, Scottish, terms.

The handful of Scottish works, outside the North British tradition, which in one way or another did reach America before the Revolution have already been mentioned in Chapter Two. *The Gentle Shepherd,* after its initial American publication in New York in 1750, remained popular beyond the Atlantic. Other editions followed at Philadelphia in 1771, 1795, and 1798, at Carlisle in 1805, at Pittsburgh in 1812, and at Philadelphia once again in 1813. The importance of Ramsay's play, as the first piece of writing largely in the Scottish vernacular to be circulated in America, is considerable, but two other works, neither of which was a 'pure' product of the native Scottish literary movement in the eighteenth century, were of the highest importance in launching and promoting the new literary image of Scotland: John Home's *Douglas,* and James Macpherson's *Ossian.*

Lacking the roots in the native literary or folk traditions which characterised the poetry and songs of the vernacular, these works represent the growth of a new, more self-consciously Scottish, tradition. Such terms as 'ersatz' or 'contrived' or 'artificial' have been applied to it, but their use is quite tendentious. Whatever may

E

be said of the language and style of such works, the impulse behind them—as for example in the case of *Ossian*—could be genuine enough. And it should be remembered that what now appears artificial in these writings certainly enhanced the immediacy of their appeal with the result that, in America as elsewhere, their impact was at least as great as that of the productions of the vernacular tradition. *Douglas* may in a sense be regarded quite correctly as a North British work; John Home himself, was a life-long member of the North British group. But the play itself must have appeared, in 1756, significantly non-Augustan in background, plot, and sentiment. Based on the old Scottish ballad of 'Gil Morrice', its central characters, Randolph, and particularly Young Norval, seem to prefigure the grand, heroic protagonists of the Ossianic poems. It was the ease with which the play could be romanticised in this way, could be assimilated to the developing romantic image of Scotland, which best accounts for its enduring popularity throughout the eighteenth, and early part of the nineteenth centuries.

No American edition of *Douglas* earlier than that published at Philadelphia in 1790, or thirty-four years after the play's first performance in Edinburgh, has been found. But while this might seem to support the common view that American literary taste consistently lagged about forty years behind that of England, the American response to *Douglas,* like that to so much of Scottish literature, cannot in fact be fitted into such a pattern. With a letter he sent to Sir Alexander Dick, dated at London on 3 January 1760, Franklin enclosed a copy of a Philadelphia newspaper: 'You will see in the same Paper,' wrote Franklin, 'an Advertisement of the Acting of Douglas, one of your Scottish Tragedies, at our Theatre, which may show the regard we have for your Writers.' The paper referred to was *The Pennsylvania Gazette* which on 12 July 1759 advertised the performance 'At the Theatre, on Society-Hill', of '*Douglass*, a new Tragedy, written by the Reverend Mr. Hume, Minister of the Kirk of Scotland.'[1]

In 1777, a Philadelphia edition of *Alonso and Ormisinda* described the play as 'A new tragedy in five acts. . . . Written by Mr. Home, author of the Tragedy of Douglas.' From its first performance in Philadelphia before 1760, *Douglas* held its place on the American stage for at least the next sixty years: the title-page of the 1790 Philadelphia edition reads, 'American Edition. Douglas, a Tragedy.

As performed by the American Company, at the theatre, in Southwark, Philadelphia.' This performance, we gather, was very popular; another edition of the play, in the next year, at Philadelphia, was headed, 'Douglas, A Tragedy As performed with Universal Applause by the American Company.' Numerous editions of the play appeared in succeeding years. It was published at Baltimore in 1803; at New York in 1806, 1810, 1814, 1819, and 1823; at Philadelphia probably in 1810; and at Boston in 1823.

Further evidence of continuing American interest in Home's play is provided by a discussion of Witherspoon's writings in Brockden Brown's New York magazine, *The American Review and Literary Journal*, in 1801. The article notes the occasion of Witherspoon's pamphlet, *A Serious Inquiry into the Nature and Effects of the Stage*, describes *Douglas* as 'a celebrated tragedy', and presumes that few readers 'are ignorant of the noise which that performance made on its first appearance, and of the uneasiness which it excited in many serious minds, as the production of a clergyman'.[2] Reviews of performances of the play occur in the *Port Folio* in 1801 and 1805;[3] it was performed in New Orleans in 1819;[4] and as late as 1825, the weekly *New York Literary Gazette* printed a long account of the play, detailing its plot, and describing it as 'one of the best modern tragedies'.[5]

The popularity of the tragedy of *Douglas* was largely a consequence of the ease with which it could be fitted into the developing romantic image of Scotland. In the creation and definition of that image no single work compares in importance with Macpherson's *Ossian*. The case of *Ossian* is a more complex one than that of *Douglas*. The simple fact of the immense popularity throughout all of Europe of Macpherson's work should be enough to convince the modern critic and reader that this is so; to dismiss the Ossianic poems as simply a successful literary fraud is to miss the point entirely. Genuine or fraudulent, a product of the Gaelic bardic tradition, or an artificial literary exercise, there is a note in these poems which found a response in contemporary readers everywhere, and which lingers there for the unprejudiced reader of today. Beneath the posturing and the rhetoric, the artificiality of language and style, there it remains: the elegiac note which so often characterises a great epic poem, the lament for an age, a civilisation that is passing, for the old way and the old way's order, which the present is destroying.

Recognising this elegiac note in the Ossianic poems, George Pratt Insh, the Scottish historian, relates it specifically to the situation of Macpherson's native Scottish Highlands after 1746. Clearly the battle of Culloden represented more than the end of the possibility of a return of the Stuart dynasty to the British throne. It symbolised the final defeat, in political terms, of the Gaelic culture of the north by the Anglo-Saxon culture of the south, the victory of the expanding, commercial civilisation of Lowland Scotland, over an older civilisation with its own literary and intellectual traditions.[6] Insh sees the outcome of the struggle in these terms: the Scottish north-west and north-east were forced into a new alliance, 'where they now fought, not with the weapons of the flesh but with those of the mind and spirit, and where the battle-ground was no longer a windswept Scottish moor, but the ancient cities, the camps and the courts of Europe; and where the spiritual forces of the older civilisations made willing captives of the hearts and minds of soldiers, scholars, and poets'.[7]

James Macpherson was born in Ruthven, in the parish of Kingussie in Inverness-shire. When he was ten years old, he had probably seen arrive at Ruthven the remains of the Highland army after Culloden; by a strange coincidence it was at Ruthven too, that the clansmen of the rebellion of 1715 had finally disbanded. Through his father Macpherson was related to Cluny Macpherson, chieftain of the clan, and his mother also came of a family of some rank in the clan Macpherson. Brought up, then, in the midst of the Jacobite tragedy, aware of its consequences all around him, it was inevitable that a consciousness of the fate of his own people should make itself felt in his handling of the traditional subjects of the heroic Gaelic past which he brought forward for the first time upon the European scene. It is Macpherson's own awareness that strengthens and sharpens the elegiac note that pervades the Ossianic poems. According to Insh, his translation or adaptation, '... ceased to be an exercise in antiquarian reconstruction and literary exposition. It became a passionate lament for the passing of an ancient civilisation. It recalled the battles and heroes of far-off pagan centuries: but the spirit that throbbed through it was the spirit of the Scottish Highlands in the generation that followed Culloden....' This was the note that in the Europe of Macpherson's own day stirred the heart of both the soldier and the sage.'[8] Macpherson's work remains in a sense a rejection of all the forces trying to mould the life of the Scottish Highlands into the pattern of that of the south. And beyond any question of specific intention, the effect of *Ossian* was that of a counter-attack: an attempt to impose upon Scotland, as her truest and most traditional self, a romantic image created out of the wild grandeur of her Highland scenery, and the heroic simplicity of a poetic Highland past. If the Ossianic counter-attack did not win a complete success, nevertheless, in alliance with other literary productions, its impact was powerful and enduring. An account of its reception in America will help to define in more detail the nature of the image of Scotland it helped both to create and to promote.

David Hall offered *Fingal and Temora* for sale in Philadelphia in 1766, but the first American edition of *Ossian,* with Hugh Blair's highly favourable *Critical Dissertation on the Poems of Ossian*, did not appear in Philadelphia until 1790, the year, notice, of the first American edition of Home's *Douglas.* However, *Ossian* was quite widely read before that date: Thomas Jefferson, for example, was an enthusiastic reader in 1773,[9] and though John Trumbull's satire *M'Fingal* does not parody much more than the title of Macpherson's work, his title does imply some awareness of the original. Trumbull's poem was published in 1775, and before 1800 continuing American interest in *Ossian* is best shown by further imitations and parodies—by William Munford, J. M. Sewall, J. L. Arnold, Paul Allen, and others.[10] None of these, however, pre-date 1785. Hence it is reasonably clear that the *Ossian* vogue in America did not really get underway before the 1790s. The significance of the first American edition is then clear: it represents a response to a growing interest in the Ossianic poems. Further evidence of this emergence of a general popular interest in *Ossian* in the 1790s may be seen in the publication, in 1796, in both Boston and Charleston, of a theatrical work based on *Ossian,* the title-page of which is particularly significant: *Oscar and Malvina; or, the Hall of Fingal. A grand Scottish Heroic Spectacle ... The Manners, Characters, and Incidents, taken from the Poems of Ossian (translated by the late James M'Pherson, Esq.).* Just how widespread knowledge of *Ossian* had become by the turn of the century is suggested by a comment in the *Port Folio,* in 1801, which included a versified extract from *Ossian*; the contributor dispensed with any notes or explanations, because 'the source whence I draw, is in every library'.[11] American libraries must have continued to be well supplied by the editions of the Ossianic poems which appeared at New York in 1801, 1806, and 1810; Philadelphia in 1802; New Haven in 1806; and Morristown, New Jersey, in 1813, 1815, and 1823.

One of the earliest critical commentaries on *Ossian* to appear in America derived from a Scottish source: an article in *The Mirror,* a periodical which had appeared in Edinburgh under the direction of Henry Mackenzie, between 1779 and 1780. Both volumes of the magazine were published in Boston in 1792, and in Philadelphia in 1793. The article avoided the question of the authenticity of Macpherson's work, but saw in the limited range of natural images employed by the poet, and their sublimity, evidence of its antiquity.[12] In 1803, in his *Brief Retrospect of the Eighteenth Century,* Samuel Miller expressed an attitude towards the Ossianic poems which was probably shared by the majority of American readers. '...*Fingal and Temora* have been recalled from a long oblivion by the labours of Mr. Macpherson,' wrote Miller; they represent 'a work of true and uncommon genius, which, on several accounts, will probably be read with pleasure for many centuries to come, whatever opinion may be formed with respect to its origin'.[13] The closing reference to the authenticity question indicates that the debate on that subject was as familiar in America as it was in Great Britain. An article in C. B. Brown's *Literary Magazine,* in 1805, declared that Macpherson 'has taken very great liberty with the original...by no means...for the better'.[14] In the same year, the *Edinburgh Review* discussed the report of a committee headed by Henry Mackenzie, set up by the Highland Society, to enquire into the authenticity of Macpherson's work, and arrived at the conclusion that:

> ...while we are compelled to renounce the pleasing idea, 'that Fingal lived, and that Ossian sung,' our national vanity may be equally flattered by the fact that a remote, and almost a barbarous corner of Scotland, produced, in the 18th century, a bard, capable not only of making an enthusiastic impression on every mind susceptible of poetical beauty, but of giving a new tone to poetry throughout all Europe.[15]

The *Literary Magazine* reproduced this sentiment. Discussing the same topic it suggested that:

> ...while obliged to deny that Fingal lived, or that Ossian sung, it is surely sufficiently honourable to Scotland and

Macpherson, that the eighteenth century has produced, in a remote corner of the Highlands, a bard capable of making the strongest impressions on all poetical minds, and of giving a new fashion to poetry throughout Europe.[16]

The *Literary Magazine* turned again to the subject in 1806 in an article comparing Homer and Ossian: Ossian is here shown not to be genuine, as evidenced by the unreality of the metaphors employed by Macpherson.[17]

In 1806, too, the *Port Folio* made its major contribution to the controversy. As always, Dennie's magazine was more than well-disposed to a Scottish production. In fact the praise bestowed upon Macpherson's work represents a high-point in American appreciation of *Ossian*:

> Never did an investigation into the origin of any branch of science, nor a contest for the honor of having invented an art, create more interest than is felt in the poems of the Caledonian bard. The learned have divided on the question of their authenticity; the lovers of simplicity and elegance have wasted argument in endless scrutiny, and the admirers of poetic excellence have entered with enthusiasm the lists of disquisition on a subject which can never be determined: but all mankind must admire that genius, which produced the *Works of Ossian*. The son of Fingal, appears, 'like the beam of the rising sun, when he disperses the storms of the hill, and brings peace to the glittering fields.' Cherished as the Muse's darling son, he depicts the noble manners of an interesting age; and is still superior to the malice of criticism and the malignant attacks of envy, whether he paint the mistress of his soul in all the glow of beauty, or tune his harp to deeds of war, when he sings 'the tale of other times'.[18]

'Like the oak of Morven', Ossian's fame increases, as the years advance. In 1807, an article in the same magazine implicitly used *Ossian* as a touchstone in differentiating between the two kinds of earliest poetry—the softly sweet or pastoral, and the grander, wilder, more sublime. Scottish poetry exhibits the distinction perfectly: 'Compare, in this view, the poetry and musick of the north and south of Scotland, and you will see whence the difference arises. The latter, like Arcadia of old, affords the sweetest pastoral strains in the world; the former breathes of nothing but wild grandeur and melancholy.'[19]

The nature of the appeal of the Ossianic poems in America, in one of its dimensions at least, and the kinds of association which developed around them, are apparent perhaps in only slightly exaggerated form in the response of the Pennsylvanian poet, John Blair Linn.[20] In a sketch of his life, written as a preface to an edition of his poems, his brother-in-law, Charles Brockden Brown stated that Linn held Ossian 'in higher estimation than any other poet'.[21] Good evidence of this is that Linn wrote something as inappropriate as his 'Ode on the Death of Washington', in an imitation of *Ossian*'s style. It is in his poem called *The Powers of Genius,*—a poem which makes Linn's lack of that quality all too plain— first published in 1801, that Linn's feelings towards Ossian are made most explicit. After addressing Shakespeare as his first genius, and writing a few lines on Alonzo d'Ercilla, the poet moves on to the Celtic bard:

> A perfect taste dwells only in the mind,
> With manners polish'd, sentiments refin'd;
> But Genius rises from the darkest shade,
> Where never ploughshare cut the barren glade;
> Amidst his native wilds and misty plains,
> Sublimest Ossian, pours his wizard strains.
> The voice of old revisits his dark dream,
> On his sad soul the deeds of warriors beam;
> Alone he sits upon the distant hill,
> Beneath him falls a melancholy rill;
> His harp lies by him on the rustling grass,
> The deer before him thro' the thickets pass;
> No hunter winds his slow and sullen horn,
> No whistling cow-herd meets the breath of morn;
> O'er the still heath the meteors dart their light
> And round him sweep the mournful blasts of night.
> O voice of Cona, bard of other times,
> May thy bold spirit visit these dull climes!
> May the brave chieftains of thy rugged plains
> Remember Ossian and revere his strains![22]

In a note to this section of the poem, Linn expatiates on his view of Ossian's mournfulness; it is related to the nature of his native region, 'a wild picturesque and melancholy country.... There he wandered through narrow vallies, thinly inhabited and bounded by precipices, which by the light of the moon presented a landscape the

most grotesque and ghastly. There he heard on every side the fall of
torrents, the mournful dashing of the waves along the friths and
lakes. . .'.[23] Here, *Ossian*'s part in the eighteenth century tradition
of the picturesque and the sublime, and the ease with which it could
be amalgamated with that tradition, become unmistakable. In an
appendix to his poem, Linn takes up the question of the authenticity of Macpherson's work. For him, there is no question or doubt:

> It is unaccountable, that men of literature should deny the
> authenticity of Ossian's poems. There is no evidence wanting
> to convince all who are willing to believe. Poems are still
> repeated in the original Erse, by many aged persons in the
> Highlands, and by some persons whom I have seen in this
> country, who obtained them from their fathers.[24]

Ossian's genius 'ranks with Homer's, and Milton's and Shakespeare's,
and with Fingal, "yields not to mortal man"'.[25]

The romanticism of Linn's response to *Ossian* may well have
been somewhat more extravagant than that of most of his contemporaries. But the American vogue for *Ossian* is clearly to be
related to the gradual emergence within America of a romantic
sensibility. By the 1790s American readers were becoming able
to recognise in *Ossian* a successful challenge to an already dying
English neo-classicism. To express enthusiasm for *Ossian* in the
1760s would have been bold indeed; to do so in the 1790s was
perfectly proper.

Such an explanation of the vogue for *Ossian* which began in
America in the 1790s is reasonably satisfactory. But one is tempted
to offer an additional one. Changes in taste are not always best
understood in isolation from other, wider forms of change: social,
political, economic, religious, or whatever. The fundamental
change in America between the 1760s and the 1790s is of course that
represented by the American Revolution. Now the Ossianic poems
are hardly to be seen as epics of revolutionary triumph.
Rather, as we have seen, they are epics of defeat, celebrations of a
society and a civilisation that are passing away. Nonetheless they
are epics with a strongly nationalist undercurrent, and furthermore,
the cultural nationalism they celebrate is one remote from the
genteel society and culture of eighteenth century England. Perhaps
it is here that an important source of *Ossian*'s appeal for Americans
is to be identified: now politically independent of England, they

respond enthusiastically to a literary experience challenging the polite culture to which they recognise their own continuing, but somewhat reluctant, subservience.

The challenge that *Ossian* represents, however, is a decidedly muted one—and here may lie another reason for its success. By the end of the eighteenth century, and in the early decades of the nineteenth, America had ceased to see herself as a revolutionary society. Ideologically committed to the new society of the New World, her social climate or temper was nonetheless not marked by radical fervour. Her literary tastes mirror such an ethos. By the 1790s America was beginning to respond to the kinds of writing which heralded the onset of romanticism. But America preferred—and went on preferring—its romanticism to be of a reasonably safe and undisturbing nature. This perhaps is the clue to the success, in America at least, of various manifestations of Scottish literary romanticism. The Ossianic poems represent no kind of threat to the present, to the status quo and its institutions. The emotions they evoke are nostalgic, elegiac, backward-looking; the epic heroism they celebrate has nothing to do with the modern world; their moral posture is undisturbing. The reader is invited to regret the present perhaps, not to revolutionise it. The romantic emotions of regret and nostalgia released by the poems are in the end quite harmless. May this not be a source of *Ossian*'s appeal for the broadly conservative societies of America and elsewhere?

Whatever else it may have represented, a major part of the significance of the *Ossian* vogue in America was the way in which it helped to create the grand, heroic, romantic image of Scotland and the Scots—the image to which all the literature discussed in this chapter in some way contributed. A suggestion of just how, in time, *Ossian* became assimilated into this standard American image of Scotland, is provided by the journal of a precocious young American, Edmund Griffin. Born in 1804, in Wyoming, Pennsylvania, he became at an early age a brilliant student at Columbia, and subsequently a minister in the American Episcopal Church. In 1828, he sailed for Europe, but he died in 1830, soon after his return from his European tour.

When he was thirteen or fourteen, Griffin had gone on a short holiday trip to the Falls of the Passaic, in New Jersey. In a journal which he kept on this visit, he records how one night he met a stranger near the falls, playing the bagpipes:

I thought ... of the Highlands of Scotland. I saw in imagination's eye, a Wallace, or a Bruce, leading Scotia's chiefs upon
some daring enterprise. I saw the chieftains of other times, the
turf-raised monument, the four gray stones that rested on the
body of heroes; methought I heard the deserted, blind, and
mournful Ossian lamenting for his child. 'Why openest thou
afresh the spring of my grief, son of Alpin, inquiring how
Oscar fell. He fell as the moon in a storm, as the sun from the
midst of his course, when clouds rise from the waste of the
waves, when the blackness of the storm enwraps Ardannider;
I like an ancient oak in Morven, I moulder alone in my place;
the blast hath lopped away my branches, and I tremble at the
wings of the north Oscar my son! shall I never see thee
more? ...'[26]

Griffin was clearly an imaginative young American who, in addition
to *Ossian*, had almost certainly been reading Jane Porter's tale of
Scotland's struggle for independence, *The Scottish Chiefs*, but it is
fascinating that such a passage should be written in response to so
minor a stimulus. The extravagantly romantic idea of Scotland that
is present here suggests a very different kind of Scottish impact upon
America than that represented by the intellectual influence of the
North Britons.

Douglas and *Ossian* were key works in the more literary and
consciously heroic strain in eighteenth century Scottish literature.
But for its energy and vitality that literature owed most to works
produced within the vernacular tradition: the most local, and
distinctively national, productions of the entire cultural renaissance
of eighteenth and early nineteenth century Scotland. The appearance
in America of Allan Ramsay's play, *The Gentle Shepherd*, and its
frequent reprintings, have already been noted. Originally published
in 1725, Ramsay's work had an obvious appeal in a world still
governed by Augustan literary standards; the pastoral remained
a favourite Augustan genre, and Ramsay, despite his preoccupation
with peasant characters, was careful to observe the rules of decorum
and good taste. Particularly in its songs, the play's vernacular is
often rich and therefore difficult, but Ramsay's success in other
directions seem to have been enough to outweigh this
drawback. English critical approval no doubt gained for *The*

Gentle Shepherd its first American publication in 1750. But its subsequent history of republication makes it clear that American interest in the play did not decline. Critical opinion around the end of the eighteenth century is probably fairly represented by the views of Samuel Miller in his *Brief Retrospect*. Having discussed the pastoral poems of Pope, Phillips, Gay, Shenstone, Rowe, and Collins, Miller goes on:

> But inferior to none that have been mentioned is the *Gentle Shepherd*, of Allan Ramsay, a work of great and original genius, in which a happy delineation of characters, an affecting exhibition of incidents, and a captivating simplicity and tenderness remarkably prevail.[27]

Ramsay's poems, too, were neither unknown nor unadmired. They were published at Philadelphia in 1813, and a selection called *Beauties of Allan Ramsay* appeared in the same city in 1815. In 1801, the *Port Folio* had noted that, 'The Poems of Allan Ramsay, the author of "The Gentle Shepherd," a pastoral drama, which will vie with the softest scenes of the Italian school, have been elegantly edited by some rightful lover of Caledonian song.'[28] An article in Brown's *Literary Magazine*, in 1806, attests the continuing respect and popularity enjoyed by Ramsay: he 'certainly deserves to be placed first in the rank of Scottish poets', and once again *The Gentle Shepherd* receives particular praise:

> A vein of solid good sense, a nice discrimination of character, a nervous elegance, and a pathetic simplicity of expression; in a word, the genuine language of nature, of passion, and of poetry, place his pastoral comedy of the Gentle Shepherd almost beyond our praise. From the closet of the philosopher to the maid at her distaff, the poet's eloquence enraptures every heart, and irresistibly commands our tears.[29]

What is of particular interest here is the fusion of Augustan critical values with the demands of the romantic sensibility. Such an account explains the play's enduring popularity. Like the poetry of Macpherson's *Ossian* it could be seen as engagingly romantic without being disturbingly revolutionary.

There is one point, however, on which the opinion of the writer in the *Literary Magazine* needs to be qualified: few of his contemporaries in 1806 would have agreed that Ramsay 'deserves to be placed first in the rank of Scottish poets'. By 1806 in America Ramsay had long been overtaken both in popularity and critical esteem by the inheritors of the tradition in which *The Gentle Shepherd* partially stands, and in particular by the poet who represents the fullest flowering of that tradition: Robert Burns.

That Burns, the ardent democrat, should have been an admirer of the America which had successfully asserted its right to freedom is hardly surprising. More surprising, perhaps, is the fact that he wrote only two poems directly concerned with America: in 1784, the 'Ballad on the American War', which is interesting only for the knowledge it shows of the progress of the war, and the pattern of British politics, and, in 1794, an 'Ode for General Washington's Birthday', a rhetorical celebration of the presence of Liberty in America, and her disappearance from her traditional abodes in England and Scotland.[30]

There is no evidence that these poems received any particular notice in America, though this is not to say that Burns's American reception may not have been helped by his belief in the worth and dignity of the individual, irrespective of his rank or station. That Burns's poetry did make an immediate and lasting impression upon America is quite clear. The original Kilmarnock edition of Burns's poems appeared in Scotland in 1786; two years later they were published in Philadelphia, and, some months later, along with a selection of Scots poems chiefly by Robert Fergusson, at New York. American enthusiasm for Burns is attested by the number of editions that followed. Editions of *Poems Chiefly in the Scottish Dialect, by Robert Burns*, appeared at Philadelphia in 1798, at Boston in 1801, at Wilmington, Delaware, in 1804, and at Baltimore in 1812 and 1815, while editions of *The Works of Robert Burns* appeared at Philadelphia in 1801, 1804, 1807, 1811, 1814, 1818, 1822, and 1823; at New York in 1820 and 1821; at Baltimore in 1814, 1815, and 1816; at Alexandria, Virginia, in 1813; and at Salem, New York, in 1815. A work entitled *Reliques of Robert Burns*, which included letters, poems, and critical comments on Scots songs, appeared at Philadelphia in 1809 and at Baltimore in 1815. *Letters Addressed to Clarinda* appeared at Philadelphia in 1809, and at Washington City in 1818, while an edition of Burns's letters was published at Boston in 1820.

What was probably the first critical appraisal of Burns to be read in America initiated a familiar approach to Burns's poetry:

Henry Mackenzie's comments in *The Lounger*, in the course of which Burns is referred to as 'this Heaven-taught ploughman', the natural genius, of humble birth and education.[31] *The Lounger*, a periodical paper which appeared in Edinburgh during 1785, 1786 and 1787, was published entire in two volumes at Philadelphia in 1789. In the following decades, American interest in Burns continued to grow. His life, of course, came to be a major topic of discussion. In 1797 the *New York Magazine* printed an account of Burns in which both 'the *powers* and the *failings* of genius' were ascribed to the poet; the writer of this article accepted the view of Mackenzie and other British critics that Burns was wrong in writing in the vernacular.[32] In John Blair Linn's poem, the *Powers of Genius*, Burns appears alongside Ossian as another type of genius. Here too the influence of the 'Heaven-taught ploughman' approach is apparent:

> Untaught by science, not refin'd by art,
> His sole instructors Nature and the heart;
> See lowly Burns move slowly o'er the lea,
> And breathe the song of sweetest harmony.
>
> (ll. 271–4)

The interest of the *Port Folio* in Burns is reflected chiefly by its reprinting many of his poems and songs, whereas that of Brockden Brown's *Literary Magazine* took a more critical turn.[33] An article in the *Literary Magazine* in 1804 compared Burns's singing the beauties of Ayr with Smollett's similar preoccupation with his native region in the *Ode on Leven Water*. Burns's emphasis on local place and language is carefully noted; no Chloes or Phyllises appear in his poems, no Parnassus or Helicon—a perception which would seem to have an obvious significance for a future American literature.[34] In the same year, the magazine published a sketch of Burns's life taken from Currie's recent, popular edition of the poems, which had been prefaced by a biography of the poet.[35] In 1807, another article discussed Burns's character and compared his genius with that of Cowper; the writer describes the poet as 'my idol', and disregards the alleged 'failings' of his genius.[36]

These comments in the literary magazines undoubtedly suggest widespread American interest in the poetry and personality of Burns. A much more specific assertion is made by Robert Walsh in the *American Review* in 1811. Walsh argues that America is particularly responsive to Burns and other Scottish writers:

> We have often been asked in the country of Mr. Scott,
> whether the people of the United States were generally
> acquainted with the poetry of Burns and Beattie. The answer
> which we have given, and which we still give, to this query,
> is calculated to startle the credulity of those, who see in us a
> mere tilling and shopkeeping race. We are quite satisfied that
> ... the works of the two poets we have just cited and even
> of Mr. Scott, are here more widely circulated, more generally
> read, and perhaps better understood than in England taken
> separately from Scotland. The dialect of the latter is more
> familiar and more grateful to us than to the inhabitants of her
> sister kingdom. We look with more reverence upon the literary
> and scientific character of Scotland, and are always prepared to
> receive with admiration, the intellectual off-spring of her
> capital, which we consider as the metropolis of genius and
> learning.[37]

Walsh's acknowledgement of Scotland's intellectual and literary
eminence is unexceptional; his suggestion that the Scottish
vernacular is more acceptable to American than to English ears
is much more striking. On the face of it the suggestion is
extravagant at least. But, as we shall see, it may not have been
entirely without foundation. Against Walsh's 1811 comment, with
its suggestion of critical awareness, it is telling to set a notice of
a new edition of Burns in the popular and influential *Knickerbocker
Magazine* in 1833:

> We are confident, that no true son of 'Auld Caledonia;' no lover
> of the plaid and the tartan, who loves to think on days 'of auld
> lang syne,' will neglect to procure a copy of this imperishable
> monument of his country's fame.[38]

The article goes on to develop the old theme of Burns the
ploughman-poet. By 1833, the spirit of vigorous, revolutionary
romanticism which had changed the course of European art and
thought was losing its initial force. For Burns, and for the country
of his birth, one consequence was a growing emphasis on the
sentimentalism which had always been implicit in their appeal—a
sentimentalism of which the plaid, the tartan, and 'auld lang syne' are
perfect symbols. Perhaps it was a healthier instinct which induced
Mrs Mackay, an old Scotswoman, to hang out as the sign-post

of her tavern in New York's Nassau Street, where Scottish dishes could be obtained and where many Scots met, a half-length picture of Burns with the inscription:

> The night drove on with songs and clatter
> And aye the ale was growing better.[39]

One consequence of American receptiveness to Burns was the increased popularity of Scots songs. The taste for such songs was of course much older than that for Burns. Many songs crossed the Atlantic with Scottish immigrants, and in the songs scattered throughout *The Gentle Shepherd* a more purely literary source for American knowledge and appreciation is to be found.[40] Here too Franklin's early ties with the Scottish literati play a minor part. Writing from Philadelphia to Sir Alexander Dick on 11 December 1763, Franklin said:

> My Daughter has been endeavouring to collect some of the Music of this Country Production, to send Miss Dick, in Return for her most acceptable Present of Scotch Songs.... She sings the Songs to her Harpsichord, and I play some of the softest Tunes on my Armonica, with which Entertainment our People here are quite charmed, and conceive the Scottish Tunes to be the finest in the World.[41]

In 1787, a year before the first American editions of Burns, a work by Alexander Reinagle, similar perhaps to that which Franklin's daughter received from Scotland, had been published in Philadelphia: *A Select Collection of the most favourite Scots Tunes. With variations for the piano forte or harpsichord*. But the most important publication was that in Philadelphia, in 1797, of *The Scots Musical Museum*, edited by John Aitken; this 'collection of the most favorite Scots Tunes, adapted to the voice, harpsichord, and pianoforte', probably derived from the work of the same name which had appeared in five volumes, in Edinburgh, between 1787 and 1796, under the editorship, in all but name, of Burns. Into the preparation of the songs for Johnson's *Scots Musical Museum* went much of Burns's poetic energies in the closing years of his life. Versions of a large number of these songs would of course be well-known to most of the Scots in America, but Aitken's volume would help to increase their general availability. Continuing American interest in Scots songs is suggested by the appearance at Philadelphia in 1818 of a

David Steuart Erskine, 11th Earl of Buchan (1742–1829) by John Brown.
A somewhat eccentric Scottish enthusiast for America and Americans.
(Reproduced by kind permission of the Council of the Society of
Antiquaries of Scotland. The drawing is on loan to the Scottish
National Portrait Gallery.)

Professor Dugald Stewart (1753–1828) by Sir Henry Raeburn.
His philosophy of common sense was widely accepted in early nine-
teenth century America. (Reproduced by kind permission of the
Scottish National Portrait Gallery.)

Lord Francis Jeffrey (1773–1850) by Colvin Smith.
Editor of the *Edinburgh Review* which made a major contribution to
American intellectual life. (Reproduced by kind permission of the
Scottish National Portrait Gallery.)

Mrs Anne Grant of Laggan (1755–1838) by William Bewick.
Her house in Edinburgh became a popular rendezvous for American
travellers in Scotland. (Reproduced by kind permission of the Scottish
National Portrait Gallery.)

work entitled *The Scottish Minstrel: being a complete collection of Burns' songs, together with his correspondence with Mr. Thomson* (George Thomson was another collector and editor of Scots songs with whom Burns collaborated). The evidence strongly suggests that Scots songs were widely known and sung in America in a period stretching from the mid-eighteenth century well into the nineteenth. Burns's versions of the words of these songs were certainly most popular, but the words were clearly always identified with the appropriate music.

An off-shoot of Sir Walter Scott's enormous popularity in America provides evidence of another kind of American appreciation of Scots airs. In America, as in Great Britain, Scott's novels were adapted for the stage almost as soon as they appeared. In some cases, these stage adaptions took a semi-operatic form, Scottish songs and tunes providing most of the musical background. In New Orleans in 1824, for example, there was presented the 'Grand Operatic Play of Rob Roy, or Auld Lang Sine', which included the songs, 'My love is like the red rose', 'Louden's bonny woods and braes', and 'Roy's wife of Aldivallah'. This particular presentation was based upon an English text. In 1829 it was performed in New Orleans again, this time with songs which had not appeared in the English version: 'Draw the sword Scotland', 'Charlie take me home love' arranged to the popular air of 'Wha'll be King but Charlie', 'March, March, Etrick and Tevotdale [*sic*]', and 'All the blue Bonnets are over the Border'.[42] Such performances, lending them all the prestige which came from association with Scott's magic name, must have done much to maintain and develop American interest in Scots songs.[43]

An encouragement of the taste for Scots songs was not the only consequence of Burns's undoubted popularity in America. Imitation is supposed to be the sincerest form of flattery and imitations of Burns's poems began to appear in America from an early date. These imitations were not limited in their scope to considerations of style and form; even Burns's language was transferred to the American scene. However briefly, the Scottish vernacular tradition had a flourishing off-shoot three thousand miles away in the New World. Most of these American poems in the Scottish vernacular remain anonymous, and no doubt the large majority of them were written by Scottish immigrants in America, but it is not without significance that such 'local' effusions should have found their way into the standard literary magazines of the day. Such a phenomenon helps us to understand Walsh's apparently odd belief that the Scottish vernacular was better received in America than in England, and perhaps hints at American recognition of the vernacular as a viable literary language.

Perhaps the earliest example of this American branch of the Scottish vernacular tradition appeared in the *New York Magazine*, in November, 1790. Entitled 'Verses Addressed to Robert Burns, the Air-shire Poet', the poem was cast in the familiar Burns stanza. The opening lines pay tribute both to Burns and Ramsay:

> Fair fa' ye Robie, canty callan,
> Wha rhym'st amaist as weel as Allan,
> An' pleasest highlan' lads an' lawlan,
>   Wi your auld gab,
> May never wae come near your dwallin,
>   Nor scaith nor scab.

Some of the verses have at least a suggestion of Burns's liveliness, and this stanza on time does not seem less than a good imitation of the Ayrshire poet:

> Auld Time, that jinking slippery chiel,
> Ere lang will mak' us end our reel,
> And a' our fire an' spirits queel,
>   And quench the low,
> That now within our breasts we feel,
>   And bleach our pow.[44]

The poem was written by 'a lady in Gorham' in Maine; that it should have travelled down to New York is interesting in itself.

Between 1805 and 1808, the *Port Folio* published several original poems in Scots. Some of these suggest the truly popular basis of Burns's appeal. In 1805 appeared two poems, both written in stanzaic patterns regularly used by Burns, by Henry Clow, a Scot from Ayrshire, who held the position of baker at Nassau Hall, in Princeton.[45] Clow's poems were not without their effect; in a subsequent issue appeared another poem in Scots by an 'unlettered, and unknown Farmer', who had been inspired by Clow's example to write a poem on Burns. The vernacular used in this poem is particularly rich. Here is a stanza on the topic which has always been a favourite of Scots poets:

> O death, why did ye smite my Robin,
> Why stave his cogie lip and laggin.
> Why plunge the warl' in dool and sabbin,
> >   Wi your d—d scythe;
> Why stap his winsome tunefu' gabin
> >   Sae bal and blythe.[46]

In the following year appeared another poem in the Burns stanza
entitled, 'To the Blackbird in Winter':

> Poor bird! my heart is truly wae,
> Forlorn to see thee wand'rin' sae,
> Whar ilka thing's thy mortal fae...[47]

—the influence here is that of the sentimental and moralising Burns
of 'To a Mountain Daisy'—and a second 'Lament on Burns', in
which the poet is linked, as death's most recent victim, with the
older bards Ramsay and Fergusson.[48] In 1806, too, appeared another
contribution from Henry Clow: 'Scotch Verses' is largely in English,
but the poem contains some pleasantly ironic touches. The 'bonny
lasses o' this place' come under discussion:

> I dinna like ye're fauts to tell,
> For ilka ane has fauts himsel',
> Tho' faith there's some can scarcely spell
> >   Yet think they've knowledge.
> An' like to chat wi' chiels that dwell
> >   At Princeton college.[49]

Clow was almost certainly the author of verses 'In Memory of
Burns', which the *Port Folio* printed later in 1806.[50]

In 1807, another poem in Scots, apparently written by a Scottish
visitor in America, appeared in the magazine; once again the Burns
stanza is used, and the poem praises at length American freedom,
hospitality, and scenery.[51] In the following year a poem by G.
Turnbull, invoking Ossian, Burns, Ramsay, Hamilton of Gilbertfield, and King James, called 'Elegy on My Auld Fiddle', appeared,[52]
and also what was called 'A New Scotch Song' to the tune of
'Whistle o'er the lave o't'. Its concluding stanza returns to the death
theme:

> And when auld Death, wi' ruthless paw
> Shall clapperclaw us ane and a',
> We maun submit to Nature's law,
> And whistle o'er the lave o't.[53]

In 1813, the *Analectic Magazine* published a poem in Scots, in the Burns manner, by William Ingram, entitled 'To My Auld Coat',[54] and in 1821, the *Port Folio* once again, published 'Verses on Burns' Punch-Bowl' supposed to have been extemporised while that vessel was put to its original use.[55]

All the poems described have an occasional air about them, but there is little doubt that some at least represent the impingement upon the established American literary scene of the work of groups of American, or Scottish–American, rhymsters who, inspired by Burns's example, had begun to write verses in the Scottish vernacular on local and occasional themes. Such a group certainly existed in northern New England, centred in the person of Robert Dinsmoor, the 'rustic Bard'. Dinsmoor was an American of Ulster-Scots descent:

> The highest pedigree I plead—
> A Yankee born—true Scottish breed.[56]

His ancestors had moved from the Tweed area of southern Scotland to Northern Ireland. Born in 1757, he had fought against the British during the Revolution, and had been present at the surrender of Burgoyne. Most of Dinsmoor's poems originally circulated in manuscript among his friends, or appeared in local newspapers in his native New Hampshire or the adjoining province of Maine, but they were collected and published, along with some poems by rhyming friends and one or two by minor Scottish poets, at Haverhill, Massachusetts, in 1828.

Burns is clearly the leading inspiration behind Dinsmoor's verse, though if we can accept the claims made in the preface to his book of poems, he had begun to write, presumably in Scots, some time before Burns's poetry was published either in America or Scotland. A poem called 'Skip's Last Advice' on a favourite old dog of the poet's father, would seem to support the claim; it is said to have been written in the poet's seventeenth year, that is, in 1773 or 1774. The poem begins in rhyming couplets, but then passes over into the Burns stanza—suggesting that the published version is probably a revision of the original. Nevertheless, it remains true that this poem written in New England in the early 1770s, stands directly in a distinctively Scottish poetic tradition—a tradition represented by Hamilton of Gilbertfield's 'Last Dying Words of Bonny Heck', which had been included in Watson's *Choice Collection*, and

Allan Ramsay's 'Lucky Spence's Last Advice'—a tradition which
Burns was to take up in 'The Death and Dying Words of Poor
Mailie'. The direct influence of Burns, however, is also apparent:
in a poem such as 'The Sparrow':

> Poor innocent and hapless Sparrow!
> Why should my moul-board gie thee sorrow?
> This day thou'll chirp, an' mourn the morrow,
> > Wi' anxious breast—
> The plough has turn'd the mould'ring furrow
> > Deep o'er thy nest.[57]

—and in the many verse epistles, nearly all in the Burns stanza,
which Dinsmoor wrote to his friends.

Dinsmoor's talent was neither large nor particularly vigorous;
most of his poems are spoiled by a facile, sentimental, moralising
strain. But occasionally, writing in a lighter vein, he can achieve
a minor success. What is probably his best poem also falls within
the Scottish tradition of animal poems: verses about a dog, called
'Spring's Lamentation and Confession'. The opening stanzas suggest
the lightly ironic tone of the whole:

> Alas! an' I'm condemn'd to death!
> A Cobler now maun stap my breath;
> To lea' my Dame, I'm very laith,
> > Though 'tis her sentence;
> May he that caus'd it, an' she baith,
> > Soon get repentance.
>
> Lang hae I liv'd wi' kind Miss Bessy,
> Wha kept me cozie, warm an' fleshy;
> In lanely hours she would caress me,
> > An' mak' me fain,
> Baith e'en an' morn I gat a messy,
> > As though her wean.[58]

Dinsmoor was a friend of the young J. G. Whittier. In a poem
addressed to the 'Rustic Bard', Whittier too is able to turn to the
Scottish vernacular:

> Health to the hale auld 'Rustic Bard!'
> Gin ye a poet wad regard,
> Who deems it honor to be ca'd
> > Yere rhymin' brither,
> Twould gie his muse a rich reward—
> > He asks nae ither.[59]

Another of Dinsmoor's rhyming friends was the Revd David M'Gregore; his poems compare favourably with Dinsmoor's own. Here is the first stanza of a witty verse epistle:

> Did e'er a cuif tak' up a quill
> Wha ne'er did aught that he did weel,
> To gar the muses rant an' reel,
>   An' flaunt an' swagger,
> Nae doubt ye'll say, 'tis that daft chiel,
>   E'en Dite M'Gregore.[60]

Another Scottish-American poet who, like Dinsmoor, achieved something more than a purely local fame, was David Bruce, whose *Poems Chiefly in the Scottish Dialect* was published in Washington, Pennsylvania, in 1801 Bruce was an emigrant from Caithness, the northernmost county of the Scottish mainland, who had arrived in Maryland in 1784. After some years in Bladensburgh, he moved to Burgets-town in Washington County, Pennsylvania. It was there, in the 1790s, that most of the poems collected and published in 1801 were written—many of them had appeared under the signature of the 'Scots-Irishman' in the *Western Telegraphe*, a weekly newspaper printed in Washington.

Bruce's writings were largely political in character. A Federalist of strong conviction, he published numerous satirical poems on political opponents or the principles to which they subscribed. Some of these political poems are in English, many of them in Scots. On one occasion, Bruce's opponents had ridiculed his use of Scots; in reply he pretended to remonstrate with his muse, only to learn that his fame depended entirely on his use of the vernacular. But more interesting now are the poems in Scots on less local and ephemeral topics.

In 1794, soon after the Whiskey Rebellion in Western Pennsylvania, occasioned by Hamilton's excise tax on liquors, Bruce wrote 'To Whiskey', a poem which suggested that the merits of the drink were such as to make it worth any tax. Burns's influence is apparent in the spirit of the poem as well as in its form:

> Great Pow'r, that warms the heart and liver,
> And puts the bluid a' in a fever,
> If dull and heartless I am ever,
>   A Blast o' thee
> Maks me as blyth, and brisk and clever
>   As ony bee.[61]

This poem provoked a response, 'Whiskey, in answer', written, in Scots again, by 'Aqua Vitae', 'an ingenious gentleman of Pittsburgh', who was in fact Hugh Henry Brackenridge, a native of Campbeltown in western Scotland, a graduate of the College of New Jersey, lawyer, judge, and author of *Modern Chivalry*.[62] Bruce and Brackenridge continued their exchanges in subsequent poems. In one, Brackenridge compares Bruce with Allan Ramsay and suggests that the differences are due to Bruce's American situation:

> But's nae your fau't, my canty Callan,
> That ye fa' short o' the Auld Allan;
> There's neither Highland man, nor Lallan',
>   That's here the same;
> But finds him scrimpit o' the talen',
>   He had at hame.[63]

In his reply the 'Scots-Irishman' agrees. America cannot compare with Scotland as a home for the Muses:

> Whare's there a Forth, a Tweed, or Tay?
> Thro' hills and greens that saftly stray,
> Whare shepherds spen' the simmer's day
>   Sae peacefullie—
> Thir scenes gar'd Allan lilt his lay
>   Wi' sic a glee.
>
> What's here to gie the mind a heese?
> Deil het ava', but great lang trees,
> Nae flow'ry haughs or bony braes,
>   To please the een,
> Nor bleating flocks upo' the leas
>   Are heard or seen.[64]

Of special interest is the familiarity of the attitudes expressed in these poems in the context of the critical debate over the need for a national American literature. Bruce's notion of the barrenness of the American scene as a source of creative inspiration for the literary artist was soon to become a commonplace. Where America had 'diel het ava'' to offer the literary imagination, the Old World was believed to possess an exemplary richness of 'association' deriving from centuries-old literary and historical traditions. Ironically, the use of the Scottish vernacular by these two poets in America was indirectly contributing to the solution of the problem they were describing. Except as evidence of the influence of Burns in America the existence of these Scottish-American poems by Bruce, Brackenridge, Dinsmoor and the rest is of no significance: they represent no more than a rather bizarre footnote to American literary history. But in however limited a way their existence does demonstrate the viability of the Scottish vernacular as a literary medium. In this connection Burns himself is the key figure. Here was a poet who was not English, whose language was frequently vulgar, unpolished, and even unintelligible to the English reader, whose poems were often firmly tied to his native region, and whose songs owed nothing at all to the classical literature of England. Nonetheless he had been acclaimed, in England and Scotland, as a writer of true genius, an honour to his country. Particularly in his concern for place, for the individual beauties of Ayrshire and of Scotland rather than for the generalities of the classical tradition, and in the use he made of the native Scottish vernacular, Burns pointed the way forward to a national American literature.

Burns, however, was not the only poet of the Scottish vernacular tradition to be published and read in America. As has been noted, one of the earliest editions of Burns in America, that at New York in 1788, included a selection of poems by Burns's predecessor, the Edinburgh poet Robert Fergusson. An edition of Fergusson's poems was published in Philadelphia in 1815, and references to him in the periodicals are frequent enough to suggest that his place in the vernacular tradition was generally recognised. Another vernacular poet well-known in America was Hector Macneill. *The Poetical Works of Hector Macneill* appeared at New York in 1802. If Macneill is remembered at all today it is as the author of such popular songs as 'Come under my plaidie' and 'I lo'ed ne'er a lad but ane'. In 1805 the *Port Folio* printed 'Come Under my Plaidie', and also another song by Macneill, 'O Tell me how for to woo'.[65] In 1815, a second American edition of his poems appeared at Philadelphia; but the advertisement to this edition, mentioning the earlier one at New York, indicates that it had had only a small circulation.[66] Then Alexander Wilson, better known as an American ornithologist than as a Scottish-American poet, continued to write verses after his arrival in America from Scotland in 1794.[67] In 1805, Wilson's narrative poem 'Watty and Meg', Scottish in every respect including language, was printed at Philadelphia.[68]

American responsiveness to the vernacular tradition in Scottish literature is evident from the popular and critical admiration of its major exponents, the regular publication in America of their works, the wide and enduring popularity of Scots songs, and the writing and publication of poems in Scots in America. Such American interest in writing apparently so exclusively Scottish is, as has been said, of some interest as a by-way of American literary history; and awareness of it adds something to our understanding of popular and critical taste in the formative period of American literature. But the true significance of the American response to the Scottish vernacular tradition, like that to the development of Scottish literature as a whole in the eighteenth and early nineteenth centuries, was the recognition it implied of how a culturally backward and dependent nation might move towards the achievement of a worthy and truly national literature.

The Scottish vernacular tradition in poetry reached its high point with the achievement of Robert Burns. A great deal of vernacular poetry went on being written in Scotland long after Burns's death in 1797, but native energy and comic and satiric zest came increasingly to be replaced by provincial sentimentality and pawkiness. The two poets who dominated the Scottish literary scene—and to an extent the English one as well—in the first decade of the nineteenth century made only occasional use of the vernacular. But both Thomas Campbell and Walter Scott made a significant impact upon America.

The position occupied by America in the Scottish liberal tradition has already been noted. Brought up within that tradition, Campbell is the first Scottish writer whose liberal principles were recognised and welcomed in America. Throughout his life, Campbell had close, personal ties with America. His father, Alexander Campbell, had lived and worked for many years as a merchant in Falmouth, Virginia. Shortly before the Revolution, he had returned to Glasgow and had established a firm trading with Virginia; but like many other Glasgow merchants in the Scottish-American trade, he was ruined by the events of 1775. Alexander Campbell was a man of considerable ability; in Glasgow he was a close friend of both Adam Smith and Thomas Reid—it was from Professor Reid that his son, the poet, took his name. With friends such as these, it is quite probable that despite his personal involvement in the American colonies, Alexander Campbell's political views, like those of his son, were of a liberal nature. But in his son's case, the decisive influence was that of another of Glasgow's

distinguished liberals—Professor John Millar, whose lectures
Thomas Campbell attended while at Glasgow University.[69] In 1794,
when he was a sixteen-year-old student, Campbell had gone over
to Edinburgh to be present at the trial of Joseph Gerrald; for him,
as for many others, the experience was one he never forgot.
Afterwards he said that it represented an era in his life.[70]

With such a background, it is not surprising that Campbell
should be well-disposed towards America. In March, 1797, planning
to join his brothers who were already in Virginia, he was ready to
cross the Atlantic as an emigrant. But his eldest brother persuaded
him not to take such a step at that time: he needed first to
acquire more 'useful knowledge'.[71] A letter which Campbell wrote
to a friend named Thomson, almost exactly a year later, sums up the
attitude towards America he held then, and was to hold throughout
his life: 'Ever since I knew what America was, I have loved and
respected her government and state of society....'[72] Almost twenty
years later, Campbell was again thinking of emigrating to America.
In a letter to Washington Irving, in May, 1817, expressing dismay
at the political situation in Britain, he said that he might be forced to
take up his abode in 'the only other land of Liberty'.[73] Towards
the end of his life, in 1840, in conversation with an American named
Lester at the home of William Beattie, he again expressed his
admiration and love for America:

> I love America very much—and I came very near being an
> American myself. My father passed the early portion of his life
> in Virginia. My uncle adopted it as his country; one of his sons
> was district-attorney under Washington's administration. My
> brother, Robert, settled in Virginia and married a daughter of
> your glorious Patrick Henry. Yes, if I were not a Scotsman, I
> should like to be an American.[74]

America responded, in a sense, to these expressions of regard by
the poet by reading and admiring his poems. The part played in his
popularity by his Scottish nationality is difficult to estimate, but there
can be no doubt that his liberal principles and admiration for
America helped to strengthen his American reputation.[75] An article
in the *New Englander* in May, 1851, suggested that this was so;
Campbell 'was born near the opening of our Revolution,' it said,
'and the connection of his family with this country must have
familiarised him from his early years with our struggles for freedom';
he 'is the poet of liberty and humanity'.[76]

Apart from these considerations, Campbell's American reputation was promoted through his friendship with Washington Irving. In 1810, Campbell's brother, then living in New York, appealed to Irving for help in the publication of 'O'Connor's Child' and a new edition of *Gertrude of Wyoming*. Irving responded by writing a short life of the author as an introduction to the poems.[77] (Later, in 1815, Irving published a new version of this biographical sketch in his *Analectic Magazine*.)[78] The personal ties between the two writers were strengthened through a visit which Peter Irving, the brother of the American author, paid to Campbell at Sydenham, in Kent, his English home, in the autumn of 1813. Peter tried to assist Campbell in obtaining an American copyright for a work which was to appear simultaneously in both countries.[79] Washington Irving himself called at Sydenham in July, 1815, pointlessly, since Campbell was away.[80] In August, 1817, the two writers did meet there, and as a result, Irving wrote to Henry Brevoort proposing that Campbell should be invited to America to repeat a series of twelve lectures on poetry and belles-lettres, which he had recently given with great success in London. The idea was well received in America, but in the end Campbell proved unwilling to undertake such a trip.[81]

Campbell's *Pleasures of Hope* was first published in America, at New York in 1800, a year after its appearance in Britain. The poem's success is attested by the four other editions in New York, and another at Wilmington which appeared in the same year. Further publishings occurred at New York in 1804 and 1822; at Philadelphia in 1804; at Cambridge, Massachusetts, in 1807; at Boston in 1811 and 1814; at Baltimore in 1813 and 1814; at Albany in 1814; and at Richmond in 1820. *Gertrude of Wyoming* appeared in America immediately after its publication in Great Britain in 1809; in that same year it went through three editions in New York. It appeared again in Philadelphia in 1820. But by then several editions of *The Poetical Works of Thomas Campbell* had been published: at Baltimore in 1811 and 1814; at Philadelphia in 1815; and at New York in 1821.

American criticism of Campbell followed closely that of the British reviews. The Scottish poet was of course a great favourite of the *Edinburgh Review*. In 1809, *Gertrude of Wyoming* was reviewed very favourably indeed: Campbell's restraint, the refined tenderness of his sentiment, which contrasted so favourably with the extravagance of most modern poetry, was noted with particular approval.[82] An article in the *Port Folio*, in 1814, drawing a parallel between Scott and Campbell, emphasised the same qualities; in comparison with Scott, Campbell's work was more delicate, more refined, more tender; Scott was too concerned with immediate popularity.[83] Reviewing *Theodric and other Poems*, in 1824, the *Edinburgh*, noting Campbell's firm adherence to liberal principles, again praised him highly:

> Mr. Campbell is not among the number of those poets whose hatred of oppression has been chilled by the lapse of years, or allayed by the suggestions of a base self-interest. He has held on his course through good and through bad report, unseduced, unterrified, and is now found in his duty, testifying as fearlessly against the invaders of Spain, in the volume before us, as he did against the spoilers of Poland in the very first of his publications.[84]

However important his liberalism may have been, *Gertrude of Wyoming*, with its particular Pennsylvanian setting, and its semi-historical story of the American frontier, would have been enough in itself to guarantee Campbell's American popularity. Edmund Griffin, who, as we have already seen, was particularly receptive to impressions from Scottish writers, returned to his native Wyoming, Pennsylvania, in his thirteenth year. The journal he kept describes his first view of the valley of Wyoming: 'A scene more lovely than imagination ever painted, presented itself to my sight—so beautiful, so exquisitely beautiful, that even the magic verse of Campbell did not do it justice.'[85] Griffin had personal reasons for visiting Wyoming; other Americans travelled to the area only because Campbell had written of it. The Revd Mr Lester, who met Campbell at William Beattie's house, had gone on such a poetical pilgrimage. 'Every day,' he said, 'we wandered through the primeval forests; and when tired, we used to sit down under their solemn shade among the falling leaves, and read "Gertrude of Wyoming".' To this Campbell replied, 'It overcomes me to think that in that wild American scenery I have had such readers; all, too, among scenes which I never witnessed myself.'[86] By choosing to write a poem with an American setting and story, Campbell helped both to sharpen American awareness of a difference between the New World and the Old—the comparative absence of literary and romantic associations in the New—and to show American writers how to supply such a deficiency. A Scottish writer, very popular in America, may be seen here, once again, pointing the way forward for a national American literature.

The importance of Walter Scott in the literary and social history of the United States has always been recognised. From the immediate recognition he received on the appearance of the *Lay of the Last Minstrel* in 1805, until his death in 1832, his reputation, popularity, and influence in America steadily increased. His reputation and fame in America excelled that of any other writer of the time—American, English, or Scottish.[87] *The Lay of the Last Minstrel* was published at Philadelphia in 1805. Subsequent editions appeared at Philadelphia in 1807 and 1810; at New York in 1806 and 1811; at Charleston in 1806; at Boston in 1807 and 1810; at Baltimore in 1811 and 1812; and at Savannah in 1811. The story is the same for the other narrative poems. *Marmion* was published at Boston in 1808 and 1810; at Philadelphia in 1808 and 1810; at Baltimore in 1811 and 1812; and at New York in 1811. *The Lady of the Lake* appeared at New York, Boston, and Philadelphia in 1810; at Baltimore in 1811 and 1812; at Montpelier, Vermont, in 1813; and at New York again in 1813. The other narrative poems were published in due course and collected editions of Scott's poems were soon also making their appearance. Hence three years before the appearance of *Waverley*, in 1814, Scott's popularity was already such that a writer in the *American Review* could remark that,

> No poetical works, not excepting even those of Cowper and Burns, have been more widely circulated or read with more avidity in this country, than those of Walter Scott, who is now as a poet, on the highest pinnacle of fame and popularity. The 'Lay of the Last Minstrel' belongs to every private library, and is familiar to the memory of almost every man among us, who has the most inconsiderable pretensions to literature.[88]

Five thousand copies of *The Lay of the Last Minstrel* had been sold, and already, only a year after its publication, four thousand copies of *The Lady of the Lake*. These figures provide an interesting comparison with those of a later date for Scott's novels. In his *Discourse concerning the Influence of America on the Mind*, delivered in 1823, C. J. Ingersoll asserted that 'nearly 200,000 copies of the Waverly [*sic*] novels, comprising 500,000 volumes, have issued from the American press in the last nine years.'[89] Even if these figures

should not be perfectly accurate, it is obvious that Scott's novels
had reached a mass public which had no 'pretensions to literature'
at all. And the figures are in fact confirmed by an estimate made
by John Neal in 1825: 'Half a million of the great Scotch novels,
we dare say, have re-issued from the American press. They are read
by everybody—everywhere—all over the States.'[90] During his
travels in North America, between 1828 and 1831, James Stuart
noted that copies of Sir Walter's works were to be found 'even
more frequently than Mr. Cooper's novels, wherever we go in this
country'.[91]

His subsequent fame gives an especially ironic twist to Scott's
inauspicious introduction to the American literary scene. According
to the reminiscences of J. W. Francis a copy of *The Lay of the Last
Minstrel* was presented by its author to a childhood friend now
in New York, Mrs Divie Bethune. A number of the New York
literati were thus able to read the poem and a debate followed
over whether it merited publication in the city. Because the poem
was 'too local in its nature' the coterie of critics decided not to
advise publication. However Longworth printed the introduction
to the first canto of the poem in the *Belles-Lettres Repository* of 1805,
and the Scott vogue was underway.[92] Charles Brockden Brown's
Literary Magazine was the first American journal to praise Scott. In
1805, a contributor wrote of *The Lay of the Last Minstrel*, 'There has
just fallen into my hands a poem, which has given me so much
pleasure that I cannot forbear calling the attention of your readers
to it.' It is 'a very beautiful and entertaining poem, in a style which
may be just deemed original, and which affords evidence of the
genius of the author.'[93] But here again there is proof of the
influence and importance of the *Edinburgh Review*: the second
part of the quotation is taken directly from the *Review*'s notice of the
poem.[94] The *Port Folio* proceeded in a more straightforward manner
simply reprinting in its columns a large part of the *Edinburgh*'s
article.[95] In 1807, the *Port Folio* could refer to Scott's 'honourable
name', as one 'now perfectly familiar to every lover of poetical
description'.[96] And in the next year, in the course of a laudatory
notice of *Marmion*, Scott is recognised as the newest of a long line
of distinguished Scottish poets:

> Scotland has long been eminently distinguished for the
> splendour of her poetical reputation. Drummond of Haw-

thornden, Hamilton of Balfour [Bangour], Thomson, Beattie and Burns have glorified their country by the most brilliant colours of imagination. To these *time honoured* names we may now add that of Walter Scott, who in every respect is most certainly their compeer.[97]

The *Port Folio* later went through a period in which Scott was regarded with rather less than the usual favour: when *Waverley* finally appeared the editor doubted whether a work so poor could be by Scott.[98] The magazine could truly maintain, in 1815, in a review of *The Lord of the Isles* that, 'Our approbation of his [Scott's] writings ... has never been unqualified; nor has our admiration arisen to the pitch of enthusiasm.'[99] In this particular case, objection is made to Scott's descriptions of the Scottish Highlands. Too few people have seen these places, 'the beauties of such description, if indeed it possess any, must be utterly lost to all who are strangers to that romantic country.'[100] That the reference to 'that romantic country' could even be made was in fact largely due to Scott and his predecessors, and it was precisely Scott's descriptions that were making such scenes both known and appreciated. The review of *Waverley* in the *Analectic Magazine*, on the other hand, had emphasised the accuracy of Scott's presentation of Highland society and scenery.[101] And in 1818, the *North American Review*, in discussing *Rob Roy*, drew from Scott's Scottish preoccupation a quite opposite, and more accurate conclusion to that of the *Port Folio*. 'His own country is the home and school of his genius—it is familiar to him, and thus, as the scene of his stories, it gives them an air of easy reality.'[102]

However, by 1820, the *Port Folio* could describe *The Abbot* as 'another of the delightful creations of the Scottish novelist',[103] and by 1822, Scott had become, 'the first genius of our age'.[104] That judgement is one with which few American critics or readers could have disagreed. Each successive novel of Scott was received with enthusiasm. The pattern of reviews was always the same: a few introductory pages, mostly of praise, and then many pages of extracts from the work in question. Phrases such as 'the wealth of his imagination', 'the reach and majesty of his power', typify the American reaction to Scott; he 'stands upon an eminence, to which approaches have been made, but no one has placed himself by his side.'[105] If anyone at all shared Scott's lofty eminence, it could only be Shakespeare himself: 'The Novels of Scott, have become in fact, a literature of themselves, and we know not if his writings were expunged, what deeper injury could be inflicted on English literature, except sentence of oblivion were passed on Shakespeare himself.'[106]

American enthusiasm for Scott had many ramifications. In introducing an article called the 'Original of the Black Dwarf', the editor of the *Analectic Magazine* remarks on this enthusiasm:

> The public feeling is alive to all that issues from the prolific genius of the author of Rob Roy, etc. and connects with whatever is illustrative of his works, the eagerness of curiosity and the attention of interest. Under this impression we give place to the following account of The Black Dwarf. . . .[107]

Before the appearance of the novel, the same magazine had already printed an account of Rob Roy which had appeared in *Blackwood's*[108] and in 1819, again from a Scottish source, an account appeared of the originals of the Cottage of St Leonard's, Muschat's Cairn, the ruins of St Anthony's Chapel, and of Effie and Jeanie Deans.[109]

Another instance of the almost obsessional interest in Scott is related to the cloak of anonymity under which *Waverley* and the subsequent novels appeared. Among the suggestions made on the question of their authorship more than one linked the Waverley Novels with a North American author. In 1819, the *Analectic Magazine* pronounced all such suggestions worthless: 'With respect to the disputed parentage of these novels, we are positively informed, that the many stories of their "transatlantic origin," so confidently circulated in the United States, are destitute of all foundation.'[110] Only a year before, in discussing *Rob Roy*, largely on the flimsy evidence of the use of the word 'wig-wam', and in earlier writings of the term 'the plantations', the same magazine had attributed the authorship of the novels to a Dr Greenfield who had visited America some years before.[111] A more popular attribution was to Walter Scott's brother, Thomas, who lived in Montreal. Professor John Griscom, who travelled in Britain in 1818 and 1819, mentions the canvassing of this idea,[112] and a comment in the Philadelphia *Literary Gazette*, in 1821, confirms the popularity of the suggestion:

> The Quarterly Review, a few years ago hinted, that the

merit of authorship belonged to a *brother* of Walter Scott, living
beyond the Atlantic, and the same idea has been more than
once expressed in our newspapers. We understand that at
Montreal, the place of residence of Mr. Thomas Scott, the
fact is universally believed. . . .[113]

Francis also recalled hearing arguments in favour of the view that
the true author of the Waverley Novels was Scott's brother in
Canada. Charles Mathews, the English comic actor, in the course
of a visit to New York, was the first person, according to Francis,
'who gave a pretty decisive opinion that Scott was the author of the
Waverley novels'. Mathews' opinion was given five years before
Scott's own disclosure in 1827, 'and while we in New York were
digesting the argument of Coleman, of the Evening Post, and his
correspondents, who attempted to prove that such could not be the
truth, and that a Major or Col. Scott, of Canada, was the actual
author.'[114] The notion of at least a transatlantic residence for the
author of the Waverley Novels was clearly widely enough debated
for the idea to have had a substantial appeal.

Final evidence of the extraordinary esteem for Scott in America
is provided by accounts of the reaction to the news of his death. A
European traveller in America, C. D. Arfwedson, happened to be
in Charleston when the news arrived; he was present at a specially-
called meeting of the St Andrew's Society—no doubt St Andrew's
societies throughout the country reacted in a similar way—and
listened to a tribute of respect paid to Scott's memory:

> The extraordinary talents of the deceased as a poet and novelist
> were represented in colours which soon drew the most
> enthusiastic applause from all parts of the hall, and clearly
> evinced a disposition on the part of the audience warmly to
> contribute to the proposed subscription for raising, in some
> conspicous place in the city, a marble bust in commemoration
> of the Scottish bard.[115]

The most effective speaker was General Hayne, the governor of
the state. In Richmond, the newspapers carrying the news of Scott's
death appeared with black borders.[116]

Such references as these do no more than indicate the kind of
impact that Scott had upon America. The depth and pervasiveness
of that impact are beyond dispute. Explanations of it are quite
another matter. Of course a large part of Scott's appeal in America

F

must have been identical with that felt by readers in Scotland, England and the rest of Europe. The universality of Scott's success makes it obvious that there was much about his work that appealed to contemporary readers whatever their place of origin. What precisely that was is itself far from clear. Not, I should say, simply his romanticism. Broadly speaking romanticism was individualistic, progressive, revolutionary; Scott was none of these things. His romanticism was hedged around with all kinds of reservations, ambivalences, and hesitations. Even if it is true that most contemporary readers, including American readers, tended to neglect, or closed their eyes to, Scott's rationalism and Scott's realism, difficulties remain with the identification of Scott's romanticism as the key to his popular appeal. The Waverley Novels, which rocketed Scott to unprecedented heights of popularity and fame, were mostly written and published in a period of powerful social and political counter-revolution both in Europe and America. On the face of it the writer to be idolised in such a period is hardly likely to have been an exponent of revolutionary romanticism. Scott's romanticism, like that of so many earlier Scottish writers, appealed so widely probably because, however attractive, it seemed relatively safe rather than socially disruptive.

Such a socio-political explanation of the Scott phenomenon in Europe and America is clearly sufficiently fashionable. But other more literary perspectives should also be kept in mind. That there are dangers in the dissolution of literary phenomena into broader socio-political trends is certainly suggested by the most popular of explanations of Scott's fantastic vogue in America. Twain's thesis, alluded to in the note on page 170, was that Scott's romantic nationalism, his celebration of bogus aristocratic values, his advocacy of medieval notions of chivalry and nobility, had inspired the American South with a set of misguided notions about itself, what it believed in, and what it represented. The result was an inevitable conflict with the North. In other words it is the socio-political structure of the South that best explains Scott's appeal in that section of America. Now it is perfectly true that some of the more extreme manifestations of the Scott vogue in America occurred in the Southern states. It was in the South, for example, that quasi medieval jousting tournaments, modelled on that described at Ashby in an early chapter of *Ivanhoe*, became a common form of popular entertainment. Southern plantations and Southern children did often owe their names to Scott's novels. Certain words and phrases from Scott did find their way into popular, chauvinistic Southern songs. But the sociology of the South can hardly explain Scott's appeal for the rest of the United States. And there is no evidence that Scott was read with significantly greater enthusiasm in Charleston or Savannah than in Boston or New York.

The basic weakness of Twain's case, and that of all those modern commentators who have either sympathised with his view or tried to refute it, is a lack of literary historical perspective. Almost without exception these commentators treat Scott as an isolated phenomenon: the Great Unknown indeed, Scott, we gather, arrived in America like a meteor from outer space. As we have seen, of course, nothing could be farther from the truth. Significantly, Scott's strength as a writer was not that of startling originality, boldness of imagination. His achievement was to build on an existing literary tradition and, by assimilating it, bring it to a brilliant consummation. *Douglas* and *Ossian* on the one hand, Ramsay and Burns and the whole tradition of Scottish ballad and song on the other, all of these prepared the way for Scott and did much to make possible his spectacular popular triumph. The first half-dozen or so of the Waverley Novels, all of them concerned with periods in the Scottish past, sent Scott's fame and reputation soaring to unprecedented heights in America not because they represented something unfamiliar and unknown, but because they were the crown of a Scottish literary tradition whose line of descent had long been known and admired in America. What the evidence makes clear is that Scott reaped the harvest of his predecessors' sowing. If this is the key to Scott's instant American success, may it not go far to explain his success elsewhere?

In relation, at any rate, to the particular question of the popular American image of Scotland, Scott's contribution was a determining one. Just how far Scott's writings controlled and directed American responses to the experience of Scotland will appear in due course, but it is clear that Scott's main effect in America was the confirming and strengthening of a series of ideas and attitudes which his Scottish predecessors had already set in motion in the American mind and imagination. It is not too much to say that it was through Scott that the romantic aura, which it has never entirely lost, in America and elsewhere, was finally settled upon Scotland. Scotland was now indeed the land of romance; of the honourable and heroic Highlander, present in embryo in Young Norval, grander and more poetic in *Ossian*; of the earnest lowland peasant, zealous, intelligent and singer of songs; of romantic history, of Wallace and Bruce and the border ballads; and of romantic scenery, the wild, sublime, and mist-wrapped mountains and glens of the north and west, and the softer, milder beauties of Burns's Ayrshire and the Tweed. Of all the Scottish writers, Scott it was who brought Scotland to the centre of the romantic map of Europe.

Of the writers who followed Scott's lead in writing of Scottish subjects and scenes, often with frequent use of the Scottish vernacular, probably the most popular in America as both poet and story-teller was James Hogg. Hogg's career seemed to fit perfectly with all the romantic preconceptions of the Scottish peasant-poet. In 1815, a review of the *Queen's Wake* in the *Port Folio* ended by suggesting that, by this performance, and *Pilgrims in the Sun*, Hogg had surpassed the best of Scotland's 'unlettered bards', Ramsay and Burns.[117] A review of the same work in the *Analectic Magazine*, the year before, began by describing Hogg's lack of formal education and his early life in the Ettrick district of the south of Scotland.[118] In 1818, the same magazine took up the subject of Hogg's life again, emphasising once more the native genius of the bard, flourishing in an atmosphere of legend, tale, popular superstition, and border ballad, in an area which had exhibited both a Highland wildness and grandeur and a softer, milder beauty.[119] Most of this information was drawn from a memoir, by the author himself, prefaced to an edition of the *Mountain Bard*. The *Port Folio* criticised the memoir, but based a similar account of Hogg's life upon it.[120] Between 1821 and 1822, the *Ladies Literary Cabinet*, a New York weekly, and the *Literary Gazette*, both published very similar descriptions of Hogg's career.[121]

Almost all of Hogg's writings after *The Queen's Wake* (1813) received favourable notice in America. *The Queen's Wake* itself, however, probably remained his most popular work. It was published at New York in 1813,[122] at Baltimore and Boston in 1815, and at New York again in 1818. *The Pilgrims of the Sun* appeared at Philadelphia in 1815 and 1816, and the Spenserian narrative poem *Mador of the Moor* at Philadelphia also in 1816. Hogg's contribution to the tradition of Scottish song was also known in America: *The Forest Minstrel; a Selection of Songs, adapted to the most favourite Scottish airs* was published at Philadelphia in 1816. It was not only Hogg's poetry that was read in America. His prose tales were also widely known. Complete stories were sometimes re-printed in American magazines,[123] while *The Brownie of Bodsbeck* and *Winter Evening Tales*, with its portrayal of the characters and manners of the Scottish borders, appeared at New York in 1818 and 1820 respectively. Commenting on a volume of Hogg's tales in 1818, the short-lived *American Monthly Magazine* of New York described the 'Hunt of Eildon' as embodying 'in a very striking and picturesque manner, some of the wildest witcheries of a country that for ages has been known and celebrated as the land of romance.'[124] In 1834, Hogg's *Familiar Anecdotes of Sir Walter Scott* was published in New York, with yet another account of the life of the Shepherd. In recommending this work, the *American Monthly Magazine* trusted that 'the American people who have often been delighted with the works of Hogg—whose writings have cheered them in many a long night, will now come forward and, by the purchase of the book, contribute to his profit'.[125] Earlier in the same year, the same magazine had printed an account of an American's visit to Hogg in his Scottish home. The subject of the Ettrick Shepherd's works in America had been brought up:

> 'They tell me,' said he again, 'that my writings are kent in America.' I answered that they had all been reprinted there and were as well known and as much esteemed as in Scotland.[126]

Home, Macpherson, Burns, Campbell, Scott, Hogg—these were the Scottish writers best known in America, but many other lesser figures were also widely known and read.[127] As a writer of historical novels, Scott had at least one exceedingly popular predecessor: Jane Porter, author of *The Scottish Chiefs*. This tale of Scotland's struggle for independence under the leadership of Wallace and Bruce, appeared in 1810. Its success was great, both inside and outside Scotland, and it was frequently republished throughout Europe. An account of Scottish heroism and nobility, the book and its reception may be seen as examples both of resurgent Scottish national pride, and of the romantic preoccupation with Scotland's colourful and heroic past. The novel was published in America immediately after its initial appearance in Britain. In 1811, in dis-cussing what was presumably another product of the same concerns, *Wallace, or The Fight of Falkirk*, by 'Miss Holford', a metrical romance modelled on the narrative poems of Scott, the

American Review noted that 'The history of her hero has been rendered familiar to our public by the prose romance of Miss Porter, "The Scottish Chiefs", which has had so wide a circulation among us.'[128] An exceptionally wide circulation is certainly suggested by the number of editions of *The Scottish Chiefs* that appeared. The novel seems to have held its popularity even after the vogue for the Waverley Novels had got well under way. Editions appeared at Philadelphia in 1810; at New York in 1810, 1815, 1817 and 1819; at Baltimore in 1811 and 1812; at Brattleborough, Vermont, in 1814 and 1818; and at Hartford in 1822. Miss Porter's *Thaddeus of Warsaw*, another historical romance, was also published in numerous American editions, while *Bannockburn*, almost certainly a spurious work, described as a sequel to *The Scottish Chiefs*, appeared at Philadelphia in 1822.

Jane Porter preceded Scott and perhaps helped to produce an atmosphere favourable to the reception of *Waverley*; but if Scott owed something to Miss Porter, later Scottish writers owed a great deal to him. In 1823, the *Edinburgh Review* discussed the best of those writers who followed in Scott's path in an article called 'Secondary Scottish Novels':

> They are inferior certainly—and what is not? to their great originals. But they are the best copies which have yet been produced of them; and it is not a little creditable to the genius of our beloved country, that, even in those gay and airy walks of literature from which she had been so long estranged, an opening was no sooner made, by the splendid success of one gifted Scotsman, than many others were found ready to enter upon them, with a spirit of enterprise, and a force of invention, that promised still farther to extend their boundaries—and to make these new adventurers, if not formidable rivals, at least not unworthy followers of him by whose example they were roused.[129]

The novels in question are a wide selection of the works of John Galt, J. G. Lockhart, and John Wilson. Most of these were discussed in due course in *Blackwood's*, and this combined concern of the 'Scotch Critics' must have ensured American interest in them. Many in fact did come under review in the American journals.[130] And while Scott was looking farther and farther afield for the subjects of his romances, these writers wrote mostly of Scotland and the Scottish people.

Another aspect of the developing romantic image of Scotland is apparent in the many tales which began to appear in American magazines set in an exotic, Scottish scene. In these stories, the characteristics of the Scotland of *Douglas* and *Ossian*, of the songs and ballads, of Scott, Hogg, and the other story-tellers, are interchanged with increasing familiarity. In 1796, the *New York Magazine* published *The Ruins of Caithness—a Gothic Tale*,[131] and in the following year, from a Scottish source, a ballad-like tale called the *Authentic and Interesting Story of Adam Fleming and Ellen Irvine* with a poem based on the story.[132] The *Boston Weekly Magazine*, in 1802, published an untitled tragic romance of Scotland; the story opens with a traveller in Edinburgh visiting Holyrood Palace, discussing Mary Queen of Scots and other typical tourist topics, then quite skilfully moves into the tale itself.[133] The many Scottish tales published in *Blackwood's Magazine* seem to have renewed American interest in this particular kind of fiction; the American reader does not seem to have been at all dismayed by the fact that many of *Maga's* stories were written, either throughout or in part, in the Scottish vernacular. The *New York Literary Gazette*, around 1827, specialised in Scottish stories: stories of Bruce, of the Covenanters in the south-west of Scotland, of Highland traditions, of the supernatural.[134] In the same period, *The Casket*, too, published many romantic, Scottish tales of love and the supernatural.[135]

An interest in Scotland's past, her national traditions and antiquities, had been continuously a part of the native or national aspect of her eighteenth century cultural renaissance, and a similar concern soon became characteristic of the response to the romantic image: Scott's first novel was called, of course, *Waverley, or, 'Tis Sixty Years Since*. This kind of interest quickly spread out to include much of Scotland's history. Mary Queen of Scots, in particular, as a symbol of romance and tragedy, appealed to contemporary imaginations in a quite unparalleled manner. In 1795, the *New York Magazine* published an account of the murder of David Rizzio, Mary's Italian favourite, in Holyrood House.[136] In 1807, Brown's *Literary Magazine* discussed Mary in relation to Hume's historical account of her life and some papers in the library of the Scots college in Paris.[137] By the 1820s a strong movement was under way to vindicate Mary from the old charge that she had been implicated in the murder of her second husband, Lord Darnley. The subject had been raised in *Maga* in 1821.[138] In 1826, the *New York Literary Gazette* discussed Mary's life and concluded that she was 'more sinned against than sinning'.[139] Her appearance was described in *The Casket*, in 1828;[140] and in the course of a notice of a new biography, she was defended in the *Southern Review* from all the traditional charges made against her.[141] The extent to which Mary had become idealised is well suggested by the virulence of this description of Elizabeth of England: '...that royal tigress who couched her on the throne of England, thirsting for the blood of an innocent and helpless victim whom she was prepared to spring upon and devour'.[142]

Second only to Mary as a symbol of the romantic appeal of Scotland was Rob Roy. *Blackwood's Magazine* had carried an account of his career shortly before the appearance of Scott's novel in 1817.[143] In 1819, the *Port Folio* reviewed a book by Kenneth Macleay, a Scottish antiquary, on Rob Roy and the Clan Macgregor, printed at Philadelphia less than a year after its initial publication in Glasgow. The magazine was confident of the public's interest: 'Of the biography itself we shall not offer any opinion, as we believe that public curiosity can only be gratified in any tolerable degree, by an abridgment which we shall proceed to lay before the reader.'[144] In the account that follows, Rob Roy becomes a type-figure of the herioc and poetic Highlander:

> At an early period, he studied the ancient history, and recited the poetry of his country; and while he contemplated the sullen grandeur of his native wilds, corresponding ideas impressed his soul, and he would spend whole days in the admiration of a sublime portraiture of nature. The rugged mountains whose summits were often hid in the clouds that floated around them; the dark valley encircled by wooded eminences; the bold promontory opposed to the foaming ocean, and sometimes adorned by the castle of a chieftain; the still bosom of the lake that reflected the surrounding landscape; the impetuous mountain cataract; the dreary silence of the cavern, were objects that greatly influenced his youthful feelings, and disposed his mind to the cultivation of generous and manly sentiments.[145]

Another book on the Highlands, concerned in part with Rob Roy, published in Philadelphia in 1818, was reviewed in the *American Monthly Magazine*. This author's approach was apparently less romantic; the magazine suggests that his 'temperate manner', and other qualities, 'entitle him to the praise of an honourable as well as acute examiner, and induce us to consider at some length the *rationale* of a book which goes far toward destroying the high and biassed consideration with which it has long been customary among us to regard the natives of the Scottish Highlands.'[146] This form of praise well suggests the pervasiveness in America of the grandly romantic image of Scotland deriving from *Douglas, Ossian*, the poems and novels of Scott, and other products of the Scottish literary tradition.

The Jacobite rebellion of 1745 was another historical subject of considerable interest. The *Literary Gazette,* in 1821, published a review of the *Memoirs of the Rebellion in 1745 and 1746*, by Chevalier de Johnstone, one of Prince Charles's aides. A romantic American interest in the events described is once again assumed. 'This is a curious book, and though more important on the other side of the Atlantic than on this, it is not without value here, and at all events is interesting to those who are fond of the romance of real life. We shall give an abstract of its contents as briefly as possible.'[147] What follows is a lengthy account of the progress of the rising and Johnstone's subsequent adventures in Scotland. On this subject, as on that of Mary, American sympathies tended to be pro-Scots and anti-English. In 1834, in reviewing Robert Chambers's *History of the Rebellion in Scotland in 1745, 1746* (1828), published at Philadelphia in 1833, the *North American Review* discussed at length the atrocities of the Duke of Cumberland after Culloden and the contrast provided by Highland devotion and loyalty.[148] Largely through Jane Porter, William Wallace was also well-known in America as a national hero of unsurpassed nobility and heroism.[149]

American interest in such historical (and fictional) characters as Wallace, Mary Queen of Scots, and Rob Roy, along with the received idea of the peculiarly romantic and colourful quality of Scotland's heroic past, well suggests the nature of the romantic image of Scotland in America. But the literary sources of that image were sufficiently obvious to ensure that one of its consequences should be the identification of Scotland itself as a land of poetry and song. Ancient traditions of honour and nobility of character, wild sublimity and grandeur of scenery combined with pastoral beauty, ideas of an intelligent, self-taught peasantry and the untutored bard of nature, separately or taken together, were seen as producing a new home for the Muses. This was not a specifically American point of view: it could be held by Scots themselves. Here, for example, is an extract from a letter written by Alexander Wilson to a friend named Orr, in July, 1802:

> In Burns, Ferguson, Ramsay, and all our Scottish songs ... are the charms that captivate every heart. I believe a Scotsman better fitted for description of rural scenes than those of any other nation on earth. His country affords the most picturesque and striking scenery; his heart and imagination warm and animated, strong and rapid in its conceptions, its attachments, and even prejudices, his taste is highly improved by the numberless pathetic ballads and songs handed down from generation to generation. There is not an ignorant ploughman in Scotland but who has a better taste and relish for a pastoral, particularly if interwoven with a love intrigue, than most of the pretended *literati* of America. Where is the country that has ever equalled Scotland in the genuine effusion of the pastoral muse, or where so many tears of joy, sympathy, and admiration have been shed by the humblest peasants over her bewitching strains?[150]

Views similar to these of Wilson are not uncommon in the pages of the *Edinburgh Review*. The basis of the argument rested on the assumption that the aim of poetry was to 'delineate feeling'. Modern society had taught men to discipline, restrain their feelings. The Scottish Highlander and Borderer, however, had not reached such a level of sophistication. Theirs was a freer, more feeling, and hence more poetic life, in keeping with the grandeur and beauty of their native regions. By their very nature, then, such Scots were brought close to the essence of poetry.[151]

Attitudes and ideas similar to these were widely adopted in America. The best evidence of this, as we shall see in the next chapter, is provided by the books written by American travellers in Great Britain. But the concept of the unspoiled Scottish bard of Highlands or Lowlands is clearly present in such comments as these on 'The Ettrick Shepherd and Other Scotch Poets', in N. P. Willis's *American Monthly Magazine*:

> The literary history of Mr. Hogg—the Ettrick Shepherd we mean—is little other than a repetition of the history of Scott, and Ramsay, and Burns. Almost all the poets of this northern

Arcadia, in fact, have sung, as they sang in the silver ages of the ancient father-lands of poetry. They have come forth not from 'the crowded city's gay saloons', but from the river banks and vallies of the country; from the sunny fields of the lowland, and the green and fairy dells of the mountain; from the hall of the laird, and the shepherd's cottage on the shadowed hillside, and even from the humble hut of the poor farmer, built with his own hands, like that of the father of Burns.[152]

The explanations offered for the flourishing of the 'northern Arcadia' follow the established pattern; the peasantry of Scotland inherit a living tradition of poetry and song and 'passion and romance of all kinds'.[153] In Scotland, 'There has been a universal and passionate culture of imagination and taste, as well as of general intellect. The former, indeed, almost infallibly results from the latter.... But in Scotland the result has been assisted by the scenery of the country, the most animated and various, the most impressive, and the wildest on earth.'[154]

Behind all these ideas, whether expressed in Scotland or in America, one may clearly recognise the influence of several standard concepts of late eighteenth century thought: of cultural primitivism, of natural genius unconstrained by the rules of 'art', of the sublime, and of Hartleian associationism. But these are only theories: the image of Scotland as the land of song gave them a kind of ideal, practical application.

It was the impact of Scottish literature, then, which finally produced a new American image of Scotland—Scotland, the land of romance. In the course of an account of the pervasiveness of romantic attitudes and emotions in England in the period 1830–50, G. R. Kitson Clark has referred to the way in which 'Scotland was rediscovered, almost reinvented round the eccentric nucleus of the Highlander'.[155] In fact what Kitson Clark calls the 'mysterious tidal wave' of European romanticism, cast up on its Scottish shore much more than the Highlander, but the point is that what the study of the American response to Scottish writing exemplifies is the very process by which Kitson Clark's rediscovery or redefinition of Scotland actually occurred. That process certainly originated in the more native or national side of Scotland's eighteenth century cultural renaissance. Clearly, the line of descent from Watson's *Choice*

Collection to the Scotland which was the 'classic ground' of the early nineteenth century American visitor is not a direct 'one. It might be argued, as has already been suggested, that the whole *Douglas-Ossian* course of Scottish writing was part of the North British movement. But from the perspective provided by consideration of the American context, it becomes clear that this is not so. English was the only possible language for a non-Gaelic literature of the Scottish Highlands—the Scottish vernacular was of course the language only of the Lowlands—and the fact that *Douglas* and the Ossianic poems in particular were so closely identified with the Scottish Highlands is decisive. To the contemporary reader in America, and probably elsewhere, the pure Scottishness of their subjects and settings drew Home, Macpherson, and Scott closer to Ramsay, Fergusson, and Burns, than to Wilkie, 'The Scottish Homer', Blacklock, 'the Scottish Pindar', or any of the other forgotten North Britons who tried to write within the English neo-classic tradition.

The image that was created through all these distinctively Scottish works of the creative imagination may be seen as Scotland's answer to the loss of political nationality which followed from the Union of 1707; the North Britons also contributed to that answer, but, by its nature, their contribution could not take possession of both the mind and the heart, as that of the poets and novelists clearly did. The creation of the romantic image contained both good and bad elements for the future of Scottish culture. As a retreat from the present to an idealised past, and as a regional narrowing of interest and concern, it led to a debilitating of cultural vitality and to an increasingly sentimental provincialism; but as a return to the sources of artistic life in both folk and more sophisticated traditions, and in a new awareness of the minute particulars of the Scottish scene, it produced a literature of lasting vigour and permanent value.

Scotland's literary successes carried a special message for America. In creating a literature which utterly rejected any servile imitation of the standard English models in style and subject, Scotland had turned instead to her own resources, both new and traditional. Scotland had produced what Americans had been demanding since 1783—a distinctively national literature. The point did not escape writers and commentators in both Scotland and America. John Neal's articles in *Blackwood's Magazine* returned continually to the need for American literature to be American: 'It is American books that are wanted of America; not English books ... books, which, whatever may be their faults, are decidedly, if not altogether, American.'[156] And in praising Cooper, he made the comparison with the Scots: '[*The Spy*] was, at least, an approach to what we desire—a plain, real, hearty, North American story; a story, which, if we could have our way, should be altogether American— peculiarly and exclusively so, throughout; as much American to say all, in a word, as the Scotch novels are Scotch. ...'[157] A few years earlier, a writer in the *North American Review* in the course of a notice of James Wallis Eastburn and R. C. Sands's poem *Yamoyden*, had also invoked Scott in describing the native materials which were available to the American writer:

> And as to the resources, which a poet might find for description of natural scenery, he whose mind recurs,—as whose does not when poetical description is named,—to the haunt of the northern muse, ... must remember that compared with some of ours, Scottish rivers are but brooks, and Scottish forests mere thickets.[158]

In 1814, an article in the *Port Folio* on American literature cited the Scottish literary achievement as a perfect example of how a literature could develop quite suddenly:

> ... until within little more than the last fifty years, Scotland had scarcely a poet or a dramatic writer, to balance against Chaucer, Spenser, Shakespeare, Jonson, Cowley, Milton, Dryden, Pope, and twenty others, produced in England, except Allan Ramsay, a name that would hardly have risen to notice, if it had belonged to the other part of the Island. Yet, since that time, Scotland has produced its full quota of literary genius. In a very dignified species of composition, history, it is indeed unrivalled; and at the present day, the names of Campbell and Scott, stand higher on the list of poets, than any of their cotemporaries in England.[159]

And in 1820, the *Analectic Magazine* reprinted an article from Constable's *Edinburgh Magazine* (formerly the *Scots Magazine*), which had seen in Scotland's literary successes of today, an augury of American successes of tomorrow:

> England and America are both at this moment supplied, in great measure, with a literature of Scottish manufacture. We should not be much surprised were we to live to see the day

when we, in our turn shall be gaping for new novels and poems from the other side of the Atlantic, and when, in the silence of our own bards and romancers, we shall have Ladies of the Lake from Ontario, and Tales of my Landlord from Goose-creek, as a counterpart to those from Gander-cleugh. For our part, we have no kind of aversion to the augury; and we cannot but regard it as a most paltry and contemptible littleness, quite unworthy of the material majesty of England, not to look with an eye of love and delight upon all that is promising in the rising genius of America.

Scotland had to make her way against the current of English prejudice, but in the end England was forced to acknowledge merit. The moral for America, in the middle of the literary quarrel, is clear:

Notwithstanding the dull sarcasms and stupid prejudices out of which Scotland was so long forced to fight her way, the English were yet not backward in acknowledging the excellence of our distinguished writers. ... Now there is not a little distinction attached to the very name of a Scotchman, and we feel that our neighbours honour us because we have from our birth breathed the same air with Hume, Robertson, Smith, Stewart, Blair, Alison, Burns, Scott, and Campbell. The literary glory of America is yet to come; but we doubt not that it is coming.[160]

That it was recognised in America that the distinctively national path to literary glory, which American writers should follow, had been pointed out to them by the Scots, is indicated best by an address called 'The Romance of New England History', delivered by Rufus Choate, the lawyer and statesman, at Salem in 1833. The sub-title to Choate's speech shows the direction of his thinking quite clearly: 'The Importance of Illustrating New England History by a Series of Romances like the Waverley Novels'. Choate imagined a genius like Scott doing for New England what Scott had done for Scotland:

He would wish to see him begin with the landing of the Pilgrims, and pass down to the War of Independence, from one epoch and one generation to another, like Old Mortality among the graves of the unforgotten faithful, wiping the dust from the urns of our fathers, gathering up whatever of illustrious achievement, of heroic suffering, of unwavering faith, their history commemorates, and weaving it all into an immortal and noble national literature.

Beside the austere histories of New England, Choate would like to see,

> ...a thousand neat duodecimos of the size of 'Ivanhoe', 'Kenilworth', and 'Marmion', all full of pictures of our natural beauty and grandeur, the still richer pictures of our society and manners, the lights and shadows of our life, full of touching incidents, generous sentiments, just thoughts, beaming images, such as are scattered over everything which Scott has written, as thick as stars on the brow of night.

Like the *Iliad* and the *Odyssey*, the Waverley Novels are invaluable sources of history; and particularly of the kind of history that our professed history books overlook. Standard history is like '... a vast landscape ... which has no place for the enclosed corn-field, the flocks upon a thousand hills, the cheerful country-seat, the village spires, the churchyard, the vintage, the harvest-home, the dances of peasants, and the "cotter's Saturday night"'.[161] Romances such as the Waverley Novels supply the deficiencies of standard histories by speaking directly to the heart and affections and imagination of the reader. A series of North American or New England Waverley Novels would present a series of pictures, 'so full, so vivid, so true, so instructive, so moving, that they would grave themselves upon the memory and dwell in the hearts of our whole people forever'; something, Choate concludes, which would strengthen America's sense of national unity.[162]

Choate's recognition of the connections between Scott's literary achievement, Scotland's national identity, and America's need to acquire a similar sense of cultural self-definition, is particularly precise. If few other American commentators were equally perceptive, none was able entirely to resist one or other aspect of the romantic image of Scotland created by Scott, and his literary contemporaries and predecessors. Of course it was not only in America that Scotland came to exercise a peculiar, romantic fascination. The exact role that Scotland occupies in the history of the romantic movement has never been adequately defined. What is clear is that throughout Europe and America Scotland came to be associated with certain central features of romanticism to a greater degree than any other single country. Scotland in its history, its landscape, its people, and its literature, became an archetypal illustration of what romanticism meant. An attempt to grapple with the problem of the precise nature of the romantic attraction of Scotland and the Scots, for Americans at least, occurred in the *American Monthly Magazine* in 1818. The occasion is a review of Scott's *Tales of My Landlord*:

> Scotland, his own muse, has again inspired him; and, perhaps, no local genius could furnish such materials to the imagination of a writer, or such a refined, strong sympathy in a reader. And wherefore? Why do we cherish for this country feelings so peculiar? They are surely of a different nature from all our classic associations, or our political sympathies with the other people of out world!

Other nations are admired for their greatness, but Scotland's case is decidedly different:

> The natives of Scotland have achieved no conquests, and amassed no wealth; they have planted no standard on a foreign shore, nor made a diadem of power from the gold and pearls of other lands and seas; they have made no marble to think, nor canvass to speak; and their literature, mostly, is of legends and songs, hidden from us in their own language. What then do we so love and admire in this people? It is their moral dignity, their beautiful affections, and their exquisitely simple manners. They are so poetical and pastoral, so patriotic and devout, so enthusiastic and honourable; there is so much principle in their passions, so much courage and constancy in their attachments, that while things lovely and excellent awaken our imagination, Scottish history and Scottish character, will call forth an interest singularly their own; we shall delight in the torrents and the mountains that have echoed the songs of Ferguson [*sic*] and Burns, and a thousand other bards; we shall love the unsubdued race 'whose thistle sham'd the Roman bays'; whose fathers repulsed the masters of the world; and whose successive generations have offered such self-devoted lives to defend privileges and principles; we shall forgive that intolerance and superstition, so justified by conscience and interwoven with piety; we shall pity the misled zeal and inflexible faith, which cost so many sacrifices to a bad cause, and worthless princes; and shall listen with eagerness, and pleasure to the narrative which makes these virtues manifest, by recording the enchanting manners and language that exhibits them.[163]

The admirably heroic, upright, zealous, and self-sacrificing qualities of the Scottish people, the colour and excitement of Scottish history, the appeal of Scottish song, the sublimity of the Scottish landscape—all the central features of the romantic image of Scotland crowd together in such a passage.

In Charleston, South Carolina, in 1829, a receptive audience listened to a speech which tried to offer a still broader definition of what it was that Scotland had offered America, and the world, in the previous hundred years. The speaker was a Scot, the Reverend Mitchell King; the occasion, the centennial celebration of the St Andrew's Society of Charleston. Thus in one sense Mr King was engaged in no more than a useful piece of public relations on behalf of his native land. Nonetheless the sentiments he expressed, however extravagant they may seem to us, to many of his American contemporaries would have appeared no more than just.

The occasion itself was clearly a splendid one. The *Charleston Courier* reported it in terms which suggest the importance, for the history of the South, of the romantic image of Scotland and feelings of national pride, devotion and loyalty. The members of the society had marched in procession to the First Presbyterian Church in Charleston with an escort of soldiers. The soldiers wore badges appropriate to the occasion, and the officers Highland bonnets:

> We know not how these national emblems affected others— to us they were far from the least interesting part of the scene. We envy not the man who could think or feel otherwise. We envy not the cold, the callous, and contracted heart of the man, who, 'dead to the voice of minstrel fame' could, on such an occasion, survey without emotions of lively interest, far less who would feel disposed to condemn such harmless ebulitions of national enthusiasm.—They are associated with all that is great and illustrious in the history of a good and gallant people.—They cherish and keep alive a spirit, not alien, but akin to the land of their habitation.[164]

Then, in the church, 'thronged with the Beauty and Fashion of the city', Mitchell King addressed the members of the society. His speech was itself a celebration—a celebration of Scotland's intellectual and artistic achievement in the hundred years from the founding of the society. The praises of both the North Britons and the more purely Scottish writers are sung without restraint:

> As a member of this Society, as a native Scotchman, as a citizen of South Carolina, I do with the deepest feeling congratulate you, my countrymen, on the distinguished reputation and increasing glory of the land of our birth.[165]

In the last hundred years, what country has produced so many 'benefactors of mankind', as Scotland?

> Their praises are on every tongue. Their works are in every hand. They form the text books of our schools and colleges. They are found in the shop of the mechanic, in the counting house of the merchant, on the table of the physician and lawyer, in the study of the philosopher, in the cabinet of the statesman, and on the desk of the divine. There is no language or people where their voice is not heard—where they do not improve the heart, and instruct and influence the mind.

There follows the brilliant catalogue of the North Britons. First the historians—Robertson, Hume, and their successors; then the philosophers—Reid, Beattie and Stewart; the mathematical philosophers—Maclaurin, Simson, Robison, Playfair; the critics and rhetoricians—Kames, Blair, and Campbell; Smith who 'has created a new science'; the medical professors, Munro, Cullen, Hunter, Gregory, etc.; and Black who has 'paved the way for the splendid achievements of modern chemistry'. Then King turns to Scottish literature. 'Scotland is full of song and poetry', made immortal in the works of Ramsay, Burns, Macneill, and many others. Above them all towers Scott, 'the mighty magician of the north', 'with a mind replete with knowledge, an imagination fertile, inventive, boundless far beyond all Greek and Roman fame'. Next come the Scottish reviewers. 'The establishment of the Edinburgh Review alone, may almost be considered as a new era in literature.' It has served as a model for later works, and 'has maintained the principles of sound criticism, of pure taste, of enlightened liberality, of unshackled trade, of regulated freedom, of universal toleration, with so much splendor of eloquence, felicity of illustration and power of reason as to dazzle, delight and instruct every intelligent reader'.

Having thus invoked the three principal groups within Scotland's cultural renaissance of the eighteenth and early nineteenth centuries—the North British thinkers, the Scottish writers, and the Edinburgh critics—King brings them together within a single rhetorical period which symbolises, as all that had gone before had done, the impact and impression made upon America by Scotland, land of learning and land of romance. To estimate Scotland's contribution 'to the sum of human knowledge, and the means of human enjoyment' is impossible:

> But it is not hazarding too much—it is no exaggeration—to assert, that in profound, correct and original thinking—in clear, deep and conclusive reasoning—in the efforts of a fertile, chastened and vigorous imagination—in the destruction of inveterate and hurtful prejudices—in the defence of sound practical principles—in all that can ornament—in all that can dignify—in all that can purify—in all that can instruct—in all that can better society, Scotland, within these last hundred years has done more than any other nation in Europe.[166]

NOTES AND REFERENCES

1. Leonard W. Labaree (Ed.), *The Papers of Benjamin Franklin,* IX (New Haven and London, 1966), 4. That this production was a success is suggested by the following announcement in *The Pennsylvania Gazette* on 6 September 1759: 'At the Theatre, on Society-Hill, on Friday Evening, the Seventh instant, will be presented (by particular desire) *Douglass.'*

2. *The American Review and Literary Journal,* I (1801), 416–17.

3. *Port Folio,* I (1801), 406 and New Series, I (1806), 74.

4. Harold F. Bogner, 'Sir Walter Scott in New Orleans, 1818–1832,' *Louisiana Historical Quarterly,* XXI (April, 1938), 432.

5. *The New York Literary Gazette, and Phi Beta Kappa Repository,* I (1825), 91.

6. The intellectual tradition was largely maintained by the Episcopalian scholars of Aberdeen; in the seventeenth century their influence and prestige were such that the Presbyterian Church could make little headway in the area. See George Pratt Insh, *The Scottish Jacobite Movement* (Edinburgh, 1952), pp. 115–33.

7. Insh, pp. 51–52. Hugh Trevor-Roper, however, argues forcibly that the existence of the Jacobite, Episcopalian scholarly culture of the Scottish north-east also did much to make the development of the Scottish Enlightenment possible. See Hugh

Trevor-Roper, 'The Scottish Enlightenment', *Studies on Voltaire and the Eighteenth Century,* LVIII (1967), 1635–58.

8. Insh, p. 175.

9. Jefferson wrote to Charles McPherson, in Edinburgh, on 25 February 1773: 'I am not ashamed to own that I think this rude bard of the North the greatest Poet that has ever existed.' Jefferson went on to ask McPherson to send him a grammar and dictionary that he might learn the language of the originals of Macpherson's poems. Jefferson's continuing enthusiasm for the Ossianic world is suggested by the fact that his library contained Alexander McDonald's *Gaelic Songs and Poems* (Edinburgh 1751), and John Macpherson's *Critical Dissertations on the Origin, Antiquities, Language, Government, Manners, and Religion, of the ancient Caledonians* (London and Edinburgh, 1768). See *The Library of Thomas Jefferson,* items 4882, 432.

10. See Frederic I. Carpenter, 'The Vogue of Ossian in America: A Study in Taste', *American Literature,* II (January, 1931), 409–10.

11. *Port Folio,* I (1801), 151. In 1797, the *New York Magazine* published 'Two Fragments of Ancient Poetry, collected in the Highlands of Scotland. (Translated from the Gallic or Earse Language)', *New York Magazine,* II (1797), 342–3. A translation

of new songs by Ossian, recently found, appeared in the *Port Folio*, I (1801), 102. An extract from Sewall's versification appeared in the same year. Other versified extracts were printed in the *Port Folio*, V (1805), 120, 144. The earliest versified extracts from *Ossian*, however, had appeared in the *Charleston Columbian Herald* in 1785; they were the work of Joseph Brown Ladd (1764–86). See Lewis Leary, 'Ossian in America: A Note', *American Literature*, XIV (November, 1942), 305–6.

12. *The Mirror* (Philadelphia, 1793), I, 56–62.

13. Miller, *Brief Retrospect of the Eighteenth Century*, II, 187.

14. *Literary Magazine*, IV (1805), 127.

15. *Edinburgh Review*, VI (1805), 462.

16. *Literary Magazine*, IV (1805), 364.

17. Ibid., VI (1806), 264.

18. *Port Folio*, New Series, I (1806), 82–3.

19. Ibid., III (1807), 71.

20. John Blair Linn (1777–1804), minister of the First Presbyterian Church of Philadelphia, author of several plays and long poems. His literary work was highly thought of by his contemporaries.

21. John Blair Linn, *Valerian, A Narrative Poem, With a Sketch of the life and Character of the Author* (Philadelphia, 1805), p. xi.

22. John Blair Linn, *The Powers of Genius* (Philadelphia, 1802), pp. 41–2.

23. Ibid., p. 42.

24. Ibid., pp. 136–7.

25. Ibid., pp. 137–8. Linn also attempted to versify passages from *Ossian*. See 'The Farewel Song of Ossian', in *The Powers of Genius*, pp. 175–8.

26. Francis Griffin (Ed.), *Remains of the Rev. Edmund D. Griffin, With a Biographical Memoir of the Deceased by the Rev. John McVickar, D.D.* (New York, 1831), I, 21.

27. Miller, *Brief Retrospect of the Eighteenth Century*, II, 204.

28. *Port Folio*, I (1801), 207. The reference is most probably to the 1800 London edition of Ramsay's poems. I have been unable to find any evidence of an edition of Ramsay in America in 1800 or 1801.

29. *Literary Magazine*, V (1806), 111.

30. The two versions of the same poem printed as 'The Minstrel at Lincluden', and 'A Vision', were probably written as preludes to the 'Ode'. See Gustave Carus, 'Robern Burns and the American Revolution', *The Open Court*, XLVI (January, 1932), 129–36.

31. *The Lounger, A Periodical Paper* (London, 1794), II, 396–405.

32. *The New York Magazine*, New Series, II (1797), 118–19. It is possible that this periodical was suspicious of Burns's political inclinations. *The New York Magazine* was the organ of the so-called Mohawk Reviewers, who were distinguished by 'their hostility to the rising Jacobinism of the times'. See Francis, *Old New York*, p. 339.

33. See *Port Folio*, III (1803), 192, 368; IV (1804), 104, 166, 190; and V (1805), 198.

34. *Literary Magazine*, II (1804), 593–5.

35. Ibid., pp. 625–8. Currie's biography of Burns was itself prefaced by a short essay on the Scottish peasantry; with its emphasis on the Scots' intelligence and education, and their traditions of dance and song, this essay must have helped to shape the popular notion of the Scottish peasant.

36. *Literary Magazine*, VII (1807), 429–38. That other Americans were ready to idolise Burns is suggested by this comment of Dr James M'Conochie: 'I have seen Americans *weep*, when Burns and his works were the subject of conversation.' See Jay B. Hubbell, 'Dr. James R. M'Conochie's *Leisure Hours*, A Rare Book by a Scottish-American Doctor Who Knew Robert Burns', *Virginian Magazine of History and Biography*, LXVII (April, 1959), 175. M'Conochie was born in Dumfries in 1785, and studied medicine in Philadelphia under Benjamin Rush.

37. *The American Review*, I (1811), 166–7.

38. *Knickerbocker Magazine*, II (1833), 149.

39. Stuart, *Three Years in North America*, I, 442–3.

40. Scottish immigrants, of course, must have been responsible for the introduction of Scots ballads to America. Forty to fifty per cent of the 'British' ballads which survive in American oral tradition are Scottish in origin. See Herschel Gower, 'The Scottish Palimpsest in Traditional Ballads Collected in America', in *Reality and Myth* (Nashville, 1964).

41. Leonard W. Labaree (Ed.), *The Papers of Benjamin Franklin*, X (New Haven and London, 1966), 385.

42. Bogner, 'Sir Walter Scott in New Orleans, 1818–1832', pp. 468–9, 476. 'My love is like the red rose' is of course by Burns; 'Loudon's bonny woods and braes' is by Robert Tannahill (1774–1810), the Paisley poet and song-writer; 'Roy's Wife of Alldivaloch' is an eighteenth century Scots

song which appeared in Johnson's *Scots Musical Museum*. 'March, March, Ettrick and Teviotdale' is a song from Scott's *The Monastery*; 'All the blue Bonnets are over the Border' is probably part of the same song; 'Draw the sword Scotland' and 'Charlie take me home love' ('Wha'll be King but Charlie' was a popular Jacobite song) sound like adaptions or imitations of Scots songs.

Of particular interest is the manner in which these semi-operatic versions of Scott's novels illustrate how easily Scott could be assimilated within the national Scottish literary tradition. These stage combinations of Scottish songs and Scott's novels symbolise perfectly Scott's place in the Scottish literary tradition in its impact upon America. Bogner notes (pp. 441–3) that musical programmes in New Orleans in the 1820s tended to consist of Scots and English music; Scots songs and airs recur. Bogner suggests that this was another result of the Scott vogue, but I should maintain that such programmes rather reflect the older, independent interest in Scots songs which in fact made possible the kind of stage performances described.

43. Scottish travellers in America provide further proof of the American taste for Scots songs. As Scots themselves their ears were no doubt particularly well-attuned to any reminder of their home country. John Melish, for example, recalls how he was called upon to contribute to the entertainment at a party: '…as heretofore,' he writes, 'I could do nothing except in Scottish songs, and I was doubtful how they would answer on the banks of lake Erie. However, I soon found that this was one of the most acceptable treats I could give the company. They were, in fact, enthuiastic admirers of Scottish music; Burns's songs were highly relished, and one of the company anticipated me by singing my favourite song of Muirland Willie.' Melish, *Travels through the United States of America*, p. 360. John Duncan and James Stuart also describe incidents involving Scots songs. See Duncan, *Travels through part of the United States and Canada in 1818 and 1819*, I, 118; Stuart, *Three Years in North America*, I, 117, 492.

44. *The New York Magazine: or, Literary Repository*, I (1790), 668–9.

45. *Port Folio*, V (1805), 280.

46. Ibid., p. 319.

47. Ibid., New Series, I (1806), 191.

48. Ibid., pp. 175–6.

49. Ibid., p. 224.

50. Ibid., II (1806), 128.

51. Ibid., III (1807), 103–6.

52. Ibid., VI (1808), 127–8.

53. Ibid., V (1808), 47.

54. *Analectic Magazine*, I (1813), 182.

55. *Port Folio*, 4th Series, XII (1821), 485.

56. Robert Dinsmoor, *Incidental Poems accompanied with Letters, and a few Select Pieces, mostly original, for their illustration, together with a Preface, and Sketch of the Author's Life* (Haverhill, 1828), p. 13. The vernacular poem, 'Verses addressed to Robert Burns, the Air-shire Poet', published in the *New York Magazine* in 1790 (see p. 134), is reprinted in this volume; it is here (p. 160), that the writer is identified as 'a lady in Gorham'.

57. Ibid., p. 55.

58. Ibid., pp. 48–9.

59. Ibid., p. 248. Whittier was an enthusiastic admirer of Burns; he saw in Burns the strongest initial influence on his own poetic development. His friendship with Dinsmoor was responsible in part for developing his admiration and appreciation of Burns. See George Price Carpenter, *John Greenleaf Whittier* (Boston and New York, 1903), pp. 30–1. A sketch of Dinsmoor appears in Whittier's *Old Portraits and Modern Sketches: Personal Sketches and Tributes: Historical Papers* (Cambridge, 1888), pp. 245–60. He comments in particular on the rural realism of Dinsmoor's poems. Another American poet who, earlier than Whittier, tried his hand at imitating Burns was the Virginian, St George Tucker. Tucker knew Burns's work by 1789 and wrote a number of poems—for example, 'An Imitation of Burns' (1805) and 'To Genius' (c. 1811)—which followed Burns both in their vernacular and their 'passionate libertarianism'. See Davis, *Intellectual Life in Jefferson's Virginia*, p. 331.

60. Dinsmoor, *Incidental Poems*, p. 105.

61. *Poems Chiefly in the Scottish Dialect, originally written under the Signature of the Scots-Irishman, by a Native of Scotland. With Notes and Illustrations* (Washington, 1801), p. 11.

62. Ibid., pp. 15, 46.

63. Ibid., p. 18.

64. Ibid., p. 21.

65. *Port Folio*, V (1805), 352 and 359–60. Earlier, the *Port Folio* had printed 'Donald

and Flora', a ballad in English by Macneill. See *Port Folio*, III (1803), 218–19.

66. *The Poetical Works of Hector Macneill* (Philadelphia, 1815), p. v.

67. Revd Alexander B. Grosart (Ed.), *Poems and Literary Prose of Alexander Wilson* (Paisley, 1876), I, 88. Quoted here is a letter from Wilson dated 14 September, 1801: 'I have amused myself... with writing detached pieces of poetry for the *Newark Centinel,* and have grown into some repute with the editor and his readers. A song entitled "My Landlady's Nose" has been reprinted in a New York paper, and in a periodical publication called the *Museum.*' 'My Landlady's Nose' however, is in English, not Scots.

68. From time to time the American periodicals printed individual poems by Scottish poets. In the period 1801–11, when it was under the direction of Joseph Dennie, himself of Scots decent, the *Port Folio* in particular was well-disposed towards Scottish writing. Poems printed and discussed in this period include Hamilton of Bangour's 'The Braes of Yarrow' (I, 1801, 221–2) and 'Ode on the Battle of Gladsmuir' (I, 1801, 300–1); John Logan's English version of 'The Braes of Yarrow' (II, 1802, 248); 'Sir Patrick Spens' (II, 1802, 293); 'Annan Water' from Scott's *Minstrelsy of the Scottish Border* (IV, 1804, 148); John Mayne's 'Logan Water' (V, 1805, 95); Mrs Cockburn's 'The Flowers of the Forest' (V, 1805, 71); 'Blyth Davie' an early version of 'Doun the Burn Davie' by Robert Crawford, and 'Marion', a seventeenth century song (New Series, III, 1807, 221). Brown's *Literary Magazine* published 'The Murder of Red Cuming', a ballad in Scots in 1806 (V, 1806, 237–9). The *Port Folio*, also published a number of poems in English inspired by Scottish subjects. On Burns: see *Port Folio*, I (1801), 360; New Series, V (1808), 8. On ballad subjects: 'Ellen Irwin, or the Braes of Kirtle', I (1801), 391–2; 'The Maid of Donalblayne', II (1802), 184; 'Osric and Ella', II (1802), 208. This last poem is introduced thus: 'He, who venerates the valiant spirit of a Scottish warrior, or who delights in Caledonian imagery, will peruse with no languid emotions, a ballad, descriptive, natural and pathetic.'

69. William Beattie (Ed.), *Life and Letters of Thomas Campbell* (New York, 1850), I, 180.

70. Ibid., p. 91. An account of the trials of Gerrald and his fellow Reformers will be found in the Appendix.

71. Ibid., p. 194.

72. Ibid.

73. Pierre M. Irving (Ed.), *The Life and Letters of Washington Irving* (New York, 1862), I, 364.

74. *Life and Letters of Thomas Campbell*, II, 499. The Revd Mr Lester was an American delegate at the London Anti-slavery Congress of July, 1840.

75. In 'Thomas Campbell and America', *American Literature*, XIII (January, 1942), 346–55, Charles Duffy claims that Campbell, 'by virtue of his nationality', 'escaped whatever lingering rancor might have persisted in the young republic against Englishmen' (p. 349). He does not consider the possibility of any such rancour against the Scots, though, as we have seen, anti-Scottish feeling was once particularly strong. However, Duffy may well be right; by the first decade of the nineteenth century, America's awareness of Scotland's traditional spirit of independence was perhaps already much stronger than her awareness of Scotland's dubious part in the Revolution.

76. Quoted by Duffy, p. 350.

77. *Life and Letters of Washington Irving*, I, 252–3.

78. See *Analectic Magazine*, V (1815), 234–50.

79. *Life and Letters of Washington Irving*, I, pp. 303–5. The work was Campbell's *Specimens of the British Poets* which did not appear until 1819.

80. Ibid., p. 334.

81. Ibid., pp. 371–3.

82. *Edinburgh Review*, XIV (1809), 1–19.

83. *Port Folio*, 3rd Series, IV (1814), 504–6.

84. *Edinburgh Review*, XLI (1824–5), 281.

85. *Remains of the Rev. Edmund D. Griffin*, I, 15.

86. *Life and Letters of Thomas Campbell*, II, 498.

87. Since Mark Twain asserted in *Life on the Mississippi* that it was the impact of Scott on the South that produced the Civil War, Scott's popularity and influence in America have been widely studied. A somewhat restrained version of Twain's thesis is advanced by H. J. Eckenrode in his 'Sir Walter Scott and the South', *North American Review*, CCVI (October, 1917), 595–603. Eckenrode describes the South as 'Walter Scottland'; but he does not mention any earlier Scottish writer. Grace Warren Landrum in 'Sir Walter Scott and His Literary Rivals in the Old South', *American Literature*, II (November, 1930), 256–76,

defends Scott from Twain's charge, and argues both that Scott was not accepted quite uncritically in the South and that he had popular literary rivals in Bulwer and Byron. Again no reference is made to any of Scott's predecessors. The most penetrating analysis of Scott's influence on the social history of the South is to be found in Rollin G. Osterweis's book, *Romanticism and Nationalism in the Old South* (New Haven, 1949). See in particular, chapter four: 'The Theme from Abbotsford', pp. 41–53. G. Harrison Orians in 'The Romance Ferment after Waverley', *American Literature*, III (January, 1932), 408–31, indicates how Scott provided American writers with an example of a successful national literature. In his 'Literary Tastes in Virginia before Poe', *William and Mary College Quarterly*, XIX (January, 1939), 55–68, Richard Beale Davis describes the literary circle in Richmond headed by William Wirt (1772–1834), later attorney-general of the United States, at the beginning of the nineteenth century. Over bowls of punch the circle discussed Ossian, Scott and the *Edinburgh Review* (p. 57). Of these commentators upon Scott's impact upon America, Davis alone suggests that American receptiveness to Scott had been prepared for: 'Scott would never have been enjoyed had not the Virginian been prepared for him by Ossian and *Tristram Shandy* and *Scottish Chiefs*...' (pp. 55–6). Finally H. F. Bogner's study of Scott in the New Orleans theatre, reference to which has already been made, provides excellent evidence once again of the strength and pervasiveness of Scott's American impact. Bogner describes presentations of plays based on *Guy Mannering* (1820), and subsequently of others based on *The Chronicles of the Canongate, The Lady of the Lake, Marmion, Rob Roy, The Talisman*, and *Peveril of the Peak*. French versions of some of these were also performed in New Orleans. Thomas J. Dibdin's dramatisation of *The Lady of the Lake*, originally performed in London and Edinburgh in 1810–11, was acted in Richmond on 31 October 1811 and repeated several times. See Davis, *Intellectual Life in Jefferson's Virginia*, p. 241.

88. *American Review*, I (1811), 166.
89. *North American Review*, XVIII (1824), 162.
90. Pattee, *American Writers*, p. 196.
91. Stuart, *Three Years in North America*, I, 82.
92. J. W. Francis, *Old New York*, pp. 348–50. Mrs Divie Bethune, born Joanna Graham, had been brought to New York by her mother, Isabella Graham, in 1789. A widow, Isabella Graham had set up a private school in Edinburgh in 1780. Her friends and patrons included Mrs Walter Scott, the poet's mother—a circumstance which lends credence to Francis's account of the presentation copy of *The Lay of the Last Minstrel* dispatched to New York. Mrs Graham's decision to return to America where she had resided briefly with her husband was partly arrived at through the influence of John Witherspoon whom she met in Edinburgh in 1785. See *The Power of Faith: Exemplified in the Life and Writings of the late Mrs. Isabella Graham of New York* (Edinburgh, 1817), pp. 22, 30.
93. *Literary Magazine*, IV (1805), 99.
94. *Edinburgh Review*, VI (1805), 2.
95. *Port Folio*, V (1805), 306–8, 313–15.
96. Ibid., New Series, IV (1807), 134.
97. Ibid., New Series, VI (1808), 302.
98. Ibid., 3rd Series, V (1815), 326–33.
99. Ibid., VI (1815), 59.
100. Ibid., p. 66.
101. *Analectic Magazine*, V (1815), 89–110. The article is taken from the *British Critic*; it is probably based on the notice in the *Edinburgh Review* which had attributed the success of *Waverley*, 'composed, one half of it in a dialect unintelligible to four-fifths of the reading population of the country', to its adherence to nature, and to the truth and vivacity of its colouring. See *Edinburgh Review*, XXIV (1814–15), 208.
102. *North American Review*, VII (1818), 149.
103. *Port Folio*, 4th Series, X (1820), 370.
104. Ibid., XIII (1822), 73.
105. *Southern Review*, VIII (1831–2), 46.
106. Ibid., IV (1829), 499. Cf. *North American Review*, XXXVI (1833), 312–13.
107. *Analectic Magazine*, XI (1818), 332.
108. Ibid., pp. 130–9.
109. Ibid., XIV (1819), 1–3, *The Heart of Midlothian* is the novel referred to.
110. Ibid., XIII (1819), 123.
111. Ibid., XI (1818), 309.
112. John Griscom, *A Year in Europe, Comprising a Journal of Observations in England, Scotland, Ireland, France, Switzerland, the north of Italy, and Holland, in 1818 and 1819* (New York, 1823), II, 355.
113. *The Literary Gazette: or Journal of Criticism, Science, and the Arts*, I (1821), 129.
114. Francis, *Old New York*, p. 242.

115. C. D. Arfwedson, *The United States and Canada, in 1832, 1833, and 1834* (London, 1834), I, 383. The memorial service for Scott held in New York was no doubt paralleled by similar ceremonies in other cities. The memorial address in New York was delivered by John McVickar, professor of moral, intellectual, and political philosophy, rhetoric and belles-lettres, at Columbia.

116. Osterweis, *Romanticism and Nationalism in the Old South*, p. 69.

117. *Port Folio*, 3rd Series, VI (1815), 505.

118. *Analectic Magazine*, III (1814), 104–25.

119. Ibid., XI (1818), 414–21.

120. *Port Folio*, 4th Series, XII (1821), 191–204.

121. *Ladies Literary Cabinet*, IV (1821–2), 57–9. *The Literary Gazette*, I (1821), 295–9.

122. Shaw and Shoemaker list an edition dated 1812; as the work was not written until 1813, the 1812 date must be a printer's error.

123. For example, two stories from *Winter Evening Tales*, in the *Analectic Magazine*, New Series, II (1820), 66–80; or *The Brownie of Black Haggs* in *The Casket*, II (1828), 558–64.

124. *American Monthly Magazine and Critical Review*, III (1818), 353–4.

125. *American Monthly Magazine*, III (1834), 177.

126. Ibid., p. 89. The single exception was *The Private Memoirs and Confessions of a Justified Sinner* which was not in fact reprinted in America.

127. I have not been concerned with those writers, born in Scotland, whose works were written in English exclusively, and who were assimilated into the English, eighteenth century literary world, though several of these were very popular in America. James Thomson's *Seasons*, for example, was reprinted at least sixteen times in America, between 1777 and 1805. The poems of James Beattie were also highly regarded; there were at least four editions of his poems between 1784 and 1802. Henry Mackenzie was another popular Anglo-Scottish writer; all his novels were republished in America in the 1780s and 90s.
Perhaps the best evidence of the development of American taste for the Scottish poets is provided by the contents of early American anthologies. I have been able to examine six of these collections:
(1) *The Beauties of Poetry, British and American* (Philadelphia, 1791). With poems by Milton, Pope, Addison, Parnell, Goldsmith, Shenstone, etc., this contains poems by Beattie and Thomson, and 'Despondency', a poem in English by Burns.
(2) *The American Poetical Miscellany, Original and Selected* (Philadelphia, 1809). Along with twenty or so poems by the standard English authors, this volume contains a song in Scots attributed to a son of Burns, 'Scots Wha Hae', and 'A Bard's Epitaph' by Burns, two poems on the death of Burns, 'Independence' by Smollett, Ossian's 'Address to the Sun', poems by Campbell and Thomson, and 'Lady Ann Bothwell's Lament', a seventeenth century Scots poem.
(3) *The Wreath, a Selection of Elegant Poems from the Best Authors* (New York, 1813). The collection contains twenty-two poems; included are Burns's 'Man Was Made to Mourn', two poems by Beattie, and one by Thomson.
(4) John Evans, *The Parnassian Garland, or, Beauties of Modern Poetry* (Philadelphia, 1814). This is an English collection of about two hundred poems, including works by Beattie, Michael Bruce (1746–67), a Scots poet who wrote in English, Burns—'Man Was Made to Mourn', and an Anglicised version of 'John Barleycorn', Scott—including 'The Patriot'—Macneill, Blacklock, Mrs Grant and Logan.
(5) *Beauties of Poetry* (Albany, 1814). This volume contains about sixty poems in all, mostly by the standard eighteenth century English writers; included are 'Leven Water' and 'The Tears of Scotland' by Smollett, Beattie's 'Minstrel', and thirteen poems in English by Burns—in 'The Cotter's Saturday Night' all the Scots words are carefully footnoted.
(6) *The Wreath, a Collection of Poems from Celebrated English Authors* (New York, 1821). The collection contains twenty-six poems; twelve of these are by Scottish authors. Included are Beattie's 'Minstrel', Burns's 'Man Was Made to Mourn' and 'Despondency', Smollett's 'Leven Water', and Scott's 'Boat Song'. While these anthologies reflect a growing taste for the Scottish poets, they all show a marked distrust of poems in the Scottish vernacular.

128. *American Review*, I (1811), 175. 'Miss Holford' was Mrs Margaret Hodson, (1778–1852).

129. *Edinburgh Review*, XXXIX (1823–4), 160.

130. For example, see the *Port Folio*, 4th Series, XIII (1822), 52–66; and XIV (1822), 320–9; *North American Review*, XXXI (1830), 380–96.

131. *New York Magazine*, New Series, I (1796), 380–3.

132. Ibid., II (1797), 510–12.

133. *Boston Weekly Magazine*, I (1802–3), 169, 173–4.

134. *New York Literary Gazette and American Athenaeum*, II (1826), 59–60, 205–8, 255–7; III (1826–7), 4–7, 15–18, 253–4.

135. *The Casket*, II (1827), 304–6, 330–1, 420–2; IX (1834), 146–50. These stories were by American authors: *The Casket* identifies the sources of stories reprinted from *Blackwood's* and other magazines.

136. *New York Magazine*, VI (1795), 748–9.

137. *Literary Magazine*, VIII (1807–8), 128–9.

138. *Blackwood's Magazine*, IX (1821), 194–6.

139. *New York Literary Gazette*, II (1826), 34–5.

140. *The Casket*, New Series, I (1828), 425.

141. *Southern Review*, VIII (1831–2), 345–82.

142. Ibid., pp. 378–9. At least two plays about Mary were performed in America: *Mary of Scotland; or the Heir of Avenel*, in New York in 1821, and *Mary Stuart; or, The Castle of Lochleven*, in Philadelphia, in 1835. See Arthur H. Quinn, *A History of the American Drama, from the Beginning to the Civil War* (New York, 1943), pp. 463, 464. Both plays may well have been stage adaptations of Scott's novel *The Abbot*, which had appeared in 1820. *The Abbot* itself must have done much to encourage Mary's vogue.

143. *Blackwood's Magazine*, II (1817–18), 74–80, 149–55, 288–95.

144. *Port Folio*, 4th Series, VII (1819), 148.

145. Ibid., p. 149.

146. *American Monthly Magazine*, IV (1818–19), 3. The work under discussion was entitled, *Memoir relative to the Highlands: with Anecdotes of Rob Roy, and his Family*.

147. *Literary Gazette*, I (1821), 534.

148. *North American Review*, XXXVIII (1834), 425–55.

149. Cf. 'William Wallace, the Hero of Scotland', *The Casket*, II (1827), 378–80. Campbell's poem the 'Dirge of Wallace' was probably also quite well known. It had been printed in the *Port Folio*, (1802), 357. But the most interesting evidence both of Wallace's fame, and Jane Porter's part in creating it, is provided by a work by a Peter Donaldson, apparently written in America, published in New York in 1823, and re-published at Hartford in 1833. This biographical account is headed: 'The history of Sir William Wallace, the governor general of Scotland and hero of the Scottish chiefs, which may be deemed the first regular prose edition of the life of our illustrious hero ever published in the English language.'

150. Grosart, *Poems and Literary Prose of Alexander Wilson*, I, 92.

151. See *Edinburgh Review*, I (1802–3), 399; XVI (1810), 280; XXIV (1814–15), 159.

152. *American Monthly Magazine*, I (1829–30), 522–3.

153. Ibid., p. 528.

154. Ibid., p. 529.

155. G. S. R. Kitson Clark, 'The Romantic Element, 1830 to 1850', in J. H. Plumb (Ed.), *Studies in Social History* (London, 1955), p. 232.

156. See Pattee (Ed.), *American Writers*, pp. 200–1. Neal was writing in September, 1825.

157. Ibid., pp. 209–10.

158. *North American Review*, XII (1821), 484. Quoted in part by G. Harrison Orians, 'The Romance Ferment after Waverley', p. 414.

159. *Port Folio*, 3rd Series, IV (1814), 58.

160. *Analectic Magazine*, New Series, I (1820), 342–3.

161. Rufus Choate, 'The Romance of New England History', in *Old South Leaflets*, V (Boston, 1902), 202, 205.

162. Ibid., pp. 209, 222. In his *Quest for Nationality* (Syracuse, 1957), Bernard T. Spencer recognises Scott's importance as an example and guide to American literary nationalists. See in particular pp. 39, 93–5. Spencer also comments on the part played by Witherspoon, Blair and Kames in the loosening of the neo-classic ties upon American writing: see pp. 10–11, 33–4.

163. *American Monthly Magazine* (1818–19), 81–2.

164. Easterby, *History of the St. Andrew's Society in Charleston*, pp. 98–9.

165. *St. Andrew's Society of the City of Charleston, South Carolina, Founded in the year one thousand seven hundred and twenty nine. Incorporated in 1798, Rules of the Society, List of Officers and Members from 1729 to 1892, Centennial and other Addresses, Poems, and Historical Sketch* (Charleston, S.C., 1892), p. 77.

166. Ibid., pp. 81–5.

--VI--

Classic Ground

The American Revolution marked more than the end of an era in British imperial politics. To contemporaries in both Europe and America the declaration of independence by Britain's American colonies, and its successful military defence, had enormous symbolic value. Europe's attempt to recreate America in its own image had failed. The Old World's tyrannical institutions, social, political, and religious had been cast off; a New World of freedom and hope had been born. The Atlantic Ocean thus came to be more than a physical barrier between the two continents; the existence of the Atlantic proclaimed the difference between the corrupt societies of Europe and the new society of America. Such a mythology was hardly one likely to encourage Americans to visit the Old World. And in fact in the Revolutionary period it was seriously argued that loyal Americans would do much better staying at home than sojourning, even briefly, in decadent Europe. In 1785, for example, no less a figure than Thomas Jefferson could maintain that young American students had nothing to gain and everything to lose by coming to Europe in pursuit of knowledge.[1]

Such a complete rejection of Europe, while heralding continuing American distrust throughout the nineteenth century and beyond, was short-lived. Even Jefferson had been forced to admit that Americans who wished to study medicine would do well to go to Europe, and for many Americans the cultural, intellectual, and even more the educational appeal of Europe, soon proved irresistible. Thus by the opening of the nineteenth century the American traveller in Europe was already a comparatively familiar figure. And inevitably nowhere was this more true than in Great Britain.

At this particular date, however, the Scottish impact on America was such that Britain meant a great deal more than London, Oxford and Cambridge, and Stratford. Such indeed was Scotland's intellectual and romantic appeal that no American traveller could imagine that his European experience was complete unless it had included a journey to Scotland. That Americans should have felt that this was so is itself the finest proof of the depth of the Scottish impression upon America in the period after the Revolution; the Scotland of Scott, Jeffrey, and Dugald Stewart had come to radiate a magnetic attraction which few American travellers were able or inclined to resist. But of course the arrival of numbers of Americans in Scotland was nothing new. As we have already seen, even before the Revolution, the Scottish universities, and in particular the medical school at Edinburgh, had drawn many young Americans across the Atlantic. And whatever injurious effects the Revolution may have had on certain aspects of Scottish–American cultural relations, it certainly did not sever this particular international link. Indeed after the war, as the reputation of the University of Edinburgh continued to grow—in 1791 Jefferson referred to Edinburgh as the finest university in the world—American students of medicine and other subjects arrived there in increasing numbers.[2]

Early in the new century, however, at the same time as the achievements of the North Britons and their influence upon America's intellectual life were beginning to win full recognition beyond the Atlantic, a new kind of American began to arrive in Scotland. He did not come for education quite in the literal sense; he came instead to experience something of the intellectual vigour which he recognised as characteristic of the Scottish capital in particular. Probably he was aware that he was returning to the place in which many of the threads that had been woven into the pattern of his own intellectual life had originated.[3] Certainly he was aware that in visiting Edinburgh, he was visiting what was perhaps the pre-eminent cultural capital of Europe. Few Americans who published an account of their European travels failed to make this point explicit. Benjamin Silliman, professor of chemistry and natural history at Yale, and one of the leading American scientists of the early nineteenth century, stayed in Edinburgh for six months during 1805 and 1806. Of the Scottish capital, he wrote: 'Edinburgh presents a constellation of scientific and literary men, and, in proportion to its population holds, in this respect, a rank superior to that of any town in Britain, or perhaps the world.'[4] Another American man of science, Benjamin Rush, who had enjoyed Edinburgh's intellectual life a generation earlier, was still prepared to endorse Silliman's opinion. Writing in 1809 to his son James, a student at the University of Edinburgh, he described Edinburgh as 'the most rational and perhaps the most enlightened city in the world'.[5] In the following year, he returned to the same theme:

> However wishfully you may cast your eyes across the Atlantic and long for a seat at your father's fireside, be assured you will often lick your fingers in reviewing the days and hours you are now spending in the highly cultivated society of Edinburgh. Perhaps there is at present no spot upon the earth where religion, science, and literature combine more to produce moral and intellectual pleasures than in the metropolis of Scotland.[6]

A third American scientist, John Griscom, professor of chemistry in the New York Institution, who travelled in Europe in 1818 and 1819, exhibited a similar enthusiasm on leaving the Scottish capital. 'I shall leave Edinburgh', he wrote, 'highly gratified with my visit, and with regret that I cannot longer remain to become more intimately and extensively acquainted with persons of so much talent, intelligence and polish, and withal so hospitable, as one finds in this city. There are few places in the world, where literature and luxury,—where the arts and elegancies of life, have made such rapid advances.'[7]

Griscom's recognition of Edinburgh's distinctive combination of both the intellectual and social graces—a combination particularly appealing to the American intellectual usually debarred from the higher levels of European aristocratic society—was matched by that of many other American visitors to the city. George Ticknor of Boston, the distinguished American scholar and man of letters, who was in Edinburgh at the same time as Griscom, saw the combination as 'the secret of the fascination of society' in the Scottish capital.[8] In his tribute to Edinburgh's cultural pre-eminence in 1825, Nathaniel Carter, a New York editor and journalist, again refers to this distinctive quality of the city's society:

> The capital of the North was perhaps never more flourishing, nor more prominent in the great republic of letters, than at the present moment.... A literary spirit is predominant in the metropolis, and constitutes the controlling principle in its associations. Every body reads, and a great many write. It is

fashionable for both sexes to be numbered among the *literati*, and it would be extremely difficult for a person, who has not some pretensions of the kind, to find a passport to good society....[9]

And the same combination of social and intellectual distinction is noted once again by Emma Willard, the American educator and champion of the cause of women's education, as she salutes the city in a letter to her sister written in 1831:

> To-morrow I leave Edinburgh—I might say, tear myself away from it,—for I am completely fascinated by its wild and wonderful scenery, and with the general tone of society which I have met here,—combining the heart's warmth in all its best affections, with high intelligence, and wit, and shrewdness, in all common affairs.[10]

Emma Willard, however, mentions something other than Edinburgh's intellectual and social attractions: the appeal of the city's scenery. Miss Willard's is a timely reminder. The American who began to arrive in Scotland soon after 1800 was not drawn there solely by Scotland's reputation as the land of learning; the land of romance exercised an equal, and in the end, a stronger, attraction. It was the impact upon American of *Ossian*, Burns and Scott, as much as, or more than, that of the North British thinkers, and the Scotch reviewers, that directed American steps to the north. It was Scotland's writers, her poets and novelists, who had made her hills and moors and glens classic ground.

Again and again American travellers and critics point to the richness of association which her history and her writers had brought to Scotland. It is as if their recognition of the barrenness of so much of the American scene in this respect had sharpened their awareness of its presence in every corner of Scotland. Silliman expresses his sense of it in very personal terms. Writing of Edinburgh Castle he says:

> I am afraid you will be sick of ancient castles; I am not yet tired with visiting them, for I contemplate these venerable monuments of the heroic ages with real and unaffected emotion. How can it be otherwise with an American in whose country there are no such monuments, and whose early curiosity has been fired with the history of ages, when heroes and castles and feats of gallantry and personal valour threw an air of romance

over the whole course of events. What boy on the other side
of the Atlantic has ever read of feudal barons, and of thanes and
clans and border warfare, and has not longed to see a castle![11]

Washington Irving, who toured Scotland in 1817, jotting down this
contrast between the feelings awakened in him in Italy and Scotland,
establishes the principle on a more general level:

> Scotch situations [?] come nearer to my heart. witching songs
> of the nursery earliest days of my childhood—my puir buried
> sister—auld lang syne—nothing remarkable in scenery of the
> country to the luxuriant scenery I have beheld—but they have
> tied [?] the charms of poetry on every river [?] hill & grey rock
> made [?] the desart to blossom as the rose—old buildings—
> clothed with poetry as with ivy—.[12]

Similarly Emma Willard, describing her sail round Loch Lomond,
commented on how 'the most exquisite gratifications' deriving from
the natural beauty of the scene 'were heightened by the poetical
associations, which the names of the glens and mountains, were ever
and anon bringing to our minds'.[13]

The special part played in this enriching of the Scottish scene by
Sir Walter Scott was defined in 1832 by Calvin Colton, American
journalist and economist who, between 1831 and 1835, served as
European correspondent of the *New York Observer*. 'The genius of a
single man', wrote Colton, 'has consecrated those wide regions, as
modern classic ground, and the history of that country as a classic
legend. Italy and Greece have at this moment, if possible, less interest
in the eye of travellers for their classic associations, than the land
which gave birth to Walter Scott.'[14] Orville Dewey, an American
cleric who travelled in the Scottish Highlands in the summer of 1833,
reiterates the theme. In Glasgow on 20 July, he describes the tour he
has just completed:

> From Edinburgh, I have come round through the Highlands to
> this place. Every step of the way has been on classic ground; the
> beautiful windings of the Forth with the Grampian Hills on the
> north; Stirling Castle; the wild grandeur of the Trosacks; Ben
> Nevis and Ben Venue, and the haunted waters of Loch Katrine,
> every rock and headland garlanded with romance; the bold and
> majestic shores of Loch Lomond; the haunts of Rob Roy, the
> Lennox country, and the soft scenery of the Leven.[15]

American critics, too, recognised Scott's particular accomplishment. An article in the *North American Review* on the Waverley Novels noted both the transformation wrought by Scott upon the face of Scotland, and the impetus his writings had given to travels in the Scottish Highlands. Scott's fiction 'has given a charm to the rocks and mountains of his native land'. His genius has cast its light 'on every city, castle, and tower, from the Solway to the Shetland isles'. 'A hundred years ago, the Highlands of Scotland were as little known as the Rocky Mountains', but Scott's pen 'has thrown them open as completely as a thousand military roads, and travellers will wander over them in all generations to come'.[16] It was to this particular aspect of his achievement that allusion was constantly made in American tributes to Scott after his death. A characteristic example occurs in an article by an American visitor to Scotland published in the *American Monthly Magazine* in 1834:

> How completely with the name of Scott is every river, hill, and ruin, in the land of his birth associated—he has given them names—he has made them immortal. Every stream in Scotland has a memorial of him: in every shire of Scotland where the traveller sojourns, they may point out to him some ancient castle or tower, of which the works of Scott have furnished a chronicle. . . . In a word, from Thule to the Tweed, travel where you may, at every step there is something to remind you of Scott. When a king dies, his name adds but a line to the tables of chronology, and the same hour which mourns his death rejoices in his successor. But 'the Minstrel of the North,' though his remains slumber in this narrow cell, has a fame bounded only by the poles, and a memory not likely to be outlived by time.[17]

The eloquence of these remarks was equalled, or even surpassed, by that of an article on Scott in the *North American Review*, in 1833, which insisted that '. . . no traveller will visit Melrose or Flodden . . . hereafter, without recollecting their departed minstrel, or gaze upon a lake or mountain of Scotland, without bidding his gentle spirit rest. It is a great prerogative of genius, thus to write its name upon every hill and valley of its native land, so that all coming generations shall read it there.'[18] A few pages later, the article underlines the theme by introducing the religious image which has so often appeared to be about to be invoked:

> And for whom should Nature mourn, if not for him, who has made her dear to many hearts,—who has thrown a charm over

all the scenery of his native land, which shall live when ages
shall have passed away? On every one of her mountains he has
set a crown of glory, like that which is flung upon them by the
morning sunbeam; he has converted her valleys into a holy
land, towards which the footsteps of the literary pilgrim
tend....[19]

Many indeed were the Americans who made a literary pilgrimage
through Scotland. And it is apparent from their journals, letters and
accounts that these American visitors did not come to Scotland out of
any sense of duty or requirement; their attitudes and feelings are still
in a sense closer to those of the earnest, interested and practical
Franklin of 1759 than to those of the Baedeker tourist of a later age.
Certainly, very soon there were clearly established routes to follow
and places to visit, but in most cases these routes were followed and
places visited with an eagerness of expectation which was not always
to characterise the American tourist in Europe.

The explanation of this eagerness is not hard to find; and present
in it is a criticism of the rather rigorous and schematic manner in
which, in the interest of clarity of interpretation, the two sides of
Scotland's cultural life, and the corresponding American images of
intellectual and romantic Scotland, have been differentiated. The
Americans who travelled in Scotland in the early part of the
nineteenth century did not come merely to gaze upon scenes of
natural beauty or historical interest; their awareness of Scottish
tradition and history, and in particular their enthusiastic knowledge
of Scottish literature, were such that the ground they covered was
already familiar to them. The physical journey was no more than the
exciting confirmation of the imaginative one experienced long
before. In this sense, the impulse to make the tour through Scotland
was as much a part of an intellectual response to the Scottish
achievement as that which directed the American to Edinburgh in
the first place. If the appeal of Scotland was largely a romantic one,
then the romanticism was of an active and vigorous kind, not at all
incompatible with a lively intellectual concern. This is not to say, of
course, that in the early decades of the nineteenth century, it is not
possible already to find suggestions of the sentimental approach to
the Scotland of auld lang syne of a later age, but such an attitude
was not typical of those Americans who journeyed over Scotland's
classic ground in the period when its 'classic' status had been but
recently acquired.

In this period, indeed, one can only with difficulty distinguish between Americans drawn to Scotland by one of her associated images rather than the other. Certainly looking at the first three decades of the new century, one may see the gradual supplanting in priority of appeal of the intellectual image by the romantic one: a change indicated, as we shall see, by the difference between the several winter months in Scotland passed by the American towards the beginning of the period, and the several summer weeks passed by his successor towards its end. But during the period as a whole, intellectual eminence and romantic glamour both exercised their appeal, and it was to both that the American visitor responded. Edinburgh itself stands as the perfect symbol: city of romantic history and unparalleled beauty, but city too of a famous university, of Scott and Jeffrey, of the *Edinburgh Review* and *Blackwood's Magazine*. For every visitor Edinburgh seemed to encompass all aspects of Scotland's attraction, and it was to Edinburgh first that every American hurried his course.

In the Scottish capital, as in Scotland generally, Americans were received with uniform cordiality. Few found reason to complain of their welcome. In a letter which she wrote to an American friend in 1835, Mrs Anne Grant of Laggan, herself hostess to many an American in Edinburgh, explained how both in Scotland and America the claims of personal hospitality rose superior to any feelings of national prejudice:

> We talk of your apathy, your national vanity, and, above all, your utilitarianism, your little apprehension of the ludicrous, etc.; but, when a live American comes among us, we feel as if it were kindred blood stirring, and treat him with warm kindness. On your side, again, there is not even a novel written without some reflection on the English, their pride, their artificial manners, and all the traits that are the necessary faults resulting from over-refinement. Yet one of us goes among you, and if tolerably and properly introduced, he is sure to be well received, and even caressed.[20]

Of course there is no need to take Mrs Grant's assumptions at their face value. Mrs Grant was a Tory, and though her career gained her the attention of almost all the members of Edinburgh's literary circles including Jeffrey and the other Whigs, there is no reason to believe that she did not share the normal Tory attitude towards

America. Consequently, there is no need to accept the view that the Scottish cordiality extended to individual visiting Americans existed always along with a hostile attitude towards America in general. What has already been said of the *Edinburgh Review* and the Scottish liberal tradition in relation to America is in itself sufficient to discredit such a notion. But in addition, the more particular evidence of American visitors themselves may be offered.

Benjamin Silliman, for example, who stayed in Edinburgh between November, 1805, and May, 1806, became particularly intimate with a family whose name he does not reveal.

> I was present to-day at a dinner in this family [he wrote] with an American friend; we met a large party, and were much gratified with their cordial manners. 'Perpetual peace and friendship between Great-Britain and the United States' was given as a toast by the head of the family, and was promptly echoed by the company. The Scotch appear to be very averse to the idea of war with us, and all those with whom I converse, express their wishes that the existing differences may be amicably adjusted. Our host, alluding to my companion and myself, remarked that it was a very delightful thing to see people born and educated 3000 miles from each other, sitting down in friendship at the same table, and finding a common language, mutual feelings, and identical manners.[21]

Perhaps Silliman had this experience partly in mind when a little later he wrote in general terms of the low opinion of the United States he found prevalent in Great Britain:

> A few, (I am sorry to say, that as far as my observation extends they are very few) possess correct information and make that rational and candid estimate of the United States, which an unprejudiced American can hear without displeasure. People of this description are less numerous in England than in Scotland, where there is much more kindness towards us, and some share of real knowledge, concerning the American republics.[22]

Although Silliman immediately qualifies this statement by saying that, even in Scotland, such enlightened individuals are relatively rare, it is difficult not to see in such a passage confirmation of the suggestion of a traditional Scottish awareness of, and concern for, America, originating in the pre-Revolutionary years and persisting down to the early years of the nineteenth century.

The cordiality and hospitality with which Silliman was received in Scotland was in due course extended to all those Americans who followed in his footsteps. We shall see how, in Silliman's case, as in that of his successors, the warmth of his Scottish welcome extended far beyond the limits of social decorum and good manners; throughout the period, no Scottish intellectual or literary circle was necessarily closed to the properly introduced visiting American. In these circumstances it becomes evident that the personal experience of Scottish cultural life enjoyed by Benjamin Rush and all the other American students in Scotland, both before and after the Revolution, was shared by a great many more Americans in this later period. What this situation represents is a renewal and strengthening of personal intellectual ties between Scotland and America.

How far this is so will emerge from an examination of the accounts of four American travellers in Scotland in the early nineteenth century: Benjamin Silliman, Washington Irving, George Ticknor, and N. P. Willis. Silliman and Willis arrived in Scotland towards the beginning and end of the period under consideration; and their accounts of their European travels were exceptionally popular in America. Irving's account is of interest because of his literary stature, while Ticknor too occupied a distinguished place in the intellectual life of his time. The differences between the attitudes and responses to the Scottish intellectual world of these representative Americans will also indicate the changes which begin to occur, as the nineteenth century goes on, in this particular area of Scottish–American cultural relationships.

As we learn from his journal, Benjamin Silliman arrived in Edinburgh on 23 November, 1805, and soon joined two fellow-countrymen in lodgings in the city.[23] Silliman remained in Edinburgh until the end of April, 1806, when he left the Scottish capital for Glasgow and the Clyde, whence he sailed for home. At no point in his account of his European travels does Silliman explain the long duration of his Scottish stay, but it is clear that if he did not come to Edinburgh like so many Americans before him, to enrol as a student at the University, he came nonetheless to study, probably in preparation for his assumption of his Yale professorship in chemistry and natural history.

His studies seem to have taken up most of Silliman's time.[24]

Between entries in his Journal there are often lengthy periods which pass unremarked — one presumes that these periods were occupied by scholarly activities which Silliman thought would not interest the general reader. But whatever the reason, it is clear that Silliman did not take part in Edinburgh's winter social season. This is not to say, however, that he enjoyed no social life of any kind. He did spend many entertaining evenings in the company of Edinburgh families with whom he had become friendly, and he was impressed by the ease and cordiality with which he was invariably received. At the University he naturally made many friends among the faculty; as a result, subsequent transatlantic visitors were going to arrive there, carrying letters of introduction from Professor Silliman.[25]

The high point, however, in Silliman's social life in Edinburgh, was the evening he spent with his two American friends at the home of Dugald Stewart. The party consisted of both men and women and Silliman was impressed by the informality of the occasion; instead of sitting solemnly in chairs, the company had stood in little groups in the room, eating in the buffet style. Silliman was apparently much surprised by this, but he admired the way in which it removed restraints, and encouraged everyone to talk with everyone else.[26] Dugald Stewart's manner and appearance are both described in flattering terms.[27]

Silliman's account of his Scottish sojourn also provides us with evidences of the continuity of Scottish-American relationships from the years before the Revolution. He met, for example, an early friend of John Witherspoon to whom Witherspoon later addressed his Letters on Education. The same man had also been a friend of Benjamin Rush, when that American had been a medical student in Edinburgh. And Silliman met other Scots who remembered Rush with admiration and respect.[28]

In Edinburgh, too, Silliman discussed the topic of American literature. In the course of his soirée Dugald Stewart had expressed a polite but apparently unenthusiastic interest in the subject; to Silliman it was soon clear that neither Stewart nor his guests were acquainted even with the names of such poets as Timothy Dwight, Joel Barlow, and John Trumbull. One morning in April, 1806, Silliman called on a 'literary man' and American writing again came under discussion. The Americans were allowed 'much genius, much keenness and energy of intellect, and a considerable share of information', but they had 'not yet *attained to taste*', and most of their literary productions 'were turgid and bombastical'.[29] Though he found such comments annoying, Silliman was constrained to admit, at least tacitly, that they were but too well founded. Here again, however, he ends his description of the conversation with the thought that many of America's finest literary productions had been little read on the European side of the Atlantic.

From his account of the more intellectual and social side of his Scottish experience, Silliman emerges as in a sense an intermediary figure. His experiences in these respects are not so very different from those of Benjamin Rush. While Silliman did not come to Edinburgh as a degree-seeking student, his attendance at lectures and classes at the University—lectures and classes which he rarely mentions in his book—was clearly the controlling factor during his stay. But in another sense this transitional quality of Silliman may only have been a reflection of the transitional state of the Edinburgh of his day. In 1805, all the North British giants had passed from the capital's scene, while the new generation was still in the process of establishing itself. Some of Edinburgh's most famous hostesses had not yet appeared. Mrs Anne Grant's arrival, for example, of special significance to subsequent American travellers, was still five years distant; had Silliman been able to know this lady, his experience of Scottish intellectual society might have been even more varied and exciting.

Mrs Grant's role in Scottish–American personal intellectual relationships is significant enough to warrant her a brief digression at this point. After her arrival in Edinburgh in 1810, her house quickly became familiar to many of the most famous members of the city's literary and intellectual circles. Hence she was in an excellent position to facilitate the introduction of strangers to these circles. Her ties with America dated from her childhood years. She was the daughter of Duncan Macvicar, an officer in the British Army who had been stationed in America in the pre-Revolutionary period. When she was three years old, she and her mother had joined her father in America. The next ten years were passed in the American colonies, mainly in New York, near the town of Albany. It was in this period that the young Anne Macvicar became a protégé of Madame Schuyler of Albany, a member of one of the most influential families in the province of New York; it was this experience with Madame Schuyler that she was later to describe in her *Memoirs of an American Lady*.[30]

The Macvicars returned to Scotland in 1768. Duncan Macvicar

had retired from the Army but was soon persuaded to accept the post of Barrack-Master of Fort Augustus in Inverness-shire. It was while living in the Highlands at Fort Augustus that Anne Macvicar met the Revd Mr Grant of the parish of Laggan, whom she married in 1779. In the years that followed, Mrs Grant settled down to the active life of the wife of a Scottish Highland minister. But this era was brought to a close by the death of her husband in 1801.

Mrs Grant was now faced with the problem of finding a means of support for her large family. (Her eldest son had died shortly before his father; her youngest child was born two weeks after his brother's death.) It was to writing that she turned. She had earlier won for herself among her friends something of a reputation as a poet. Through the patronage of the Duchess of Gordon, her poems were now collected and edited by George Thomson, friend and correspondent of Burns, and published in 1802.[31] The success of the venture was assured by the three thousand subscriptions which had been obtained prior to the volume's appearance. The publication of *Letters from the Mountains*, a selection of Mrs Grant's correspondence from Laggan, followed in 1806. *Memoirs of an American Lady*, appeared in 1808; *Essays on the Superstitions of the Highlands of Scotland* in 1811; and finally, *Eighteen Hundred and Thirteen: a Poem*, in 1814.

The success of her *Poems*, and of her next two publications in particular, quickly established Mrs Grant as a figure of some note upon the Scottish literary scene. In 1803 she left Laggan and went to live in Woodend, a few miles outside Stirling; in 1806 she moved into Stirling itself, and finally, in 1810, to Edinburgh. It was near the time of her arrival in Edinburgh that her ties with America were renewed.

In 1806, Charles Lowell, who had recently completed his theological studies in Edinburgh, brought home with him to America a copy of *Letters from the Mountains*.[32] The book passed into the hands of his sister who communicated her interest to a circle of her friends. Probably moved in the main by the story of Mrs Grant's life, these Boston ladies arranged for the republication by subscription of her work; an edition of eight hundred copies was produced, and Mrs Grant soon received one hundred pounds as the result of this American sale of her book. In a letter to John Hatsell, Clerk of the House of Commons, dated 17 March 1810, she mentions the receipt of a second hundred pounds from Miss Lowell of Boston.[33] In 1809, too, *Memoirs of an American Lady* was republished at New York.[34] These American editions of her books, together with frequent allusions to her in the American literary journals, were sufficient to establish Mrs Grant's reputation beyond the Atlantic.[35]

It was her connection with the Lowell family, however, that was of most importance in making Mrs Grant's home the rendezvous of so many visiting Americans in Edinburgh. Her tie with Miss Lowell was brought to an end by the latter's death in 1810. At a time when she knew her death was near, Miss Lowell, in a letter to Mrs Grant, spoke nonetheless of the future: 'But should my intercourse with you soon terminate, there are others who shall long cherish your remembrance, and who are worthy of your friendship.'[36] The implications of this passage were in fact fulfilled. To the end of her long life, Mrs Grant remained a close friend of the Lowell family.[37] This tie was sufficient to guarantee that she should come to know many other Americans. It was of course standard practice for Americans travelling in Europe to arrive armed with introductions, wherever possible, to whatever social circles they wished to penetrate. After her rise to literary eminence, Mrs Grant's position in Edinburgh was such that an introduction to her amounted to an introduction to most of Edinburgh's literary and intellectual society. An article in the *North American Review* in 1815 noted the friendship she invariably displayed towards Americans: 'She appears ... to be aware of the patronage she has received [in New England], and her attentions to all Americans, who are made known to her, are very constant and of the kindest description.'[38] Many Americans must have been 'made known' to Mrs Grant by the Lowell family; and no doubt the more Americans Mrs Grant received in Edinburgh, the more she was likely to meet in future years. Apologising for her delay in answering an English friend's letter, in 1819, she wrote: 'You must know that, in the summer, which is the season to which I look forward for the repose which the demands of society preclude in winter, many tourists come from London, from America, and from Ireland, with letters of introduction to me'.[39] It is impossible to estimate how many Americans did arrive in Edinburgh carrying letters of introduction to Mrs Grant. But apart from Dr Robert Anderson, that other friend and correspondent of the Lowells, it is evident that no other individual did so much to encourage and develop personal ties between Americans and Scots.

To set the scene for Washington Irving's Scottish visit it is necessary to say something of Henry Brevoort, his friend and correspondent, who largely prepared the way for Irving's visit in 1817.[40] Brevoort, whose experiences and reactions reveal him as a more typical American intellectual visitor in Edinburgh than his distinguished friend, was in the Scottish capital during the winter of 1812–13. The long letters he wrote to Irving make it clear that he came in contact with all the leading figures in Edinburgh's literary and intellectual circles. He has little to say of Edinburgh's appearance, and if he visited any of the city's places of romantic or historical interest then again he did not consider the fact worth mentioning. It is of the famous names among Edinburgh's literati that he writes to Irving.

As is made clear by his first letter to Irving, dated at Edinburgh, on 9 December 1812, Brevoort's interests in Edinburgh were quite as serious as those of Silliman. 'We are busily employed', he wrote, 'in various studies, which are charmingly enlivened by the kind attentions of a most intelligent circle of acquaintances.... We attend the lectures of Prof: Playfair on Nat: Philo: Prof: Jameson, on Nat: History & Geology—Dr. Hope on Chemistry & Dr. Brown, on Moral Philosophy.'[41] At this stage it is Playfair whom Brevoort describes in the warmest terms: 'Prof: Playfair is decidedly the Luminary of Edinburgh; he is universally beloved & looked up to, & is not less distinguished for the simplicity of his manners than by his genius & profound knowledge.'[42] Attendance at a meeting of the Royal Society of Edinburgh had enabled Brevoort to encounter 'a full divan of the savans of Scotland'.[43] During the winter his 'circle of acquaintances' widened to include many such 'savans'. A letter to Irving, dated 1 March 1813, describes a dinner which he had attended at Walter Scott's two days before. The company included Henry Mackenzie, Francis Jeffrey, and Kemble, the famous actor: 'the conversation turned upon dramatic poetry and upon the art of acting [and] was kept up for several hours with very extraordinary ability.'[44] By this time, Brevoort, who writes throughout as a sophisticated observer of the Edinburgh scene, had been completely captivated by the personality of Scott. In the same letter to Irving he wrote: 'I am now pretty well acquainted with the luminaries of Edinburgh and confess that among them all, Scott is the man of my choice; he has not a grain of pride or affectation in his whole composition.... I would not give the Minstrel for a wilderness of Jeffreys.'[45] We have seen, however, in a later letter to Irving, how his opinion of Jeffrey was to be considerably revised. But the confidence and familiarity with which he writes of these figures is in itself a good indication of his successful penetration of Edinburgh's intellectual circles.

Significant in his own right as an early example of the young intellectual of the American republic, less easily impressed than a Silliman, but combining an air of cultural maturity with an eager desire to learn and to know, Brevoort acquires an added importance through his relationship with Irving. In 1813, and even at his arrival in Scotland in 1817, Irving was not a well-known figure in British literary circles: it was only with the appearance of the *Sketch Book* in 1819 that his reputation was established. However, before leaving Edinburgh in 1813, Brevoort presented Scott with a copy of the second edition of his friend's *History of New York*. Scott was much impressed by the work, and immediately addressed a letter of praise to its author.[46] Jeffrey too, through Brevoort, knew of Irving: when the editor sailed for America, soon after Brevoort's Edinburgh sojourn, one of the letters of introduction he carried with him from Brevoort was to Irving in New York.[47] When Irving arrived in Scotland then, in August, 1817, having previously travelled in England and Wales, and in France and Italy, he was not completely unknown in his father's native land.[48]

As Irving quickly found, August was not a good month for finding the Edinburgh literati at home. On 26 August 1817, the day after his arrival in the city, Irving wrote to his brother: 'I dined to-day with Mr. Jeffrey, [*sic*] Mrs. Renwick's brother. He informs me that Mrs. Fletcher is in Selkirkshire ... Mrs. Grant is likewise in the Highlands. Water Scott is at Abbotsford.'[49] However, not all of Edinburgh's luminaries were out of town. On the next day, 27 August, Irving walked out to Craigcrook to dine with Francis Jeffrey. He found Jeffrey 'very pleasant & hospitable in his own house, and apparently very amiable & happy in his domestic character'—sentiments which seem to reveal very clearly Irving's preconception of Jeffrey, the ferocious and slashing critic. The conversation at dinner turned upon Jeffrey's opinions of America, formed during his visit: 'Speaking of America, Jeffrey observed that he found more Luxury & comfort in the style of living than he had expected. Disliked the virulent political discussions that prevailed at table—the Violent party feeling that prevented gentlemen of different parties from associating.'[50] Jeffrey went on to take exception to the early age at which American girls were brought into society, and to mention some individuals in New York whom he had met and admired. Irving also notes that Jeffrey was 'delighted with Scotts novels— thinks them the best things that have appeared in his time.'[51] At a larger dinner party next day, Irving again was Jeffrey's guest. Among the company were Dugald Stewart's wife and daughter, and Lady Davy, the wife of Sir Humphrey Davy, the natural philosopher and inventor. Dugald Stewart himself had been expected and Irving was much disappointed by the eminent philosopher's inability to be present.[52]

A day or two later, on 30 August, 1817, Irving left Edinburgh to visit Scott, to whom he had been given a letter of introduction by Campbell. After spending a night in Selkirk, he hired a chaise, and drove out to Abbotsford; Campbell's letter was sent down, and 'in a few minutes Scott himself appeared limping up the hill'.[53] The warmth of his welcome made Irving immediately feel at home; Scott insisted that he should stay for several days, and in every way treated his American visitor with such hospitality that Irving found it difficult to express the depth of his appreciation. He wrote to his brother Peter, from Abbotsford on 1 September: 'I have rambled about the hills with Scott; visited the haunts of Thomas the Rhymer, and other spots rendered classic by border tale and witching song, and have been in a kind of dream or delirium.' Of Scott himself he said, 'I cannot express my delight at his character and manners.'[54] Irving's days at Abbotsford, largely taken up by trips roundabout with Scott—including one to call on that stalwart friend of America, the old Earl of Buchan—passed quickly. In a letter to his brother from Edinburgh, on 6 September, he summed up this experience: 'I left Abbotsford on Wednesday morning, and never left any place with more regret. The few days that I passed there were among the most delightful of my life, and worth as many years of ordinary existence.'[55]

Next day, Irving left on his tour of the Scottish Highlands, but on 19 September he was back in Edinburgh to be met by further evidence of Jeffrey's concern for him. On 20 September, he described to his brother the attentions the editor had paid him: 'On my return to Edinburgh, I found a most friendly note from Jeffrey, dated some time back, inviting me to dinner on the day after, to meet again Lady Davy and Sir Humphrey; or three days after to meet Dr.

Mason, of New York.'[56] Two days later he wrote to Peter Irving again, expressing very generously both his sense of obligation towards Jeffrey and his delighted appreciation of his Scottish experience:

> I dined yesterday with Jeffrey, and found a very agreeable party of Edinburgh gentlemen there; I cannot but repeat how much I feel obliged to Jeffrey for his particular attentions, and the very friendly manner in which he has deported towards me. He has made his house like a home to me. I have had many kind invitations to return and pass part of the winter in Edinburgh, when the fashionable world will be here; and, indeed, I have met with nothing but agreeable people and agreeable incidents ever since I have been in Scotland.[57]

Despite his concern to meet Scott, Jeffrey, and Dugald Stewart, Irving does not emerge from this account quite as a typical American visitor to Scotland at this time. Irving was a writer rather than an intellectual or a scholar, and his interests and activities in Scotland reflect the difference. If Irving 'learned' anything in Scotland, it was through his meetings with Scott. But perhaps in proportion to Irving's lack of representativeness in his response to Scotland's intellectual attraction is, as we shall see, the exemplariness of his response to her romantic, poetic appeal. It was Scotland, the land of poetry and song, and Scotland, above all else, the land of Walter Scott, that stirred and delighted Irving.

And here again, perhaps, the indefiniteness of the division between Scotland's intellectual and romantic appeals is manifest. Brevoort's admiration of Scott was as great as Irving's, and we see it matched once again by that of another American visitor in Scotland: George Ticknor of Boston.

George Ticknor, who was to become one of America's most distinguished scholars, was a figure well known in the great houses of Europe and America, having studied in Germany and travelled in France, Italy, Spain and England. He arrived in Edinburgh on 10 February, 1819.[58] Before his arrival in Scotland, Ticknor had already met so many influential Scots that few Americans can have been so well introduced to Edinburgh's intellectual society. Some years before, in June, 1815, he had spent a day at Sydenham with Campbell; and in January, 1819, just before his Scottish trip, at Lord Holland's famous house in London, he had met Sir James Mackintosh, Sydney Smith, and Henry Brougham. In fact, Ticknor's journal makes it clear that during his Scottish stay he moved more freely in intellectual circles than any other American who kept a record of similar experiences.[59]

Like so many of his countrymen, Ticknor was much impressed by Edinburgh's appearance; it is certainly, he wrote, 'one of the beautiful cities of Europe'.[60] But his early days in the Scottish city were not happy ones. He entered no capital of Europe, he says, 'with a lighter heart and more confident expectations of enjoyment.... And yet it was there I was destined to meet the severest suffering my life had yet known.' On 11 February, the day after his arrival, he received letters announcing the death of his mother on 31 December.[61]

For the next few days Ticknor felt unable to meet or see anyone. When he did begin to move in society, his first call was on Mrs Grant. On 15 February 1819, he told his father that the first person he had gone to see was Mrs Grant. 'I had not yet seen her, but when she knew why I did not call, she sent me a note which touched me very deeply.... The hour I passed with her was very pleasant to me.'[62] This was the first of many hours that Ticknor was to spend in Mrs Grant's company. A later entry in his journal describes his relations with her in more detail: he went quite often, he says, to Mrs Grant's, 'where an American I imagine, finds himself at home more easily than anywhere else in Edinburgh. She is an old lady of such great good-nature and such strong good-sense, mingled with a natural talent, plain knowledge, and good taste, derived from English reading alone, that when she chooses to be pleasant she can be so to a high degree.'[63] At Mrs Grant's, Ticknor met Robert Owen, then engaged in his New Lanark scheme, John Wilson of *Blackwood's Magazine* whom he described as 'a pretending young man, but with a great deal of talent', and James Hogg, whose rude manner must have offended the Bostonian's fastidiousness: Hogg is described as 'vulgar as his name'.[64]

Although it is clear that Mrs Grant had made a good impression on the American, it is equally clear that he had made a good impression on Mrs Grant. A letter which she wrote to a friend in America, in June 1819, indicates both the opinion she had formed of Ticknor and the extent to which her house had indeed become a rendezvous for Americans in Edinburgh.

> The American character has been much raised among our literary people here, by a constellation of persons of brilliant

talents, and polished manners, by whom we were dazzled and delighted last winter. A Mr. Preston from Virginia, and his friend from Carolina, whose name I cannot spell, for it is French, Mr. Ticknor, and Mr. Cogswell, were the most distinguished representatives of your new world. A handsome and high-bred Mr. Ralston from Philadelphia, whose mind seemed equal to his other attractions, left also a very favourable impression of transatlantic accomplishments. These were all very agreeable persons—Mr. Ticknor pre-eminently so; and I can assure you ample justice was done to their merits here.[65]

Ticknor also paid many visits to the house of Edinburgh's other distinguished hostess—Mrs Fletcher. His description of his experiences there provides us with excellent evidence of Mrs Fletcher's high standing in Edinburgh society:

[She] is the most powerful lady in conversation in Edinburgh, and has a Whig coterie of her own, as Mrs. Grant has a Tory one. She is *the* lady in Edinburgh by way of eminence, and her conversation is more sought than that of anybody there. I have heard Sir James Mackintosh and Brougham speak of it with enthusiasm.... This was, therefore, a delightful house to visit, and during the latter part of the time I was in Edinburgh, I went there often.[66]

Like Mrs Grant, Mrs Fletcher reciprocated Ticknor's admiration: in her *Autobiography* she speaks of him in terms of warm approbation. Writing of a house she had taken in Callander in the summer of 1820, she talks of encounters with several Americans: her family party

was often enlivened by the arrival of agreeable English and American strangers, introduced to us by different friends. I think it was that year we first became acquainted with George Ticknor, from Boston, U.S., and a friend of his Mr. Cogswell. We thought them among the most cultivated and agreeable Americans we had ever known, and have since kept up our friendship by occasional correspondence with Mr. Ticknor.[67]

Ticknor's contacts with Edinburgh's intellectual society were not limited to these visits to the salons of the city's leading literary ladies. He spent two or three afternoons with Playfair, and, like Brevoort, was much impressed by the old professor's elegance both of mind and manner.[68] One morning he breakfasted with the venerable

Henry Mackenzie at Lady Cumming's. 'He is now old,' he wrote, 'but a thin, active, lively little gentleman, talking fast and well upon all common subjects, and without the smallest indication of the 'Man of Feeling' about him....'[69] He met and visited Mr Pillans, the headmaster of Edinburgh's famous High School, and, as must have been inevitable for a Bostonian, Dr Robert Anderson; he also met Thomas Brown, George Thomson, the editor and song-collector, Dr Alison, author of the *Essay on Taste*, and of course Jeffrey, 'who was everywhere, in all parties, dances, and routs, and yet found time for his great business, and was, on the whole, rather pleasant in his own house....'[70] Dugald Stewart was then in Devon for his health. At the house of Count de Flahault, a Frenchman married to a daughter of Lord Keith, Ticknor met some of Scotland's young noblemen, as well as several of Edinburgh's leading lawyers: Cranstoun, Clerk, Thomson, and Murray.[71]

Despite all these gratifying encounters, Ticknor was not entirely satisfied with Edinburgh society. In a letter to his father, dated 1 March 1819, he complained that the society of men of letters in the city was not quite what he had hoped it would be, or that at least he was 'not in a situation to understand or enjoy it'. Conversation too, at dinners and on other occasions, was not all it should have been; it tended to consist of a series of speeches, and so lacked vitality and continuity. The Edinburgh literati only lived up to their reputations when talked to individually.[72]

Ticknor's concern with the quality of Edinburgh's intellectual life was a particularly pointed one; he sought the society of men of letters because, as he explained rather solemnly to his father, 'it saves an immense amount of time; for a question, addressed to one who has thoroughly studied a subject you are just beginning to investigate, often produces an answer that is better than a volume, and perhaps serves as a successful explanation to half a dozen.'[73] Like Silliman and Brevoort, Ticknor had not come to Edinburgh solely for entertainment, intellectual or otherwise. This is made clear by the first letter he wrote to his father after arriving in the city. Besides wishing to share in the active intellectual life here, as elsewhere in Europe, he wrote, 'I desire to learn something of Scottish literature and literary history, and pick up my library in this department and in English.'[74] To satisfy his first desire, he went initially to Dr Anderson, 'the person, perhaps of all now alive, who best knows English literary history, to say nothing of Scotch, which was, as it were, born with him. He received me with all the kindness I had been taught to expect from him, and to-morrow morning I am to breakfast with him and explain to him all I want to do and learn here, and get what information he can give me.'[75]

In his next letter home, Ticknor explains that he has been unable, despite his efforts, to get himself in the proper frame of mind for study. Nonetheless, he has 'been to see nearly, or quite, everybody that would have interested me, if I were in the proper state of mind to be interested.' On the subject of Scottish literature, at least, his endeavours have not been without success:

> I have received all the kindness and assistance possible in this, from the four persons in Edinburgh best qualified to give them, Walter Scott, Mr. Jamieson, Dr. Anderson, and Mr. Thomson. Mr. Jamieson comes to me every morning, and we have read Scotch poetry together, from the earliest times down to our own day, until it has become as easy to me as English.[76]

Scott is mentioned here as one of those who helped Ticknor in his study of Scottish literature, but the novelist played a much greater role than this in Ticknor's Scottish experience. Ticknor's journal makes it clear that for him, as for so many Americans both before and after, the meeting with Scott was the high point of his visit in Edinburgh. None of the Scottish literati with whom he became acquainted made an impression upon him which in its depth or its favourableness, even compared with that produced by Scott. 'He is, indeed,' wrote Ticknor, 'the lord of the ascendant now in Edinburgh, and well deserves to be, for I look upon him to be quite as remarkable in intercourse and conversation, as he is in any of his writings, even in his novels.'[77]

Ticknor dined with Scott on more than one occasion. One evening, after dinner, he accompanied Scott and his family to the theatre to see a dramatisation of *Rob Roy*.[78] Another morning, Scott conducted Ticknor on a walk around the town; he pointed out the houses of Fergusson, Blair, Hume, Smith, Robertson, Black and others. He had an anecdote for each and a story about every lane and close they passed. The main theme of his conversation was that the days of the North Britons were the true golden days of Edinburgh; but Ticknor writes that he was never more inclined to deny this than at that moment.[79]

Impressed as he was by Scott, it is not surprising that the one trip away from Edinburgh that Ticknor records should have been to Abbotsford. Ticknor left Edinburgh on the morning of 15 March 1819, and with his friend Cogswell, drove as far south as Kelso. Next day the two Americans continued on to Abbotsford. They were received with kindness and hospitality. In this setting, Scott proved even more entertaining than in the city: 'He seemed, like Antaeus, to feel that he touched a kindred earth, and to quicken into new life by its influences.'[80] Here too, he was an inveterate storyteller: 'for every big stone on his estate, as well as for all the great points of the country about, he has a tradition or a ballad, which he repeats with an enthusiasm that kindles his face to an animation that forms a singular contrast to the quiet in which it usually rests.'[81] During dinner, a piper played a pibroch outside the windows, and after the meal was over the company danced Scotch reels in an adjoining room. The rest of the evening was taken up by animated conversation. So Ticknor and Cogswell passed two pleasant days at Abbotsford. 'But the visit that began so happily, and continued for two days so brightly, had a sad close.'[82] Scott suffered a sudden attack of illness, and the two Americans were forced to leave a day sooner than they had intended. Ticknor continued south towards the Lake District, where he was going to visit Southey and Wordsworth.

What had brought Ticknor, Brevoort and Silliman to Scotland was essentially a question of intellectual opportunity. In his intellectual sophistication, however, his refusal to be satisfied with anything less than the best, Ticknor clearly has more in common with Brevoort than with the older Silliman. If Ticknor implicitly recognised that in Edinburgh, as elsewhere in Europe, there were opportunities available to him that he would not find in Boston or New York, still he did not grasp these opportunities quite in the spirit of the provincial colonial. If he shared with his colonial predecessors their ardour to learn, that ardour now co-existed with a new sense of assumed intellectual equality. No more than his contemporaries in Boston who were producing the *North American Review* was Ticknor willing to bow down before the shrine of European culture. He was ready, eager, and determined to learn; but this readiness was not uncritical, this determination not indiscriminate. The change in attitude towards the dominance of English culture between the *Edinburgh Review* of 1755 and that of 1802, and between the first and second generations of Scotland's cultural renaissance, has already been remarked upon; it is this change that should be kept in mind when one notices that the *North American Review* was modelled on the *Edinburgh Review*, and when one reads in the *Port Folio* that her young intellectuals—of whom George Ticknor would be one—were 'making Boston in our hemisphere what Edinburgh is to the British Isles'.[83] In their attitude towards European culture in general, Boston's young intellectuals, and their magazine, were but following the path suggested by their Scottish prototypes.

The literary quarrel itself is of course an excellent indication of the growing self-confidence of American intellectual life. If, on the one hand, the acute sensitivity of Americans to criticism of any kind indicates a lingering sense of inferiority before the older culture of England—an inferiority which the young republic was unwilling to admit even to itself—on the other, the vigour and effectiveness with which the quarrel is conducted in, for example, the *North American Review*, suggests a developing intellectual maturity.

The significance of the literary quarrel in this period is suggested again by a story told by the writer and journalist N. P. Willis. Since 1832 Willis had been touring in Europe, at the same time writing a series of very popular articles on his experiences for the *New York Mirror*.[84] Early in September, 1834, he sailed from London for Edinburgh. On board the ship were two very noisy women; a Scotsman suggested to Willis that they must be American; Willis replied that to him they sounded Scotch: neither man had been in the other's country, but the Scot had read Mrs Trollope, the American, *Cyril Thornton*.[85]

Few Americans in Britain early in the nineteenth century were welcomed into British aristocratic society. America's republican status, and its democratic institutions which were very little to the taste of upper-class British society in general, are sufficient to explain this. Willis, however, was an exception. Both in England and Scotland he was received and entertained by the nobility. In Edinburgh in particular, however, Willis did not turn his back upon the intellectual stratum of Scottish society. In the city one morning, he breakfasted with John Wilson. While breakfast, much to Willis's dismay, cooled upon the table, Wilson spoke to his guest of American poetry; the poets to whom he gave particular praise were Percival and Pierpont, while he also expressed pleasure at the criticisms of his own works that had appeared in the American papers and magazines.[86] The remainder of the 'several hours of the highest pleasure' that Willis passed in Wilson's 'fascinating society', was taken up with discussions of the origins of the *Noctes*, of Lockhart as a critic, of Wordsworth and Southey, and of Thomas Hamilton and the literary quarrel. On the last topic Wilson remarked that Hamilton was greatly annoyed by the *North American Review*'s notice of his *Men and Manners in America*; he also remarked that he had always had the idea that he would be the best traveller in America himself.[87]

On the day he breakfasted with Wilson in Gloucester Place, Willis dined with Jeffrey in Moray Place. A large party was present, including many names distinguished in the law, as well as Lady Keith and her husband Count de Flahault; to Willis's disappointment, however, Henry Brougham was unable to be present. The great Grey dinner had been held the day before, and not surprisingly politics was the sole topic of conversation. Since his arrival in Britain, Willis had moved in exclusively Tory circles—he was staying at present just outside Edinburgh with the Tory Earl of Dalhousie—hence he felt a trifle 'out of it' among so many enthusiastic Whigs. His sympathies in the 'great and glorious' occasion were slower than those of the company, and on his admission that he had not been present at the dinner, he was rallied upon having fallen into bad company. Nevertheless, Willis went on to the ball which followed the dinner; Brougham and Lord Grey were both present, though Willis noted that the Scottish nobility was for the most part conspicuous by its absence.[88]

Willis was in Edinburgh at a time when Scotland's cultural renaissance was drawing to its close. The differences between his experiences and those of the earlier Americans discussed are marked; Willis had come to observe, not to participate. He reports what will be of interest to his readers—hence the account of his interview with *Maga*'s famous editor and the rehearsal of his opinions on American poetry and the literary quarrel. But Willis's reporting never suggests the 'engagement' with the Scottish intellectual scene that still so clearly characterises the accounts of Silliman and Ticknor, of Brevoort and John Griscom.

Their published accounts make it clear that American visitors to Scotland in the early nineteenth century were well able to enter Scottish intellectual and social circles. With the proper introductions no doors were barred to them. It is worth emphasising that the number of Americans who published accounts of their European sojourn or tour, including their stay or visit in Scotland, could only have been a fraction of all those who made the Atlantic crossing. From the remarks of Mrs Grant, from Griscom's observation of four or five compatriots at a meeting of the Edinburgh Royal Society, and from the chance encounters of other travellers, apart from any logical deduction, it is clear that the experiences recorded by those travellers we have discussed were duplicated by a great many others. Support for this point of view—and a suggestion of its importance— is contained in an article on the *Remains* of the Revd Edmund Griffin which appeared in *Blackwood's* in 1832. Having suggested that great numbers of the ablest young Americans are continually carrying home from Europe, 'not only the accomplishments, but the knowledge and the wisdom which are the fruit of judicious foreign travel', the article turns to Americans in Scotland:

> Not a few are with us every year in Scotland; and were we to form our opinion of their countrymen in general from the young Americans with whom we have made acquaintanceship and friendship, we should think almost as highly of our brethren across the western wave as of ourselves.[89]

Read even in isolation, comments such as these would make one hesitate to accept the view that the Revolution finally cut off all personal cultural interchange between Scotland and America. Read as the confirmation of much of what has been said above, such comments encourage one to take quite a different view of the state of personal cultural relations between the countries after the American Revolution. What was lost on the strictly executive, political level—the departure of Scottish governors and other government representatives—was eventually made up on the purely intellectual one. The flow of American students to the Scottish universities did not end with the Revolution, and the new kind of personal contacts which developed from the beginning of the nineteenth century represents a continuation of Scotland's intellectual impact upon America. The examples of Silliman, Brevoort, Ticknor, and Griscom, who came to Scotland with a passionate desire to study and to learn, may not have been entirely typical, but having spent some time in the lively and stimulating intellectual atmosphere of Edinburgh in the first three decades of the nineteenth century, few Americans could have returned to Boston, or New York, or Philadelphia or wherever, without retaining some of the 'knowledge and wisdom which are the fruit of judicious foreign travel'.

Few Americans came to Scotland solely because of the country's intellectual distinction; the atmosphere of romanticism in which her writers had shrouded her also exercised a strong fascination. That the two appeals supported, rather than worked against each other, is shown by the fact that several of the travellers who have been discussed or mentioned in relation to Edinburgh's intellectual life also made a point of making a pilgrimage over Scotland's classic ground, while those who did not, were not entirely immune to the country's romantic appeal.[90] But, as has been suggested, the balance between the two kinds of appeal was not, throughout the first three decades of the nineteenth century, a stable one. The pattern is rather that of a gradual weakening of the intellectual appeal, a gradual strengthening of the romantic one. The American visitor who arrived, like Silliman, early in the nineteenth century, did not venture far beyond the cities of Edinburgh and Glasgow.[91] Towards the end of the period under consideration however, Americans are being drawn to Edinburgh mainly by the city's beauty and by the richness of its associations.[92] And for travellers such as these, of course, an extended tour through the Highlands and other parts of Scotland was an essential part of their Scottish visit.

For Scotland itself this pattern of development is of the greatest significance. It heralds the fate of Scottish culture in the nineteenth century. What it implies is the approaching defeat of one image by the other: the yielding of the land of learning to the land of romance. There is nothing particularly idiosyncratic about the American response to Scotland. The Scottish history and the Scottish literature read with such enthusiasm by the Americans appealed almost as strongly to most of Europe. Hence the changing pattern of the American response to Scotland is almost certainly an accurate mirror of that of the world at large. The consequence of the change, of the coming to power, as it were, of Scotland's romantic identity, was no doubt almost inevitable: a gradual acceptance by the Scots, increasingly self-congratulatory and self-regarding in tone, of the romantic image of their country and themselves. It was this development above all perhaps that brought to an end a distinguished period in Scotland's cultural history by transforming what had once been vigorous and healthy in Scottish culture into a sentimental, self-indulgent provinciality.

The 1830s were early days, however, and in this period it is easy to see that the American response to romantic Scotland was firmly based on a first-hand knowledge of Scottish writing. As we have seen, almost all Americans who came to Scotland were irresistibly drawn in the first place to Edinburgh. To reach the city easily the most popular route was the east coast one running through the northern counties of England, entering Scotland at Berwick-upon-Tweed. Other possibilities were the west coast route via Carlisle, or the sea-passage from London direct to Edinburgh. Once in Edinburgh, the tourist hurried to see Holyrood Palace and the Castle; in the Palace he would behold with particular awe Queen Mary's chamber, and the indelible bloodstains upon the floor of Rizzio, her murdered favourite. But Edinburgh had much else to offer; the wonder of the bridges, under which not water, but other streets ran; the houses in the Old Town more than ten stories tall; the New Town with its imposing, formal elegance; and the wonderfully-varied prospects of the city and its beautiful environs, from Calton Hill, Arthur's Seat, or the Castle. And there was hardly a corner or close or wynd of Old Edinburgh which did not have some historical or literary or romantic association. The American tourist, however, rarely failed to comment on the dirtiness of Edinburgh's Old Town.

Having spent a week or more in and around Edinburgh, the tourist would probably begin his tour over Scotland's classic ground by sailing up the Forth from Edinburgh to Stirling, perhaps on board the 'Stirling Castle' or the 'Victory' or the 'Ben Lomond'. From Stirling, rich in its associations of the struggle for Scottish independence under Wallace and Bruce, the next stage was usually by coach—perhaps the 'Highlander', with its portrait of Rob Roy on the door-panels—to Callander. From Callander the route led through the Trossachs to Loch Katrine over land hallowed by Scott in the *Lady of the Lake*. Loch Katrine was crossed by row-boat—a landing of course being made on Ellen's Island. The few miles across to Loch Lomond were covered on foot. There the steamer was boarded which sailed around the Loch; a boat would be taken down the River Leven, with its associations of Smollett, to Dumbarton, and finally another steamer up the Clyde to Glasgow. This comparatively short route—it could be covered in two days—was easily the most popular one; it was sometimes followed in the reverse direction, the tourist starting out on the Clyde and ending at Stirling.

Many Americans, however, chose to make a more extended Highland tour. Having reached Stirling, they would turn north to Perth; then continue north through the mountains and moors of Perthshire and Inverness-shire to the town of Inverness, the capital of the Highlands. Inverness stands at the eastern end of the Caledonian Canal which, stretching diagonally across the centre of Scotland, links the Atlantic and the North Sea. From the Highland capital, then, the tourist could take a steamer, perhaps the 'Maid of Morven', or the 'Comet', down Loch Ness, through the canal, giving him the choice of either disembarking at Ballachulish and proceeding overland through Glencoe to Loch Lomond and the Scott country again, or of sailing on out to visit Iona and Staffa before eventually arriving at the Clyde. This route too, could be reversed, or altered by proceeding from Inverness east along the Moray Firth to Aberdeen, and then down the east coast once again to Edinburgh. Inadequate roads and accommodation, combined with an absence of compelling literary associations, explain why no tourist ventured north of Inverness, while what are probably the grandest and most spectacular areas of Highland scenery, in Wester Ross and western Sutherland, remained far outside the popular tourist routes.

After his arrival at Glasgow, at the end of either a short or an extended Highland tour, several possible routes were open to the tourist. He could go south to Ayrshire to visit the Burns country subsequently crossing back into England by way of Dumfries. More popular was the southerly route back to Edinburgh by way of Hamilton and Lanark and the picturesque Clyde valley, which allowed visits to the Falls at Stonebyres, Bonniton and Corra Linn, and to Robert Owen's community at New Lanark. Occasionally this route was extended as far south as Abbotsford, but Scott's Border home was more commonly visited on a special expedition from Edinburgh.

Once again only a few of the travellers of the many who left descriptions of their journeys over Scotland's classic ground, will be discussed at any length; Silliman, Irving and Willis for the same reasons as before—Irving because of his literary interest, Silliman and Willis because they stand at either end of the period under consideration—and two 'professional' American travellers, Nathaniel Carter of the *New York Statesman*, and Calvin Colton, foreign correspondent of the *New York Observer*, whose accounts were widely read.

Benjamin Silliman was, as we have seen, a studious and hard working chemist; but he was in no way immune to Edinburgh's romantic charm. In the first place, like so many others, he was much impressed by the grandeur of the city's setting and appearance. He compared it favourably in these respects with the English capital: 'In the vicinity of London,' he wrote, 'one may find beautiful scenes, without number, but there is nothing grand or sublime.'[93] A day or two after his arrival, Silliman visited Holyrood House. There is no doubt about what he particularly wanted to see:

> I hastened with eagerness to that part of the palace which contains the apartments of that unhappy queen, whose history will ever excite the strongest sympathy, and cause every one to regret that she had not been as innocent as she was beautiful and unfortunate. No one can fail to be deeply interested in her tragical story, while compassion for her fate, and indignation at the hypocrisy and meditated cruelty of her rival, aided by the peculiar interest which is excited by her beauty and accomplishments, naturally induce us to wish to conceal the blemishes of her character.[94]

Silliman duly details for his readers the furnishings of Queen Mary's apartment, and recounts the story of David Rizzio's murder.

Silliman was in Edinburgh before the full impact of Scottish writing had been felt in America, but even so, he was neither unaware of nor uninterested in Scottish literature. One house he visited was that of Allan Ramsay, 'the sweet pastoral bard'. Of his *Gentle Shepherd*, Silliman only complains that much of its beauty is obscured by 'the frequent introduction of words and phrases entirely local to Scotland'. As in Burns's case, however, knowledge of these peculiar forms leads to the discovery of new beauties.[95]

On his way to Glasgow, Silliman paused to view the ruined palace of Linlithgow, the birthplace of Mary Queen of Scots. At Falkirk he remarks on the battles fought there in 1298—the defeat of Wallace by Edward I—and in 1746—the successful stand made by the retreating Jacobite forces.[96]

Here again Silliman appears as an intermediary figure. As compared with the Franklin of 1759, his interests are far more literary and historical. In comparison with those of later travellers, however, the geographical limitations of his travels well indicate their circumscription. But Silliman's account, nonetheless, does have a special significance: his response to Holyrood House, his comments on Edinburgh Castle, his knowledge of Wallace, and of Allan Ramsay all go to show that even in America it was not Scott alone who created the romantic image of Scotland. Silliman's romanticism, however subdued, indicates quite clearly that Scott, in America as in Great Britain, was the inheritor, not the creator of a tradition.

This is not of course to deny the tremendous influence and impact of Scott's achievement. By the time that Irving arrived in Scotland in 1817, the wizard's wand had been waved and whole areas of Scotland had been transformed in a way that Silliman could never even have imagined in 1805. For Irving, as for many more Americans, the appeal of Scotland was hardly to be differentiated from the appeal of the land of Scott.

Irving sailed from London to Berwick near the end of August, 1817. Off the coast of Northumberland, as the castles of Dunstanborough and Bamborough, and Holy Island, were passed, he jotted down in his notebook the appropriate lines from *Marmion*.[97] On board ship, he met an old Scot named Willie Symes, a shepherd in the Grampians, who claimed to have seen Macbeth's castle at Dunsinane and the grave of Norval, the hero of Home's *Douglas*.[98]

Irving found Edinburgh 'remarkably picturesque & romantic in its general appearance'.[99] Having visited the Castle—he disapproved of the style of the modern additions—he proceeded down the High Street, past John Knox's house, to Holyrood. The association with Mary Queen of Scots again provided the main interest. Here are Irving's notes:

> Queen Marys rooms the effect in thus treading on the heels of antiquity—seems to obliterate the space of time between us— as if we hear the very sound of the steps of former ages— like Pompeii—[100]

From Edinburgh Irving went by chaise to Linlithgow. Having viewed the palace, he went on to Falkirk from where he walked to Stirling. Passing the field of Bannockburn, he inspected the stone in which Bruce's standard was supposed to have been planted.[101] At Stirling, Irving turned north for Perth and Dunkeld; from Dunkeld he proceeded to Aberfeldy and the Falls of Moness where, as he noted, Burns wrote his song, the 'Birks of Aberfieldie'.[102] From

Killin on Loch Tay he turned south to Callander, and journeyed from there down through the *Lady of the Lake* country to Loch Lomond and Dumbarton.

Having sailed up the Clyde to Glasgow, Irving set out for Ayrshire on the final stage of his literary pilgrimage—a visit to the Burns country. Associations with Wallace and Queen Mary were again noted on the way, and in Ayr itself, Irving met a stone-mason who had known and drunk with Burns.[103] From Ayr Irving returned to Glasgow, and from Glasgow, via Lanark and the Falls of Clyde, to Edinburgh. At the conclusion of his two-week tour, he wrote to his brother from the capital on 20 September, 1817:

> I arrived here late last evening after one of the most delightful excursions I ever made. We have had continual good weather, and weather of the most remarkable kind for the season— warm, genial, serene sunshine. We have journeyed in every variety of mode—by chaise, by coach, by gig, by boat, on foot, and in a cart; and have visited some of the most remarkable and beautiful scenes in Scotland.[104]

For Silliman, visits to Holyrood House, Edinburgh Castle, Linlithgow Palace, and his viewing of scenes rich in associations of Scottish history and literature, were no more than fascinating diversions during his Scottish stay. For Irving, such experiences, multiplied many times over, have become primary. Wherever he went every river, hill and rock spoke to him of poetry and romance; touched by the poetry of association, the bleakest scene bloomed like the rose. Scotland had become a continual appeal to the imagination, and to the literary imagination in particular. His meeting with Scott was for Irving but the climax of that appeal.

But even Irving's tour was relatively circumscribed in area. Although much of the ground he covered was never to lose its primacy of appeal, it was soon to be no more than a stage of more extended tours. Nathaniel Carter, for example, travelled much further afield.[105]

This New York journalist entered Scotland by the east coast route from Berwick-upon-Tweed on 24 September 1825. His first night was spent not far across the border in an inn at Renton. His romantic musings on this occasion well suggest his attitude towards Scotland:

> The moon was bright and nearly full. A century or two ago, her orb might have lighted the borderers to their predatory

incursions, or have witnessed the gambols of fairies upon the banks of haunted streams. But the age of barbarous warfare and of superstition has gone by; and although we slept upon classic and poetical ground, no unusual visions disturbed our slumbers.[106]

Due deference was, however, shown to the 'classic and poetical ground': 'Burns' Cotter's Saturday Night was read as a kind of homily before going to bed'.[107]

Of Edinburgh Carter gained a particularly striking first impression. He was fortunate enough to enter the city in the early evening when the sun was still bright, the skies cloudless, and the atmosphere possessed that distinctive, sharp translucence, which makes every building stand out clear-cut: 'it is in external appearance the most beautiful city I have ever seen, or ever expect to see, should my travels extend the world over. Nothing can surpass it in grandeur and beauty'.[108]

It was Edinburgh's literary and intellectual history that Carter found particularly fascinating. He visited the graves of Hume, Adam Smith, Blair, Maclaurin, Gregory, Allan Ramsay, and Playfair. He sought out the homes of Ramsay, 'the celebrated Scotch poet', Hume, and Boswell.[109] He found Johnny Dowie's tavern in Liberton Wynd, which had been a favourite resort of Burns. There he spoke to Dowie's widow, a seventy-four-year-old woman, who told him many tales of Burns and his drinking companions sitting late over their ale, singing Burns's songs; she claimed too, to remember David Hume and the other great men of that era.[110] And Carter inspected 'the far-famed residence of Jenny Deans', though making the comment that it was not his intention 'to furnish illustrations of the Waverly novels, which would be an endless task; for there is scarcely a rood in Scotland, to which the pen of this popular and voluminous writer has not imparted a charm.'[111]

Carter left Edinburgh for Perth by coach on 30 September 1825. From Perth he proceeded north to Inverness. An impression of the wildness and desolation of the Highland moors and mountains predominates in his account of this part of his travels:

Farther from the road, the aspect of the waste is still more cheerless. Hill rises above hill, and range after range, in perfect desolation. The eye searches in vain for a dwelling of any kind. Sometimes a smoke is seen curling above the heath, and a group of Highland shepherds, perhaps the descendants of 'Young Norval,' are wrapped in their plaids and encamped by the fire, with their dogs sleeping by their sides.[112]

Shortly before arriving at Inverness, Carter passed 'Belleville, the seat of James M'Pherson, Esq., son of the translator, or author, as the case may be, of Ossian's Poems.'[113]

Having completed a survey of Inverness itself, Carter rode out to inspect the field of Culloden. His references to the battle make it quite clear where his sympathies lay; here, before an army led by the 'infamous Duke of Cumberland', 'fell the flower of the Highland Clans, whose valour deserved a more gallant leader and a better fate'.[114] In a footnote, Carter quotes Smollett's *History of England* on 'the ravages and atrocities' perpetrated by the 'monster' Cumberland after the battle. Campbell's poem on Culloden is described as 'one of the sublimest compositions in the English language'.[115]

On 4 October 1825, Carter left Inverness in a steamer which was to carry him down the length of the Caledonian Canal. A comment he makes on the unnecessarily expensive lock system employed in the canal again points up his romantic Jacobite sympathies:

> But it is no concern of mine, how much money the British government squandered for the benefit of the Highlanders. Other millions might have been expended without making full reparation for the wrongs and outrages inflicted upon a gallant people, by carrying a war of desolation into their peaceful vales.[116]

The steam-boat docked in the evening near the end of the canal at the foot of Loch Lochy. From his inn, Carter had an excellent view of Ben Nevis. His description of the scene, with its strong romantic emphasis, is typical:

> Directly in front of the inn, and at the distance of not more than three quarters of a mile, Ben-Nevis swells from the vale to the altitude of 4370 feet above the sea, being the loftiest mountain in Great-Britain. The scenery in the vicinity is in the highest degree wild and romantic, showing off this stupendous mass of rocks to the best advantage. To the west of the chain of lakes, as far as vision extends in both directions, peak rises after peak, frowning upon the waters below. The basin is skirted with dark and desolate heaths, and sprinkled with a few turf

cottages, so rude in construction that grass and wild plants are seen growing from the roofs. A lake opens on either hand, and between them flows the river Lochy, on the banks of which are seated the ruins of two or three old castles. Upon such a scene, this monarch of the Caledonian hills looks down from his throne in gloomy grandeur.[117]

A few miles further down Loch Lochy, Carter and four other members of his party left the boat, having decided to proceed overland through Glencoe down to Loch Lomond. The journalist recognised that he was now in an area rich in associations with Ossian. The ride inland 'was one of the most pleasant which this romantic region has afforded'. 'In one direction the traveller surveys, across a wide expanse of waters, Morven and other hills celebrated by Ossian, while towards the east, he looks up the glen which was the birth-place and residence of the poet himself.'[118] Carter and his party spent their first night after leaving the boat in a small inn near Ballachulish. There they were able to listen to Gaelic songs, one of them ascribed to Ossian: 'The voices of the trio were melodious, and the music was soft and melancholy, stealing over the mind like the dying cadence of an Aeolian harp.'[119]

Next morning Carter journeyed through Glencoe. On the way the river Cona was passed, 'which is said to be the native stream of Ossian, and to which his poems contain such frequent allusions'. In Glencoe itself, Carter recognised the origins of much of the imagery of the Ossianic poems:

> The two principal mountains which rise on opposite sides of the narrow pass, are called Marmor, and Con-Fion, or the hill of Fingal, whence the great Highland bard drew some of his wildest and sublimest imagery. Here may be seen the originals of those rocks, solitudes, clouds, mists, storms and torrents— all those grand and terrific forms of external nature, on which his muse was so fond of dwelling. From the striking coincidence between some of his figures and the features of Glencoe, an argument might be drawn to strengthen the popular tradition, that this was the place of his nativity and abode.[120]

All in all, Glencoe seemed to Carter to surpass 'in solitary, gloomy and romantic wildness' anything he had seen in Scotland.[121]

Loch Lomond was eventually reached and crossed by row-boat. Carter and his party, as was not unusual, then covered the few miles that led to Loch Katrine on foot. Here again a row-boat was hired and a landing was made on Ellen's Island, 'in the identical little bay, where the far-famed heroine was wont to moor her skiff'. Ellen's Bower, 'fashioned exactly according to the description of the same object in the Lady of the Lake',[122] was duly visited. From Loch Katrine the party proceeded to Callander 'through the former dominions of Rhoderick Dhu'.[123] On the road to Stirling from Callander, Doune Castle was passed and Carter tells the story of John Home's imprisonment there; he also had a glimpse of Blair Drummond, 'formerly the seat of Lord Kames, author of Elements of Criticism. It was a subject of regret, that no opportunity presented of examining the residence of a writer, whose excellent work had afforded me so much instruction and pleasure'.[124]

Having surveyed the prospect from Stirling Castle—Edinburgh's Arthur Seat and Castle Rock in the distance, the broad windings of the Forth, and the scenes of many battles close at hand—Carter set off to inspect the field of Bannockburn.[125] The rock in which Bruce's standard was planted was noted and the comment made that 'the muse of Burns has imparted scarcely less celebrity and glory to the field, than the sword of Bruce'.[126] Carter and his friends reached Glasgow by sailing down the Union Canal which links the Firth of Forth with the Firth of Clyde.[127]

From Glasgow Carter and an American friend set off on an excursion to Ayrshire. Carter noted that Irvine was the birthplace of the Scots-Irish poet James Montgomery, and of the novelist John Galt, and also that it was a temporary residence of Burns. Of Burns however, he was able to learn much more than this. The two Americans were able to meet the physician to Lord Eglinton who had been a personal friend of the poet. The doctor showed them the originals of poems and songs, and of a verse epistle addressed to himself.[128] They also were able to meet the poet 'Davie', to whom Burns addressed two of his best known verse letters. With 'Davie' too, the Americans spent a sociable evening listening to his poems and songs, hearing stories about Burns, and once again seeing many original manuscripts. A day or two later the old poet accompanied them on a visit to the banks of the Ayr and the Doon.[129] Seeing the new and old bridges at Ayr, the subject of a poem by Burns, Carter comments that 'the personification is so vivid, that the *dramatis personae* seemed something beyond inert matter, and to be endowed with a portion of animated nature'.[130] Visits were paid to

Burns's cottage and to Alloway kirk, 'which the poetical tale of Tam O'Shanter has made immortal'.[131]

On 31 October, Carter left Glasgow again for New Lanark. After inspecting Owen's community—Owen himself had recently left for the United States—he visited the Falls of Clyde at Bonniton and Corra Linn.[132] Above the latter part of the falls he found 'a pretty little tenantless lodge or temple' furnished with 'seats, tables, and mirrors hung from the ceiling in such a way, as to present a full view of Corra Linn, increasing the effect too by making the torrent seem to pour from the skies'. Here there were several visitors' books, and among the signatures Carter saw that of 'John Randolph of Roanoke' as well as those of several New York friends.[133] The journalist and his friend left Lanark and set out for Dumfries on the last stage of their Scottish travels. In Dumfries they demonstrated once again the extent of their interest in Burns by addressing letters to the widow of the poet who still lived in the town. The Americans described themselves as 'two gentlemen from the United States ... among the transatlantic admirers of the Scottish bard'.[134] They were informed that Mrs Burns would be very happy to see them, and were able to spend a pleasant and interesting half-hour in her company.[135]

Carter's tour had been much longer and more extended than Irving's: the Scott country, the Burns country, the Ossian country. Carter—and his readers—had been everywhere. Every scene and every encounter had been graphically described; no romantic note or suggestion had been omitted. In Carter's account we see the full flowering of Scotland's romantic impact upon America; it is all there, from the reverence for the sword of Bruce to the strong Jacobite sympathies, from the rapt attention paid to the widow of Johnny Dowie and her stories of Burns and the great days gone by, to the awed response to the Ossianic sublimities of Glencoe, and the fascinated inspection of Ellen's Bower on the island in Loch Katrine. To turn the pages of Carter's account of his Scottish travels is to turn the romantic pages of Scottish literature and history.

In 1832 Calvin Colton, foreign correspondent of the *New York Observer*, covered much the same ground as Carter had done seven years before.[136] But Colton's account is of particular interest in that much of what he writes is an explicit commentary upon Carter and all the other American travellers in Scotland: a long and detailed definition of the appeal of Scotland to the American imagination.

Colton begins his account by saying that the physical appearances of Scotland and England are quite unlike, as are also the characters of the peoples. The Scots' native land is such that they are bound to be extraordinary:

> A people born and bred among such hills and vales, familiar with such mountains and lakes, challenging the stronger emotions of the soul, and the bolder flights of fancy, ought to be extraordinary. I never looked out upon the face of that country, but my mind was quickened—equally by what strikes the eye, and by historical associations.[137]

The face of Scotland exhibits great natural beauty, but in addition, 'she is venerable for the projects which have been conceived by the mind of man, and for the scenes in which man has enacted a part'. Ossian is then invoked:

> [Scotland] has been the cradle of warrior chieftains, whose exploits in heathen story would have given them rank among the gods—and even as it is, they are famed as more than mortal. The wild and romantic rhapsodies of Ossian had their natural occasions and just provocations in the *physical* and *moral* of the regions, where they were conceived.... Human beings, tenanting such a part of the world, must be bold and aspiring—must be men of high endeavour, and sometimes of mighty achievements. When war was the fashion, they must have been heroic in arms.... When poetry has moved them, they have sung wild and sweetly, and being themselves charmed, have charmed the world.

Intellectual achievements, too, have been Scotland's: 'When chastened learning and sober science have challenged their attention, they have claimed to lead the rest of mankind—at least they will not be led.' Scotland and the Scots have a distinctive character:

> Look at her warriors of times gone by, but not to be forgotten—look at her poets, her men of science, her metaphysicians, her theologians, and her universities—look to her arts and cities—and say, if Scotland has not a character of her own? She is not stamped by the rest of the world, nor by any part of it, even though for want of a political importance, the world is not stamped by her.

So Scotland has asserted her nationality. Her achievements in every field of human endeavour have compensated for her loss of political independence:

> In intellectual greatness, in moral virtue, in commercial tact—
> in literature and science—in the pulpit, in the forum, in
> parliament, and on the bench—in the drudgery of common
> life, in affairs of state—at home and abroad—on the sea and
> on the field—whenever brought into competition with the
> English in any of these pursuits and in all others, they have
> generally excelled and carried off the palm.[138]

In Edinburgh, Colton inspected Holyrood House in a mood of
high romantic enthusiasm. The associations with Mary he found
particularly appealing:

> —the *very* apartments which she occupied, and the *very*
> furniture which she used, and the *very* work of her own fingers,
> *all in statu quo*, as she used and left them ... —these, as might
> well be imagined, were the things most attractive.[139]

Of the Queen herself he wrote, 'While her fate will for ever claim
and receive the sympathy of those who read her story, her faults
shall not remain unwept.'[140]

From Edinburgh, Colton sailed up the Forth to Stirling. From
Stirling he went to see the village of Dollar beside the River Devon
which Burns had celebrated in his song 'The Banks of Devon'. Near
Dunkeld, Colton paused to admire the River Braan, a branch of the
Tay. His guide brought him to a small house or temple, beside a
waterfall, apparently like that built at Corra Linn. Inside was a large
painting of Ossian singing to his two greyhounds and the maidens
who stood around him. This picture was suddenly drawn aside by
some mechanical means to allow the spectator to look straight out
upon the cataract which dashed down forty feet in front of him. A
mirror was placed in the ceiling creating the impression that the falls
were immediately overhead.[141]

Travelling north through the Grampians towards Inverness,
Colton was appalled by the wild barrenness of the scene, and by
the meanness of the Highlanders' homes. But even as there is 'a
world of poetry and the deepest soul of song' in the music of their
bagpipes, so the Highland people have a distinctive nature:
'Certainly there is character—and not a little of character in the rude
people, inhabiting such a rugged region of the globe. It is not

difficult to believe that they have done such exploits, as are ascribed to them in the historical legends of that classic ground.'[142]

From Inverness, Colton sailed down the Caledonian Canal to Fort William, and on out to visit Fingal's cave on Staffa, and the ancient cathedral on Iona.[143]

Colton's Scottish reporting supplements that of Carter. Of particular interest is the manner in which his general comments on the nature of Scotland's attraction reveal so clearly certain features of the basic structure of the romantic image. The old combination of associationism and primitivism is still present; the wild Highlands are 'a world of poetry' and 'human beings, tenanting such a part of the world, must be bold and aspiring—must be men of high endeavour, and sometimes of mighty achievements'. Scotland's achievement is a distinctively national one: a successful assertion of her independence and importance in every field except the political one. For many of his readers Colton must have brought into focus feelings about Scotland which had previously perhaps remained only implicit in their interest in the country.

That interest is still present in N. P. Willis's account of his Scottish travels but it now co-exists with a new note of American sophistication; an occasional suggestion of the fading of the glamour of Scotland's classic ground. But the suggestion is certainly rare; normally Willis writes with the same enthusiasm that had characterised his predecessors, and indeed with the same apparent conviction that he is the first person ever to have seen and described these scenes.[144]

Willis arrived in Scotland, by sea from London, early in September, 1834. The view of Edinburgh from the water he found second only to that of Constantinople. When later he climbed up to the Castle to see the sunset: 'Oh, but it was beautiful!' he wrote, 'I have no idea of describing it; but Edinboro', to me, will be a picture seen through an atmosphere of powdered gold, mellow as an eve on the Campagna.'[145] A tour of Holyrood made Willis recognise 'the melancholy romance' of Mary's life as he had never done before: 'if Rizzio's harp had sounded from her chamber, it could not have seemed more tangibly a scene of living story'.[146]

Willis sailed from Edinburgh to Aberdeen. Once again his host was an aristocratic one: the Duke of Gordon, in whose castle at Fochabers he stayed for several days. From Fochabers he proceeded by coach to Inverness. Passing over the field of Culloden, and seeing

H

the castle in which the Young Pretender slept the night before the battle, he comments:

> The interest with which I had read the romantic history of Prince Charlie, in my boyhood, was fully awakened, for his name is still a watch-word of aristocracy in Scotland; and the jacobite songs, with their half-warlike, half-melancholy music, were favorites of the Dutchess of Gordon, who sung them in their original Scotch, with an enthusiasm and sweetness that stirred my blood like the sound of a trumpet.[147]

In Inverness Willis met several young Highland aristocrats; they had a style about them—'a free, gallant, self-possessed bearing, fiery and prompt, yet full of courtesy'—which reminded him of 'our high-bred Virginians'.[148] At Inverness Willis boarded the steamer and sailed down the Caledonian Canal. In describing the appearance of Loch Ness and its surroundings, he draws the familiar contrast between Scotland and America in terms of richness of association: 'You might have had the same natural scenery in America, but the ruins and the thousand associations would have been wanting; and it is this, much more than the mere beauty of hill and lake, which makes the pleasure of travel.'[149] These associations must have taken on an extra sense of reality when he discovered that a fellow-passenger, to whom he spoke, was a granddaughter of Flora Macdonald.[150]

Willis left the boat at Fort William in order to proceed overland down to Loch Lomond by way of Glencoe and Tarbet. At the inn at Ballachulish, he found in the travellers' book the names of several Americans he knew.[151] Loch Lomond he saw under particularly favourable circumstances. His comment is the most ecstatic of those his readers encountered:

> As we came in sight of the lake, ... the water looked like one sheet of gold leaf, trembling, as if by the motion of fish below, but unruffled by wind; and if paradise were made so fair, and had such waters in its midst, I could better conceive than before, the unhappiness of Adam when driven forth.[152]

After his extended tour through Scotland, Willis looked upon the final, most popular, stage of his journey with aristocratic disdain: 'We had now reached,' he wrote, 'the route of the cockney tourists.'[153] He did, however, follow that route, even landing on Ellen's Island in Loch Katrine to inspect the Bower. From Callander he rode to Stirling on the 'Highlander', then sailed down the Forth to Edinburgh on board the 'Victory'. The sail down the river was enlivened by a race between the 'Victory' and the 'Ben Lomond'; the latter was eventually successfully run aground. From Edinburgh he went to see Abbotsford. Of Scott, 'the greatest spirit that has walked the world since Shakespeare', he writes with deep feeling. Even the trees of Abbotsford are sacred: 'planted every one by the same hand that waved its wand of enchantment over the world! One walks among them as if they had thoughts and memories.'[154]

The note of sophistication which is occasionally to be sensed in Willis's account of his Scottish tour is well suggested by his rather condescending reference to the 'cockney' tourists. It is after all an American who speaks so disparagingly of the route followed by so many English tourists in Scotland; it is as if a Scotsman today touring in America, and writing in a Scottish newspaper, were calmly to dismiss all those Americans who have never been west of the Mississippi. Willis—and so vicariously his thousands of American readers—can, out of his wider experience, feel greatly superior to these cockneys. Nonetheless, in his response to Edinburgh's beauty, to Holyrood, to the Highlands and to the Highlanders, Willis is as fresh and enthusiastic as his predecessors. Perhaps by this date Americans could afford to be condescending towards the Scott country tourists; perhaps they were more familiar with Loch Lomond than with Lake Champlain, with the Falls of Clyde than with the Falls of the Passaic, with the Scottish Highlands than with the New York Highlands.

The impression of the Scots that Willis formed was a very favourable one. 'Instead of a calculating and cold people,' he writes, 'as they are always described by the English, they seem to me more a nation of impulse and warm feeling than any other I have seen. Their history certainly goes to prove a most chivalrous character in days gone by, and as far as I know Scotchmen, they preserve it still with even less of the modification of the times than any other nations.'[155] Willis supports his estimate of the character of the modern Scots by a reference to their chivalrous past. It was an identical emphasis, with its essentially literary background, developing through the final decades of the eighteenth century and the early decades of the nineteenth, which finally dissolved the much less favourable image of the Scot which prevailed during the American Revolution.

The recorded experiences of American travellers in Scotland reinforce many other of the general conclusions to be drawn from the development of the romantic image of Scotland in America. Again and again one gains the impression that the American travellers in Scotland knew beforehand what they would find. Perhaps not all of them could have defined their preconceptions quite with the readiness suggested by these comments of the Revd C. S. Stewart of the U.S. Navy on crossing the Scottish border:

> The hills and mountains, swelling on every side, are as bare and uncovered as can be imagined, and the few dwellings scattered over them, as black and weather-beaten as if they had withstood the blasts and tempests of a thousand years. Still I felt, in every vein, that it was the land of romance, and of song, the land of heroism and of genius, the land of letters, and of religion, the land of my blood and of my name; and gazed upon it with an enthusiasm I have never before known.[156]

One feels, however, that few would not have shared his initial enthusiasm. And few again, one imagines, would have found much to disagree with in this second comment by Stewart, made when his travels in Scotland were nearing their close:

> My prejudices have always been strongly in favour of Scotland and the Scots. I am an enthusiast in the history of the nation, tragic and bloody as for the most part it is, and were you with us, dear V——, you would find that I am now likely to become equally the admirer of its wild scenery and everything associated with it.[157]

Where the Americans went, what they wished to see, even their response to the varied scenes, all were clearly controlled by their enthusiasm for Scottish history, 'tragic and bloody' as for the most part it was, and for Scotland's wild scenery and the literature which had graced and adorned it. So it is that traveller after traveller writes of identical things: of Scotland's history, of her ancient castles and palaces, of Wallace and Bruce and the heroic struggle for Scottish independence, of the tragic figure of Mary Queen of Scots, and of the Highlanders' devotion to the Stuart cause, and equally of the almost inexhaustible richness and variety of Scotland's literary associations, of the classic ground which her poets and writers had made her moors and glens.

The intimate knowledge of Scottish history and literature revealed by these various Americans was not something acquired on the Atlantic crossing. It was the result of an enduring, well-established, and enthusiastic American response to Scottish writing; in other words, it was the direct consequence of the impact of the more native or national side of Scotland's eighteenth century renaissance upon America. Without that impact, the American traveller would never have come to Scotland; if he had he would not have ventured far beyond Edinburgh. As it is, an American in Edinburgh could reflect that, '... through these streets Queen Mary was brought after her defeat at Carberry Hill, in degradation, and disgrace, and tears— ... upon these very pavements, Robertson, and Hume, and Mackenzie, and Burns, and Scott have walked; a holy air of antiquity seems to breathe from every wynd and close, and touching memories are inscribed on every stone...'[158]—and be angered by the people round about him who have allowed familiarity to dull their response to these scenes. That sacred past, perhaps, he regarded as as much his own heritage as theirs. Certainly it was a heritage in which she shared that Emma Willard sensed in Edinburgh:

> The very graves of some of the fathers of my mind, who here repose, awaken feelings which I have never experienced on similar occasions,—except it might have been in visiting the tomb of Washington,—and convince me of what I have never thought of before, that I cherish a more intimate affection for the Scottish, than the English writers, though not a livelier admiration.[159]

It is this sense of in some way sharing in Scotland's heritage that enabled the American traveller in the early nineteenth century to write so intimately of Mary Queen of Scots, of Bruce and Wallace, of Falkirk and Culloden and the rest; but even his awareness of that heritage—as its selectivity clearly shows—was literary in origin. It is the *romantic* history of Scotland the American knew: that colourful past which we have already encountered in America itself as one element within the developing romantic image of Scotland.

And what was true of the American's knowledge of Scottish history was equally true of his knowledge of Scottish literature. The literature he knew so well, the associations and settings of which he pursued so tirelessly on his Scottish pilgrimage, was no other than the literature which had begun to make itself felt within America even before the Revolution. From Allan Ramsay's *Gentle Shepherd* through *Douglas* and *Ossian* it had run, until in Burns and Scott, with its associated image of Scotland, it had finally taken possession of the American imagination.

No better proof of that possession could be offered than this record of American travellers in Scotland in the early nineteenth century. It may be argued that these travellers are exceptions, that the fact that they came to Scotland demonstrates their special interest in that country and its culture. But such a position cannot be maintained. The visit to Scotland was normally only part of a much more extensive European tour; and there was clearly nothing exceptional about it—it was the rule, not the exception. Furthermore, the writings of the American travellers on Scotland imply their audience: an audience as interested, concerned, enthusiastic—and informed—as the travellers themselves. A reference to Young Norval needs no explanation; no more than one to Fingal, or to 'the big ha' Bible', or to Muschat's cairn, or to 'Gray Benvenue' and Loch Katrine. In this sense Scottish literature had indeed become part of the American heritage.

The literary pilgrimage to Scotland of a Washington Irving one might imagine to be a special case; but the examples of Carter and Colton and Willis, and all the others, show how wrong such a conclusion would be. For one and all, their progress through Scotland was exactly a literary pilgrimage. On Loch Lomond Emma Willard was complimented on her knowledge of Scottish poetry and song and told that 'our Scottish women' did not know half so much about the Scottish poets; asked whether her knowledge was exceptional she replied that American women were generally well read in the Scottish writers, many of them much better than she.[160] One need not conclude from this that all Americans in Scotland, and their readers at home, knew more of Scottish literature than most Scots, but it is clear that a great many did know 'the Scottish writers' very well indeed.

On the literary pilgrimage Scott is of course the controlling figure; but *Ossian*, Burns, and the whole Scottish literary tradition of story and song may clearly be seen directing both route and response. If a scene is beautiful in itself, then it is many times more beautiful because of its poetical associations; even the birds and the flowers have an extra charm because they are the birds and flowers made familiar by Scottish song. Comments as generalised as those on the appearance of the Highlands, and on the Highlanders themselves, constantly reveal their direct descent from the Highlands and the Highlanders of Home, Macpherson, and Scott. The projected literary image of Scotland had been recognised and accepted within America in such a way as to ensure that the American traveller coming to Scotland knew that he would be travelling over 'classic ground'. His Scottish experience served only to confirm the accuracy and appropriateness of that description.

NOTES AND REFERENCES

1. 'It appears to me, then, that an American, coming to Europe for education, loses in his knowledge, in his morals, in his health, in his habits, and in his happiness.'
Jefferson to John Banister, Jr, October, 1785. In Julian P. Boyd (Ed.), *The Papers of Thomas Jefferson*, VIII (Princeton, 1953), p. 637.

2. Between 1749 and 1812, 139 Americans took medical degrees at Edinburgh, and probably as many again studied there for a time without taking a degree. Of the 139, 86 came from the South, 65 of these from Virginia—perhaps an indication of the influence of the old tobacco link. See Wyndham B. Blanton, *Medicine in Virginia in the Eighteenth Century* (Richmond, 1931), pp. 86–7. A study of the records of the Speculative Society reveals the admission of only one American—Benjamin Smith Barton—in the period immediately after the War. Barton, who became president of the Royal Medical Society, was admitted to membership in 1788. But in 1790 according to an Edinburgh man in a letter to a friend in Philadelphia, there were twenty-four Americans at the university; 'two are from New York, and one or two from Pennsylvania—all the others are from the southern states.' See the *Gazette of the United States*, Wednesday, 25 August 1790. In the winter of 1805–6, according to Benjamin Silliman, professor of chemistry at Yale, who was in Edinburgh at that time, there were present twenty-five American medical students alone. See Benjamin Silliman, *A Journey of Travels in England, Holland, and Scotland, and of two Passages over the Atlantic in the years 1805 and 1806* (New York, 1810), II, 325. Again, 'an American young gentleman, now in Scotland' wrote in a letter dated 13

December 1818: 'The lectures in the University commenced early in November; 1779 students have already matriculated. They are from every quarter of the globe, and among them are about twenty-five Americans, mostly from the southern states.' See *Ladies Literary Cabinet*, I (1819–20), 110.

3. In 1806 Charles Lowell of Boston wrote to Dr Robert Anderson, whom he had met during his residence in Edinburgh from 1802 to 1804, introducing his fellow Bostonian clergyman, J. S. Buckminster: 'He visits Great Britain for the benefit of his health, and Edinburgh particularly, for the purpose of becoming personally acquainted with those men, whom, for their writings, he has long been accustomed to reverence.' (Original in National Library of Scotland, Adv. MSS 22.4.16.) Anderson, a literary historian, mainly through his contact with the Lowells, was host to numerous Americans in Edinburgh in the period 1805–30. Charles Lowell would introduce an American friend to Anderson; a year or two later that American would be writing introducing his friends; Anderson seems to have greeted all his transatlantic visitors with the same unfailing courtesy.

4. Silliman, *Journal*, II, 323.

5. Butterfield, *Letters of Benjamin Rush*, II, 1018.

6. Ibid., p. 1038.

7. John Griscom, *A Year in Europe*, II, 373.

8. George S. Hillard (Ed.), *Life, Letters, and Journals of George Ticknor* (Boston, 1876), I, 277.

9. Nathaniel H. Carter, *Letters from Europe, comprising the Journal of a Tour through Ireland, England, Scotland, France, Italy and Switzerland, in the years 1825, '26 and '27* (New York, 1829), I, 246–7.

10. Emma Willard, *Journal and Letters, from*

France and Great Britain (Troy, N.Y., 1833), p. 365.

11. Silliman *Journal*, II, 282. In 1824, Nathaniel Wheaton, an American cleric, sought for Holyrood House 'with an imagination excited by recollections of what I had read in childhood of this palace of Scottish kings'. Nathaniel S. Wheaton, *A Journal of a Residence during several months in London* (Hartford, 1830), p. 445.

12. Stanley T. Williams (Ed.), *Tour in Scotland 1817, and other Manuscript notes by Washington Irving* (New Haven, 1927), pp. 38–9. Irving's father was a Scot, a native of Orkney; he emigrated to America in 1763.

13. Willard, *Journal and Letters*, p. 345.

14. Calvin Colton, *Four Years in Great Britain. 1831–1835* (New York, 1835), II, 11.

15. Orville Dewey, *The Old World and the New; or, a Journal of Reflections and Observations made on a Tour of Europe* (New York, 1836), I, 64–5.

16. *North American Review*, XXXII (1831), 392.

17. *American Monthly Magazine*, III (1834), 226.

18. *North American Review*, XXXVI (1833), 304–5.

19. Ibid., p. 315.

20. J. P. Grant (Ed.), *Memoir and Correspondence of Mrs. Grant of Laggan* (London, 1845), III, 261.

21. Silliman, *Journal*, II, 336. The evidence of Silliman may be compared with that of another scientist, John Griscom, the Quaker chemist from New York, who was in Edinburgh during March, 1819. Of Thomas Brown, the moral philosopher, one of the many members of the university faculty with whom he had become friendly, Griscom wrote: 'He, as well as most of the savans whom I have met with here, appears to entertain very friendly feelings toward the United States, and looks with much interest to the progress of our institutions. It has been gratifying to me, to hear them speak in flattering terms of the Americans who are here, either as travellers, or as medical students.' (*A Year in Europe*, II, 354–5.) And again with that of the Revd Edmund Griffin, whose mind and imagination, as we have already seen, had been filled with romantic images of Scotland from an early age. Griffin spent three months in Scotland towards the end of 1829. Near the end of his stay he wrote, 'I would with great satisfaction remain at Edinburgh the whole winter, instead of going to London. The Scotch are the kindest, the most hospitable, and most agreeable people in the world.' (Francis Griffin (Ed.), *Remains of the Rev. Edmund D. Griffin*, II, 253.)

22. Silliman, *Journal*, II, 348–9.

23. Silliman's *Journal* was published in New York in 1810, and quickly established itself as a minor classic. It probably served as a guide to subsequent keepers of European journals; Benjamin Rush certainly saw it in such a light—in 1810 he wrote to his son James in Edinburgh, noting the popularity of Silliman's work and suggesting that it was an excellent model for a journal. (See Rush, *Letters*, II, 1051.) In 1818 John Duncan, the Scottish traveller, met Silliman in New Haven, and wrote of his book: '...it is calculated to flatter our national vanity, that two editions have been sold off, so completely, that I found difficulty in procuring in New Haven even a used copy.' (Duncan, *Travels through Parts of the United States and Canada in 1818 and 1819*, I, 149.) And as late as 1825, John Neal wrote in *Blackwood's* of Silliman's work: 'It is a very fair picture of what he saw, here; and a work, which deserves to be, as it is, popular in his country.' (Pattee, *American Writers*, p. 177.)

24. 'My Edinburgh life was one of constant effort, and my exertions, while in that city, pressed hard upon my health.... No five months of my life were ever spent more profitably; and this residence laid the top stones of my early professional education.' George P. Fisher, *Life of Benjamin Silliman* (London, 1866), I, 168. From Silliman's account of his Edinburgh residence, printed in Fisher's biography, we learn that at the University he attended the lectures of Dr Gregory, Dugald Stewart, and Dr Hope, then professor of chemistry.

25. John Griscom, for example, arrived at the University in March, 1819, carrying letters of introduction from Silliman to Thomas Brown and Dr Hope.

26. Silliman's surprise is matched by that of Griscom at a party given by Thomas Brown in 1819; the affair did not begin until nine in the evening, and instead of the 'select literary few' that he had expected, Griscom found a room so crowded with fashionable men and women—all, however, 'persons of some literary reputation,'—that there was no room to sit down. (*A Year in Europe*, II, 338.)

27. Silliman, *Journal*, II, 332. Stewart is never

mentioned by name, but Silliman's reference to 'the distinguished professor' who is 'the pride and ornament of the University, and of Scotland' makes the identification certain.

28. Ibid., pp. 342–3. Witherspoon's *Letters on the Education of Children* do not name the person to whom they are addressed.

29. Ibid., pp. 350–1. The 'literary man' in question was Dr Anderson, the literary historian; his house was for many years one of the literary centres of Edinburgh, and, as we have noted (p. 219), a favourite resort of American visitors. Those present on the morning of Silliman's call included the Earl of Buchan. See Fisher, *Life of Benjamin Silliman*, I, 181.

30. Margarita Schuyler (1701–82), a member of the famous New York family, married her cousin Philip Schuyler; they lived north of Albany and their house became the social centre of the Northern frontier. The Schuylers had no children of their own, but Madame Schuyler brought up and educated many nephews and nieces.

31. This and other details of Mrs Grant's biography are taken from the sketch of her life written by herself and prefaced to the edition of her letters prepared by her son, J. P. Grant, and published at London in three volumes in 1845.

32. See *North American Review*, LX (1845), 145. Ferris Greenslet, however, in *The Lowells and their Seven Worlds* (Boston, 1946), pp. 115–16, states that Charles Lowell had first met Mrs Grant in Edinburgh during the season of 1803–4. The *North American Review* wrongly dates his return to America as 1809.

33. *Memoir and Correspondence*, I, 227.

34. *North American Review*, LX (1845), 146.

35. An article in the first volume of the *North American Review*, in 1815, on the Edinburgh cultural scene which, though marred by the intrusion of a note of laboured sarcasm, recognised to the full the city's literary and intellectual eminence, said of Mrs Grant that she 'is very much known in Old England and in New England by her two first publications, and very little any-where by her two last', *North American Review*, I (1815), 193. See too the *Port Folio*, 3rd Series, II (1813), 213; and 4th Series, VII (1819), 249–52.

36. *Memoir and Correspondence*, I, 237.

37. John Lowell (1799–1836) lodged with Mrs Grant while he was a student at the Edinburgh High School in the period 1810–13.

38. *North American Review*, I (1815), 194.

39. *Memoir and Correspondence*, II, 224. Famous Americans who visited Mrs Grant in Edinburgh include John Randolph of Roanoke (see *Memoir and Correspondence*, II, 317), and Professor Norton of Harvard (*Memoir and Correspondence*, III, 133–4.) To another American friend she wrote in October, 1833: 'I have seen several Americans lately, chiefly Bostonians, all interesting, as being branches from the Lowell family, with whom I was very intimate. When I first came to Edinburgh they were here, and their society was my greatest enjoyment at the time, and we have never ceased since to correspond.' (*Memoir and Correspondence*, III, 232.) As we would expect, references to Mrs Grant appear in the pages of many American books of travels in the early nineteenth century. John Griscom met her in her Princes Street home on 13 March 1819. They talked of America of which Mrs Grant seemed to retain 'a forcible recollection'. (*A Year in Europe*, II, 340.) The Revd Edmund Griffin spent three months in Scotland near the end of 1829. In Edinburgh he met Mrs Grant, 'that remarkable lady' who is 'one of the literary boasts' of the city. Describing her as now 'a venerable ruin', Griffin was deeply impressed by her cheerful resignation, and by the originality and liveliness of her conversation. (*Remains of the Rev. Edmund D. Griffin*, II, 233–4.)

40. Henry Brevoort (1791–1874) owned a large estate on Manhattan Island. He was a man of literary taste, and travelled widely in Europe.

41. George S. Hellman (Ed.), *Letters of Henry Brevoort to Washington Irving*, I, 66–7.

42. Ibid., p. 68.

43. Ibid., p. 67.

44. Ibid., p. 74.

45. Ibid., pp. 83–4.

46. Ibid., p. 99.

47. Ibid., p. 96. For an account of Jeffrey and Brevoort and Jeffrey's trip to America, see pp. 94–7.

48. In New York Irving had been a particular friend of a Scottish lady, Mrs Renwick, the daughter of the Revd Andrew Jaffrey, of Lochmaben in Dumfriesshire; her son, James Renwick, was professor of natural philosophy at Columbia. Robert Burns had known the Jaffrey family, and had addressed

several poems—including 'The Blue-Eyed Lass' and 'When first I saw fair Jeannie's face'—to Mrs Renwick, Jean Jaffrey as she then was, in her youth. Irving often visited the Renwick household in New York; according to Pierre Irving's biography, the house 'was a cherished resort of Mr. Irving'. No doubt Mrs Renwick's poetic association with Burns gave her an added charm to Irving's eyes. See Pierre M. Irving, *The Life and Letters of Washington Irving* (New York, 1862), I, 266.

49. Ibid., p. 378. 'Jaffrey' has frequently been misspelled 'Jeffrey'. Nathaniel Carter, the New York journalist and editor, found a very similar state of affairs in Edinburgh in September, 1825; he learned that 'Walter Scott was at Abbotsford . . . Mrs. Fletcher was at Roslin Castle, and Mrs. Grant in the Highlands.' (*Letters from Europe*, I, 244.)

50. Williams (Ed.), *Tour in Scotland*, pp. 30–1.

51. Ibid., p. 31. The individuals mentioned by Jeffrey were John Wells (1770–1823), a distinguished lawyer and controversialist, and Peter Augustus Jay (1776–1843), a lawyer, jurist, and state legislator. There is no evidence that Jeffrey met Irving while he was in America in 1813; and Irving's notes on their meeting in Edinburgh do not clearly suggest that this was a renewal of an old acquaintance. However, we have already seen that Jeffrey crossed the Atlantic carrying a letter of introduction from Henry Brevoort to Irving. There is at least a possibility, then, that the two had met in America.

52. Ibid., pp. 32–3.

53. Ibid., p. 40.

54. Irving, *Life and Letters*, I, 381–2.

55. Ibid., p. 383.

56. Ibid., pp. 385–6. John Mitchell Mason (1790–1829) succeeded his father, who had been sent out from Scotland in 1761, as minister of the Scotch Presbyterian Church in New York. John attended Columbia College and later studied theology at Edinburgh, graduating in 1792.

57. Ibid., p. 386.

58. George Ticknor (1791–1871) sailed for Europe in 1815 in the company of Edward Everett, later an editor of the *North American Review*. Among the famous Europeans whom Ticknor met—with some of whom he later regularly corresponded—were A. von Humboldt, Chateaubriand, Goethe, and A. W. and F. Schlegel. Near the end of 1816 he was invited to fill the new Smith professorship of French and Spanish at Harvard. To prepare himself for this post he studied and travelled in Spain. He was inducted professor in August, 1819, and held the position until 1835. His *History of Spanish Literature*, the first full-scale treatment of the subject, was published in 1849.

59. Ticknor's only rival is perhaps John Griscom, the Quaker chemist, who was in Edinburgh at the same time as the young Bostonian. Griscom moved particularly freely in university circles being entertained by Professors Brown, Hope, Jameson, and Murray, the chemist and physicist. In addition, Griscom was entertained by Mrs Grant, Mrs Fletcher, Francis Jeffrey, John Pillans, rector of Edinburgh's High School, and David Brewster, the natural philosopher and inventor. In New Lanark he met Robert Owen, and in Glasgow, Thomas Chalmers, as well as several members of the university faculty.

60. *Life, Letters, and Journals of George Ticknor*, I, 276–7.

61. Ibid., p. 275.

62. Ibid., p. 274.

63. Ibid., p. 278.

64. Ibid.

65. *Memoir and Correspondence*, II, 211. The only thing that Mrs Grant disliked about these American gentlemen was their preference of France over Great Britain; but, she goes on 'Perhaps I carry this too far; for, though these distinguished countrymen of yours were not partial to Britain in general, they seemed to like Edinburgh very much better than any other part of this country; and with that I ought to be satisfied' (p. 213). William Campbell Preston (1794–1869) was elected United States Senator from South Carolina in 1833. He had come to Edinburgh in 1817 to study law. It was at this time that he toured the Highlands with Washington Irving. Preston's friend, whose name Mrs Grant could not spell, was Hugh S. Legaré (1797–1843). Legaré had studied in Charleston with Mitchell King, author of the St Andrew's day speech described in the previous chapter. He went to Europe in 1818, and came to Edinburgh, where he lived with Preston, also to study law. Joseph Green Cogswell (1786–1871) studied and travelled in Europe between 1815 and 1820. He attended Göttingen University with Ticknor and Edward Everett. While he was in Edinburgh, Cogswell contributed two anonymous essays to *Blackwood's Magazine*:

'On the Means of Education and the State of Learning in the United States of America', and 'On the State of Learning in the United States of America'. After his return to America, Cogswell became professor of mineralogy and geology at Harvard, and also the university librarian. Later he became acquainted with John Jacob Astor, becoming adviser on the public library which Astor proposed to establish in New York. After Astor's death in 1848, Cogswell was in charge of the arrangements which led to the opening of the library in 1845. I have been unable to identify Mr Ralston.

66. *Life, Letters and Journal*, I, 279.

67. Mrs Fletcher, *Autobiography*, p. 140. Mrs Fletcher has misdated her meeting with Ticknor. Ticknor's published *Journal* makes no mention of a journey to Callander; nor was he in Scotland during the summer months.

Other evidence of the good impression made by Ticknor and his compatriots in Edinburgh at this time is provided by John Griscom. Griscom had been introduced to Francis Jeffrey and early in March, 1819, was taken on a tour of the Scottish courts then in session in Parliament House by the distinguished lawyer and editor. The face of the Clerk of the Court of Sessions, from the many prints of it he had seen in New York, was familiar to the Quaker chemist, and Jeffrey's offer of an introduction to Scott was eagerly accepted. In the conversation that followed, Griscom was invited to Abbotsford, and other Americans in the city were discussed: 'Both S. and J. spoke of the Americans who were now, or had recently been, in Edinburgh, in flattering terms; and particularly of –. –. ––––––– of Virginia, and –. –––––– of Boston.' (*A Year in Europe*, II, 327–8.) The second person referred to is clearly George Ticknor; the first is probably W. C. Preston (of South Carolina).

68. *Life, Letters, and Journal*, I, 279.

69. Ibid., p. 279.

70. Ibid., p. 280.

71. Ibid., p. 277.

72. Ibid., p. 276.

73. Ibid.

74. Ibid., p. 274.

75. Ibid.

76. Ibid., p. 275. John Jamieson, antiquary and philologist, and probably Thomas Thomson, a lawyer with legal and literary antiquarian interests.

77. Ibid., p. 280.

78. Ibid., pp. 281–2. Scott enjoyed the performance very much. His comment at its end was, "That's fine, sir: I think that is very fine;" then, 'with one of his most comical Scotch expressions of face, halfway between cunning and humor' he added, "all I wish is, that Jedediah Cleishbotham could have been here to enjoy it." At this time Scott had yet to acknowledge his authorship of the Waverley Novels.

79. Ibid., p. 282.

80. Ibid., p. 283.

81. Ibid.

82. Ibid., p. 284.

83. *Port Folio*, 4th Series, IX (1820), 463.

84. The trip to Scotland provided the final sketches in 'Pencillings by the Way', which had begun to appear in the *New York Mirror* in January, 1832. Willis wrote in all 139 articles which 'were read with eagerness in America' and which 'were copied into five hundred newspapers'. See Henry A. Beers, *Nathaniel Parker Willis* (Boston, 1885), pp. 115–16.

85. Nathaniel P. Willis, *Famous Persons and Places* (New York, 1854), pp. 12–13. The Scottish section of 'Pencillings' was not included, for reasons of volume size, in the 1852 publication of that work. The author's preface to *Famous Persons and Places*, explains that 'a portion of the original "Pencillings" is here given' (p. v).

86. Two years before, Wilson had discussed American poetry with Henry McLellan, a young American divinity student, then attending the University of Edinburgh. Wilson talked of Bryant and of Samuel Kettell's first comprehensive anthology of American verse, *Specimens of American Poetry* (1829); he praised James Gates Percival and John Pierpont's *Airs of Palestine* (1816), and expressed a desire to know more about American poets. Henry B. McLellan, *Journal of a Residence in Scotland* (Boston, 1834) pp. 214–15.

87. *Famous Persons and Places*, pp. 34–45. Wilson's remarks on the literary quarrel suggest a liberalness of attitude that is hardly characteristic of *Maga*. He said that the examples of vulgarity with which so many travellers filled their books, he could match any day in Edinburgh. His association with all classes in his own country, he believed, would have enabled him to distinguish

between what was universal and what particular to America.

Hamilton's forthcoming book had also been discussed at Wilson's in McLellan's presence; at that time Wilson had said that he saw no reason why an admirer of the English constitution might not also admire America: 'He thought on the whole, that the work of Mr. Hamilton would be favourable to us.' (*Journal of a Residence in Scotland*, pp. 348–9.)

88. *Famous Persons and Places*, pp. 46–9. Charles, Lord Grey (1764–1845) was the Whig leader during the period of agitation which finally led to the passing of the Reform Bill in 1832. After the defeat of Wellington's government in 1830, he became prime minister; he was returned to power in 1831 and headed the government which was responsible for the passing of the Bill itself. The dinner referred to here was held in Grey's honour in Edinburgh on 15 September 1834. A special pavilion had to be erected to hold the 2,800 guests. The dinner was a demonstration of solidarity by all the liberal elements in Scottish political life. See the *Journal of Henry Cockburn, Being a continuation of the Memorials of His Time, 1831–1854* (Edinburgh, 1874), I, 64–8.

89. *Blackwood's Magazine*, XXXII (1832), 94.

90. John Griscom, for example, did not find time to do any of the sight-seeing or touring of the normal visitor; he did, however, 'regret the necessity of leaving Scotland, without going further into the north, among the lakes and mountains, and observing the peasantry, collected around their native "*wee bit inkles*," and listening, if possible by stealth, to the accents of the venerable *cotter*, as they flow from his family perusal of the *big ha' Bible*.' (*A Year in Europe*, II, 409.)

91. However, one of the Americans with whom Silliman had stayed in Edinburgh, at the time that Silliman was preparing to return to America, was leaving on a tour of the Scottish Highlands.

92. Of course this is only true in a relative sense; it does not mean that no Americans can be found in Edinburgh at this time whose presence can be explained by the city's intellectual attraction. Henry McLellan, for example, studied divinity in Edinburgh during the winter of 1831–2. But the preface to McLellan's *Journal of a Residence in Scotland* is very suggestive of the changing atmosphere. McLellan died

at the age of twenty-three, three months after returning from his European trip; his account of his travels was compiled from his papers after his death. Scotland had been the base for McLellan's European tour, and the editors of his journal felt that this fact alone would guarantee interest in his account. The editorial preface suggests

> ... that the Journal of the residence in Scotland will not be uninteresting to the general reader. For no people do we feel a higher respect and more sincere affection than for the noble and warmhearted Scotch. Their great novelist has made us acquainted with them all, from the Pentland Firth to the Mull of Galloway. The pulse quickens, and the heart warms at the very mention of the silver Tweed, Loch Ketturin, [*sic*] Loch Awe, Loch Fyne and Loch Tay, Ben Venue, Ben Nevis, Ben Voirlich, and all the wild hills of the Grampians! (*Journal of a Residence in Scotland*, p. x.)

93. Silliman, *Journal*, II, 292. Silliman's reaction to his first view of Scotland is interesting in terms of the country's romantic attraction: 'The hills of Scotland now came into view. I glanced at them with strong emotion ...' (p. 272).

94. Ibid., p. 275. Almost thirty years before, George Logan, the Quaker medical student from Pennsylvania, had visited Holyrood House. He had found it 'miserably situated' and had detailed the palace's association with Mary Queen of Scots without any particular emotion. See Frederick B. Tolles, *George Logan of Philadelphia* (New York, 1953), p. 29.

95. Silliman, *Journal*, II, 311.

96. Ibid., p. 358. Silliman's comment on the more recent battle supports the contention, made in Chapter Three, that Americans tended to see in the rebellion of 1745 a national Scottish uprising: '... the English were defeated by the Scotch [at Falkirk] in 1746; this gallant people fought with great bravery in support of the prince commonly called the Pretender, whom they regarded as their lawful sovereign.'

97. *Tour in Scotland*, pp. 25–6. *Marmion*, canto 2, 10–11, 144–7, 148–51.

98. Ibid., pp. 23–4.

99. Ibid., p. 28. Cf. the letter Irving wrote to his brother soon after his arrival in the city: 'I am enchanted with the general appearance of the place. It far surpasses all

my expectations; and, except Naples, is I think, the most picturesque place I have ever seen.' (*Life and Letters*, I, 378.)

100. *Tour in Scotland*, p. 32.

101. Ibid., p. 46. A pause at this sacred spot soon became a regular procedure for the American traveller. In 1831, Emma Willard, the American educationalist, gathered a few pebbles from the rock 'as a memento'. (*Journal and Letters from France and Great Britain*, p. 355.)

102. *Tour in Scotland*, p. 57.

103. Ibid., p. 70. In 'Abbotsford', one of the sketches in *The Crayon Miscellany*, Irving describes this encounter in more detail.

104. Irving, *Life and Letters*, I, 384–5. Irving's travelling companion on his tour was W. C. Preston of South Carolina.

105. Nathaniel H. Carter, (1787–1830) had been for a time professor of languages at Dartmouth. He was the owner and editor of the *New York Statesman* in which his 'Letters' appeared. They were widely reproduced in other papers.

106. Carter, *Letters from Europe*, I, 238.

107. Ibid.

108. Ibid., pp. 241–2.

109. Ibid., p. 252. Ramsay's old home was then occupied by Principal Baird of the University.

110. Ibid., pp. 253–4.

111. Ibid., p. 258. Carter had brought with him from New York many letters of introduction to the Edinburgh literati; the winter social season, however, had not yet begun so he was unable to present many of these. He was entertained by Jeffrey and Professor Pillans.

112. Ibid., pp. 276–7.

113. Ibid., p. 278.

114. Ibid., pp. 283–4.

115. Ibid. The poem is 'Lochiel's Warning'.

116. Ibid., pp. 291–2. Carter mentions that among his fellow passengers were two other American tourists (see p. 289).

117. Ibid., p. 293.

118. Ibid., pp. 294–5.

119. Ibid., p. 295.

120. Ibid., pp. 296–7. In 1832, the Revd C. S. Stewart of the United States Navy also saw in the wild sublimity of Glencoe the natural source for the 'high-wrought and tragic poesy' of Ossian. See Charles S. Stewart *Sketches of Society in Great Britain and Ireland* (Philadelphia, 1834), II, 175.

121. Carter, *Letters from Europe*, I, 297.

122. Ibid., p. 307. The owner of the island,

Lord Willoughby d'Eresby, had had this bower built.

123. Ibid., p. 309.

124. Ibid., p. 311. Home was taken prisoner by the rebels at the Battle of Falkirk in 1746. He led a daring escape from Doune Castle in which he and a number of other prisoners had been confined.

125. Viewing the same prospect in 1832, C. S. Stewart was reminded of Hector Macneill's poem the 'Links o' Forth', which describes the scene, and quoted two stanzas. (*Sketches of Society in Great Britain and Ireland*, II, 114.)

126. Carter, *Letters from Europe*, I, 314.

127. Ibid., p. 315. In Glasgow Carter met again the American tourists who had stayed on board the steamer at the foot of the Caledonian Canal; in tempestuous weather they had sailed out to the Isle of Staffa and the Hebrides. On its next trip, this boat, the 'Comet', foundered in the Firth of Clyde with the loss of 70 lives. Mrs Grant had planned to be on board. (See *Memoir and Correspondence*, III, 66.) This was not, however, Henry Bell's famous *Comet*, the prototype steamboat—it had been wrecked in 1820—but another vessel named *Comet II* in honour of Bell's original.

128. Dr John Mackenzie (d. 1837), who first met Burns in 1783. Mackenzie was a useful friend for Burns—he introduced the poet to Dugald Stewart in Edinburgh. The poem in question is called 'Invitation to a Medical Gentleman to attend a Masonic Anniversary Meeting'.

129. 'Davie' was David Sillar (1760–1830), a local friend of Burns, and a fellow-poet; he was a member of the Bachelor's Club which Burns founded in Tarbolton, Ayrshire, in 1780. His *Poems* was published at Kilmarnock in 1789.

130. Carter, *Letters from Europe*, I, 329. The poem is of course 'The Brigs of Ayr'.

131. Ibid., p. 330.

132. Several American travellers show great interest in Robert Owen and his community at New Lanark. In 1819 John Griscom stayed with Owen for several days and was able to examine the workings of the community in great detail. With Owen himself he spent long hours in argument and discussion, 'engaged in a wordy warfare upon the best means of correcting the abuses of society, and making the whole world a band of brothers'. (See *A Year in Europe*, II, 375–93.)

133. Carter, *Letters from Europe*, I, 347.

134. Ibid., p. 348.

135. 'Mrs Burns' is of course more familiar as Jean Armour.

136. Calvin Colton (1789–1857), journalist, politician, and author. Early in his career he had been for short periods a minister in both the Presbyterian and Episcopalian churches. He came to England in 1831 where he remained for four years as foreign correspondent for the *New York Observer*. On his return to America he took up political pamphleteering on behalf of the Whigs. In 1852 he became professor of public economy at Trinity College, Hartford. He wrote the official biography of Henry Clay.

137. Calvin Colton, *Four Years in Great Britain*, II, pp. 9–10.

138. Ibid., pp. 10–12.

139. Ibid., p. 15.

140. Ibid., pp. 18–19.

141. Ibid., pp. 50–2.

142. Ibid., p. 57.

143. Colton's book does not give a detailed account of his Scottish tour; descriptions are given only of noteworthy incidents, scenes, and experiences.

144. Emma Willard's refusal to repeat the normal description of Holyrood House in recognition of the fact that 'you may read it, and I dare say have, in forty books', is quite untypical of the American travellers. As it is, even Miss Willard does not pass on from Holyrood without a word. (See *Journal and Letters from France and Great Britain*, p. 371.)

145. Willis, *Famous Persons and Places*, p. 18.

146. Ibid., p. 20.

147. Ibid., p. 74.

148. Ibid., p. 78.

149. Ibid., p. 81.

150. Ibid., p. 83.

151. Ibid., p. 85.

152. Ibid., p. 88. Andrew Bigelow, however, the Boston clergyman, even climbed Ben Lomond. 'With feelings of wonder, we surveyed the stupendous outline of mountains which undulated along the horizon from the commencement of the Ochil-hills in the east, to Ben More on the north, and Cruachan and Ben Nevis on the west.' Andrew Bigelow, *Leaves from a Journal; or Sketches of Rambles in North Britain and Ireland* (Edinburgh, 1824), p. 239.

153. Ibid., p. 89.

154. Ibid., p. 114. Willis's salute to Scott is relatively restrained. The same cannot be said of these comments of the Revd Orville Dewey, who visited Scott's Border home in 1833: '... well, I have seen it all— I have seen it! But the study!—before the desk at which he wrote, in the very chair, the throne of power from which he stretched out a sceptre over the world, and over all ages, I sat down—it was enough! I *went* to see the cell of the enchanter—I saw it; and my homage—was silence, till I had ridden miles from that abode of departed genius.' (*The Old World and the New*, I, 74.)

155. Willis, *Famous Persons and Places*, p. 75.

156. *Sketches of Society in Great Britain and Ireland*, II, 75–6.

157. Ibid., pp. 156–7.

158. Orville Dewey, *The Old World and the New*, I, 59.

159. Willard, *Journal and Letters from France and Great-Britain*, p. 365.

160. Ibid., p. 347.

Conclusion

A strong and enduring Scottish influence upon colonial America has always been recognised. The evidence which has been brought forward of the existence and importance of Scottish-American ties in the study of medicine, in education generally, and in religion, and of the part such relations played in shaping the future pattern of American intellectual life, serves mainly to support and justify that recognition of pre-Revolutionary Scottish influence upon America. But the terms of recognition—the framework within which it occurs—are important.

The Scottish-American link in the pre-Revolutionary period may be regarded as an isolated phenomenon, the product essentially of the economic tie between the countries in all its aspects including that of emigration, or of the economic link in conjunction with the 'political' one represented by the presence of Scottish governors and other officials in the American colonies. This point of view is a valid one; it can explain and account for much of the Scottish influence upon colonial America. But it has one defect. Through its concentration on the immediate economic and political factors it encourages the scholar who holds it to magnify the damage done to Scottish–American relations by the outbreak of the Revolution: because the Revolution severed the economic and political links he is inclined to say that the break opened out to include all Scottish–American relationships.

If, on the other hand, the tie between Scotland and the American colonies is not seen as an isolated phenomenon but as a part of the widening of Scottish horizons which was occurring throughout the eighteenth century, then the break caused by the American Revolution loses much of its apparent significance. The fact that the Scottish–American tie happened to be in part political and economic should not be a decisive consideration. That the economic and political link did provide an ideal means for the conveying of Scottish cultural influences to America is of course abundantly clear; but this is not at all to say that the Scottish cultural influence was a consequence of, or was even finally dependent upon, the existence of these conditions. To claim as much would be the same as to say that if John Witherspoon had not come to Princeton, then the Scottish common-sense philosophy would never have reached America. Once again such a claim could only result from the assumption that pre-Revolutionary Scottish influence upon America represented a distinct and independent cultural phenomenon. Such, however, it was not; even the economic link itself was but one manifestation of the process of expansion in all directions which characterised eighteenth century Scotland.

It was not only in New York and Boston and Philadelphia that the influence of Scottish thinkers and Scottish writers was felt in the later eighteenth and early nineteenth centuries: it was felt in London and Paris and the rest of Europe too. It is in this sense that the Scottish impact upon colonial America was not an isolated phenomenon. Hence the American Revolution caused only a temporary check to the flow of Scottish influence upon America. By 1775, Scotland's eighteenth century renaissance had hardly run half its course; in literature it was then only beginning to gather momentum. And America was extraordinarily sensitive to the influence of the later representatives of Scottish achievement; the reception accorded to, say, Dugald Stewart and Thomas Brown illustrates the point perfectly.

This particular example illustrates something more. Stewart and Brown were immediately available to Americans because the philosophical concepts on which they were building had been introduced to America long before, had been introduced in fact in pre-Revolutionary days. The true significance of the coincidence of the early period of the Scottish cultural revival with the existence of the political and economic link with America is here. The whole course of Scotland's eighteenth and early nineteenth century intellectual and literary revival would inevitably have made some impression upon America. But the width and depth of that impres-

sion, and America's continued sensitivity to Scottish influence, re-
sulted from the groundwork for such receptiveness laid in the pre-
Revolutionary period.

That the impact of Scotland upon America after the Revolution
did continue to be wide and deep is indisputable. It is clear that the
widespread American recognition of the stature of the 'North
British' achievement, which becomes evident at the end of the
eighteenth century, had been preceded by several decades of
assimilation, the most meaningful kind of recognition. The stream
of American students to Scotland alone demonstrates that this was
so. But this recognition of Edinburgh as the medical and scientific
capital of the world, of Robertson and Hume as the model
historians, of Blair and Kames as the authorities on questions of
literary style and taste, of Reid and Stewart as the outstanding
exponents of modern philosophy, of Adam Smith as the master
economic thinker—a recognition that is unmistakably implied by
the widespread republication and circulation of their books, by their
presence in the standard college curricula, and by explicit and
frequent references in American literary and intellectual journals—
in no way coincides with a decline of Scottish intellectual
influence upon America. That influence was to remain powerful
in American thinking for several decades to come.

Soon after the turn of the century such Scottish influence upon
America was renewed and reinforced by the impact of the 'second
generation' in Scotland's cultural renaissance. Continuity is again
apparent. The writings of the original North Britons had so
permeated American intellectual life that America was in a sense
as ready as Scotland herself to receive and acknowledge the
achievements of the new generation. The speed with which the
Edinburgh Review established itself as an authority to be reckoned
with, in America as in Great Britain, illustrates this receptiveness
perfectly. And as the literary quarrel swayed back and forth across
the Atlantic, the 'Scotch critics', whichever side they were on,
never lost their dominant position on the American scene. The
success of the *Edinburgh Review*, and later of *Blackwood's Magazine*,
ensured the continuation and prolongation of Scottish intellectual
influence upon America.

However, it is the impact upon America of the more native or
national side of Scotland's eighteenth century revival that has
heretofore been insufficiently recognised. The concern for Scottish

I

national traditions and antiquities, and in particular the literature which was associated with these new national interests, did make an impression upon America, an impression which, if not so immediate, was in the end as wide and deep and lasting as that produced by the North Britons. In the decades after the American Revolution, Scottish literature and the romantic history and traditions with which so much of it was concerned, were permeating the American imagination, as Scottish thinkers were helping to shape the American mind. In terms of that shaping spirit, the immense popularity of Sir Walter Scott in America is no isolated phenomenon; American enthusiasm for *Douglas* and *Ossian*, for the poetry of Burns, for Scottish ballad and Scottish song, had prepared the way for Scott, even as the North Britons had prepared the way for the *Edinburgh Review*.

Because of the nature of its appeal, the impact of Scottish literature, and hence of the more native or national side of Scotland's eighteenth century renaissance, upon America, was even more pervasive than that of the North British thinkers: the American settlers on the banks of Lake Erie who were such enthusiastic admirers of Burns's songs probably knew little of the philosophy of Hume or of the economics of Adam Smith. It was Scottish literature rather than Scottish thought that was responsible for the dissipation of the very unfavourable image of the Scot that had become widespread during the Revolution. As the conditions which had produced that image ceased to exist, it must quickly have faded before the new literary image of the heroic and poetic Scot, the inheritor of a noble and splendid past. It was Scottish literature which recreated Scotland in the American imagination; and it was out of that recreation that Scotland finally emerged as the 'classic' land of romance.

Scotland as the land of learning, Scotland as the land of romance— from the end of the eighteenth century these two images of Scotland existed in America side by side. Melville's novel *Mardi*, in which the description of Scotland I have used as an epigraph occurs, appeared in 1849. But Melville's mid-century account admirably summarises the American response to Scotland whose origins and development I have attempted to trace. His uncannily accurate reference to the romantic homeland of the heroic, zealous, metaphysical, and poetical Scot testifies to the continuing existence of major aspects of both images and shows how the Scottish impact upon America did not come to an abrupt halt in 1835. Indeed debased, residual elements of the old romantic image undoubtedly represent what Scotland means to America—and to the rest of the world—today. But up to and beyond the middle of the nineteenth century the consequences of the long period of Scottish influence upon America, which has been described, were still being worked out. A key figure here is Carlyle. Partly through his close connection with Emerson, Carlyle made a major contribution to the development of transcendentalism in America, and up to the Civil War at least it was transcendentalism that set the tone of America's intellectual and cultural life. Carlyleism and transcendentalism both represent a reaction against Enlightenment values; the connection between the two clearly owes much to a shared intellectual background.[1] A similarly shared Scottish–American intellectual background also goes far towards explaining the phenomenon of Owenism in America from the 1820s through to the 1840s.[2] As the nineteenth century goes on it is clear that the number of individual Scots—Andrew Carnegie notwithstanding—making a significant impact upon America begins to decline. But it is equally clear that in such areas as journalism, industrial technology, and labour movements, Scots continue to make important contributions.[3] And if the burning crosses of the Ku Klux Klan owed anything at all to the Fiery Cross which summoned the Highland clansmen in 'The Lady of the Lake', and even if the Klan itself did indeed find its prototype in the German secret society described by Scott in *Anne of Geierstein*, then it is equally and undoubtedly true that the Scottish liberal tradition made an important contribution to the development of the antislavery movement both in Britain and America.[4]

But whatever the significance of these future developments, the truth is that even by the 1830s the Scottish culture which had for so long exercised such a potent influence on America and elsewhere was itself on the point of disintegration and dissolution. Scotland's 'classic' status was to prove short-lived. The dangers always implicit in her emergence as a magnetic centre of literary romanticism were about to be realised. For about a hundred years her cultural history had been progressive and exciting; there had been significant achievements in a variety of areas and some work of enduring value produced. Now the great days were all but over. But striking testimony to their greatness, to the scale and scope of

Scotland's achievement in her age of enlightenment, is the depth, pervasiveness, and many-sidedness of her influence upon the United States of America.

NOTES AND REFERENCES

1. See A. Hook, 'Carlyle and America,' *Occasional Papers*, no. 3, The Carlyle Society (Edinburgh, 1970).

2. J. F. C. Harrison has shown that it was the intellectual world of the Scottish Enlightenment that contributed most to the development of Owen's notions about man and society. It is in the 'search for a science of society' in the work of Adam Ferguson and Dugald Stewart, Harrison suggests, that the origins of most of his ideas are to be found. [See J. F. C. Harrison, *Robert Owen and the Owenites in Britain and America* (London, 1969), p. 87.] Harrison argues that this Enlightenment dimension of Owen's thought appealed strongly to Americans familiar with the Enlightenment values of Franklin, Jefferson and Adams. But the link was probably stronger than this. If Harrison is right in stressing Owen's debt to the Scottish Enlightenment, then it was peculiarly in America, much influenced by the same philosophical movement, that Owenism might be expected to produce a positive reaction. Fanny Wright, befriended in Glasgow by Robina Millar, widow of Professor John Millar's son, and subsequently a leading American Owenite, then properly symbolises in her own person the close link between Owenism in Scotland and America. (For a further note on John Craig Millar see Appendix, p. 241.)

3. Frank Thistlethwaite, *The Anglo-American Connection in the Early Nineteenth Century* (Philadelphia, 1959), pp. 28–33, 57.

4. See C. Duncan Rice's unpublished PhD thesis, 'The Scottish Factor in the Fight against American Slavery', University of Edinburgh, 1969.

Appendix

SCOTTISH LIBERALISM AND AMERICA, 1793–1802

For Scottish liberals as for liberals everywhere, from the moment of the successful establishment of her independence, America remained an inspiriting example of what could be achieved in the names of freedom and democracy. Archibald Fletcher, for example, the leader of the burgh reform movement in Scotland, according to his wife 'hailed the establishment of American Independence as one of those great events that serve to teach practical wisdom and moderation to old Governments'.[1] Fletcher's views were echoed by Sir James Mackintosh who, while still a schoolboy called himself a Whig and, in an impromptu House of Commons made up of fellow scholars, delivered the speeches attacking North's war policy, of Fox and Burke.[2] All his life, Mackintosh remained an admirer and staunch defender of the United States, commonly coming to be referred to as *the friend of America* in the American press.[3] The opinions of Fletcher and Mackintosh about America typified those of a group of young men, many of them lawyers, who were at a later date to invigorate the Whig party in Scotland.

All the movements for political reform in Scotland date from the period of the American War.[4] The freedoms which the Americans had claimed, and successfully defended their right to, were essentially those which all men of liberal feelings came to demand for the people of Great Britain. In Scotland particularly, such freedoms were notably lacking. Even before the Revolution, the contrast

233

between the political conditions at home and in America had been an important factor in encouraging Scottish emigration. The pamphlet called *A Candid Enquiry into the Causes of the Late and the Intended Migrations from Scotland* ended by insisting that the desire for freedom from oppression, produced by the intolerable conditions at home, was the chief factor encouraging emigration. In the letters from America published for the purpose of stimulating emigration, the political freedom to be found in America, in contrast to the corruption and repression typical of home, was a theme constantly emphasised. Such an emphasis is present in Alexander Thomson's letter, published in Glasgow in 1774, as *News from America*:

> We have the privilege of choosing our ministers, schoolmasters, constables and other parish officers . . . and there is, I believe no part of the world where justice is more impartially administered, than in the province of Pensylvania. . . . With respect to our laws they are made by those who are, not nominally only, but really our representatives; for without any bribes or pensions they are chosen by ourselves, and every freeholder has a vote.[5]

—and again, in a pamphlet entitled *Information to Emigrants*, published in Glasgow about 1774:

> Our native soil has a strong attraction, but the means of life are more inciting than any land. The prospect of liberty invited our ancestors from a happier clime to this Island. Liberty and plenty has induced many of our countrymen to seek after more benign skies, and a more bountiful soil; they have found them in America, and now invite us to share with them in the bounties of Providence, under the mildest of Governments, in a most healthful, fertile, and delightful Climate.[6]

Any hope, however, of a quick success for liberal reform policies in Scotland which might have existed at the end of the American War, was extinguished by the outbreak of the French Revolution. Once again, like liberals everywhere, Scottish liberals greeted the onset of the revolution with enthusiasm. Whigs such as Fletcher and Henry Erskine, Dean of the Faculty of Advocates and brother of the Earl of Buchan, were naturally jubilant, but even Principal Robertson 'was dazzled by its splendour'.[7] Dugald Stewart and John Millar were two other enthusiasts. It is probably true, at this stage, that the mass of the Scottish people remained relatively immune from any powerful reforming sentiment, but it was from Scotland that there came the two best known replies to Burke's *Reflections on the Revolution in France*: Sir James Mackintosh's *Vindiciae Gallicae*, and Thomas Christies's *Letters on the French Revolution*. Christie was a native of Montrose, and that district became notorious as a centre of democratic propaganda, perhaps partly as a result of the lingering influence of Charles Nisbet.[8] In time, too, the events in France and the writings of Thomas Paine, Mackintosh, and others, began to have their effects on the people of Scotland. In 1792 riots occurred in various Scottish towns, officially put down to the seditious influence of Tom Paine, but in fact genuine expressions of popular grievances on questions of land-holding, representation, and the other issues of reform.

In the same period, Scottish branches of the societies advocating popular reforms were established. The 'Friends of the People' first met in Scotland in Edinburgh, on 26 July 1792, and similar associations were soon formed in Glasgow, Dundee, Perth, and in every town of any size. Such Edinburgh Whigs as Fletcher and Henry Erskine—the Earl of Buchan, and Thomas Erskine, the most famous barrister of the day, later Lord Chancellor, and the youngest of the three Erskine brothers, had already joined the London branch of the 'Friends'—stayed outside such organisations because they believed that the alarm they were causing in official circles would end in strengthening the government's hand. The first convention of the Friends of the People met in Edinburgh on 11, 12 and 13 December 1792; delegates attended from local societies all over Scotland. But the government was now about to strike against the whole reform, or, as the authorities viewed it, 'revolutionary', movement. Thomas Muir, an Edinburgh advocate, vice-president of the associated reform societies in and around Edinburgh, regarded by the government as the organiser of all the reform agitation, was arrested in January, 1793. Released on bail, he travelled to London, being welcomed there by Fox, Grey and the other Whig leaders, and then to France and Ireland before returning to Scotland. Tried before both a packed jury and judges who were determined to condemn him, Muir, in August, 1793, despite an eloquent three-hours' speech in his own defence in which he pleaded guilty only to the advocacy of parliamentary reform, was found guilty of sedition and sentenced to transportation to Botany Bay for fourteen years. In the following month, after an equally ludicrous trial, Palmer, another reformer, was transported for seven years. In December, three other reformers, William Skirving, Maurice Margarot, and Joseph Gerrald, were also tried and found guilty of sedition, receiving the same sentence as Muir. The indignation evoked by these trials, in particular by the conduct of Lord Braxfield, one of the judges, spread far and wide. No Scottish trials had ever produced such passionate interest and concern both at home and abroad. Finally, in 1794, evidence of what was taken to be a revolutionary plot was uncovered, and in August and September, Robert Watt and David Downie were brought to trial on charges of high treason. They were found guilty and Watt, a former government spy, was executed.

The Watt affair provided the government with an excuse to impose even stronger repressive measures upon the country. For the next few years Scotland was virtually a police state. Liberalism of even the mildest sort was looked upon as a species of disloyalty; intolerance pervaded all levels of society; proven loyalism became a prerequisite for employment, and not only in jobs under governmental control; philanthropic work of any kind was regarded as suspect or subversive; a cause such as that of popular education was actively discouraged.[9] The position of avowed democrats was particularly difficult; some, like Robert Burns and Thomas Reid, tried to conciliate opinion by temporising; others, such as Professor John Millar, and Dugald Stewart, held their ground. Equally difficult, perhaps, was the position of a group of young Edinburgh lawyers including Francis Jeffrey, Archibald Fletcher, Henry Brougham, Francis Horner, George Cranstoun, brother-in-law of Dugald Stewart, and John Millar, son of the Glasgow professor. The Speculative Society, of which many of them were members, was now looked upon with suspicion as a possible source of both Whiggery and sedition, and both Cockburn and Mrs Fletcher affirm that it was almost impossible for Whig lawyers to obtain legal work of any kind.[10]

American interest in this series of events in Scotland was considerable. Whether or not Americans felt that during the sedition trials of 1793 the ideals for which they and their country stood were being judged, it is impossible to say, but evidence of concern over the trials is not lacking. *An Account of the trial of Thomas Muir, Esq., Younger, of Huntershill, before the High Court of*

Justiciary at Edinburgh, on the 30th and 31st days of August 1793, for sedition, was reprinted at New York in 1794, followed by two further editions in the same year. In America, as in much of Europe, Muir was regarded as a martyr for the cause of freedom. His speech to the jury became a favourite piece for declamation in New England schools, and it was in an American vessel, dispatched for that purpose, that he was able to escape from Botany Bay in 1796.[11] An account of the trial of Joseph Gerrald was published in New York in 1794; and that of Margarot seems to have evoked special interest. The account of his trial, 'taken in short-hand by Mr. Ramsey', was published in New York, Boston, Philadelphia, and Norfolk, Virginia, in 1794, and republished in Philadelphia in 1796. Finally, descriptions of the trials of Watt and Downie appeared in Philadelphia and New York, also in 1794. These trials probably reminded many Americans of the accusations of popular support for British policies of tyranny and oppression levelled against the Scots in Revolutionary days, but to others the spectacle of the Scottish martyrs probably suggested a Scottish tradition of a more heroic kind.

Mackintosh's *Vindiciae Gallicae* was published at Philadelphia in 1792, the year of its appearance in Britain. In the same period, some of the American public was able to read contributions even more distinctively Scottish to the current political debate. *The Bee*, a periodical established in Edinburgh in 1790, was consistently liberal in tone. James Anderson, its editor, was an admirer of America, and this, together with the strong behind-the-scenes influence of the Earl of Buchan, ensured that the magazine should be particularly concerned with America and American affairs. Buchan's American preoccupation carried him even further, causing him to exert great efforts to establish an American circulation for the magazine. Typically, Buchan started by writing to the President of the United States. Washington's reply is interesting for the tone of great respect it displays towards the Scottish earl:

> My Lord, I received a few days ago the letter which your Lordship did me the honor to write to me on the 27th of March last; accompanied with a view of Doctor Anderson's proposed periodical publication.
>
> Anderson's plan appears judicious, and if the execution shall equal the design in goodness (as from your account of the author we have reason to expect) there can be no doubt but

his Journal will be of great utility wherever it may be circulated. For the purpose of promoting the circulation, by bringing its object and importance more generally into notice, some account of this literary undertaking will be published in the Gazette of the United States: a paper which is read extensively in America.[12]

The letter is dated 30 June 1790, at New York. A second letter to Buchan, written two years later, shows that Washington did in fact receive *The Bee*; on 20 June 1792, in Philadelphia, he acknowledges receipt, from a bookseller in New York, of six volumes of the journal, and adds, 'Considering myself as a subscriber to the *Bee* I have written to Doctor Anderson to know in what manner I shall pay the money, that it may get regularly to his hands.'[13] Buchan also wrote to Charles Nisbet at Dickinson College, on 28 June 1791, mentioning the subject of the circulation of the journal: 'I have written, in the 21st. number of the *Bee*, a monitory paper on America, which may, perhaps, reach your College. I beg leave to recommend the *Bee* to your attention and patronage in your neighbourhood.'[14] The monitory paper referred to appeared in the magazine in the form of a letter to the editor. Opening with a comment about the American distribution, the Earl proceeds to define his sense of responsibility towards the United States:

> Sir,
>   As a foundation has been laid for an extensive circulation of your excellent journal, in the States of North America, and as I have for more than five and twenty years past entered with sincere good will into the interests and happiness of that noble community, which had the honour and resolution to obtain its freedom from the tyranny of the parent state, I feel myself inclined to fulfil my good offices towards the good people of America, by inserting such papers in your useful collection as may prove of peculiar advantage to our trans-Atlantic children.[15]

The rest of this delightful letter is taken up with the Earl's first pieces of advice: Americans must remember the indissoluble union between virtue and happiness; Britain has forgotten it in allowing the slave trade to go on; Americans must pay more attention to the necessity of education; small academies should be set up to create a learned clergy; Sunday schools should be established for labourers and servants—with silver medals as prizes to encourage them; female education should be particularly attended to. Subsequent numbers of *The Bee* carried other articles on America, some by Buchan, some from American sources.[16]

The radical reform emphasis in *The Bee* reached its height in a series of articles on the 'Political Progress of Britain', which ran through the seventh, eighth, and ninth volumes. These articles were outspoken in their condemnation of the government: English politics had been consistently anti-Scots; Scottish industry had been depressed by unjust taxation; British imperialism was disreputable; the enormously costly wars fought by Britain had served no purpose. When the articles were published in pamphlet form in Edinburgh, the government finally took action. The pamphlet was declared seditious, and a warrant issued for the author's arrest. His identity, however, was difficult to establish. A man named James Thomas Callender was suspected, but he denied all connection with the work and tried to incriminate Lord Gardenstone, then the one judge in the Court of Sessions sympathetic to the reform movement. At this point, James Anderson identified Callender as the author of the articles. In the meantime, however, Callender had fled from Scotland to the United States.

Callender arrived in America in 1793. Having republished his pamphlet in Philadelphia in 1795, he became the editor of two periodicals, the *Political Register* and the *American Register*. He later edited the *Richmond Recorder*, and published a work called *Sketches of American History*.[17] His career in America was not uneventful; in 1803, the *Scots Magazine* reported that Mr Callender, 'one of the political fugitives from Scotland about eight years ago', had been sued for libel in Philadelphia, a fact which perhaps helps to explain his reputation as an originator of the indiscriminately abusive strain in American political journalism.[18]

R. R. Palmer has reminded us how in the years before 1800 a considerable number of political radicals from the British Isles made their way to the United States. But Callender is the only Scot he mentions in relation to this form of what he calls 'more or less voluntary emigration'.[19] In fact as the *Scots Magazine*'s comment implies, Callender was not the only Scottish political refugee of this period who found asylum in the United States. In December 1793, Nisbet, who had by now lost all his faith in the future of democracy, wrote to Witherspoon: 'I hear that some of the "friends of the people" have come over from Scotland this year, and published the most dismal accounts of the situation of that country, which are contrary to all the intelligence that I have from my correspondents.'[20] Nisbet had apparently discounted a letter he had received earlier in the year from John Erskine, in which the position of various Scottish ministers in this difficult period had been described. The sermons of a Revd Mr Dunn of Kirkintilloch were regarded as seditious, and he had been jailed for three months in Edinburgh for cutting out leaves from the minutes of a society of 'Friends of the People' which might have authenticated a charge of sedition against them. Erskine goes on to say that some ministers had tried to vindicate measures carried out by bribery and corruption, while others had been unjustly branded as friends of sedition.[21]

At any rate, it is possible to identify some of the refugees whom Nisbet referred to. One was James Tytler, known as 'Balloon' Tytler, on account of an unsuccessful balloon ascent, a friend of Burns in Edinburgh. Tytler had been the editor of various periodicals before taking over the *Historical Register* in 1791. The *Register* supported the popular, reform side on all occasions. After publishing a manifesto of the people's wrongs, Tytler was accused of sedition and forced to flee the country. He arrived first in Ireland, then in America, and lived out his life in Salem, Massachusetts.[22] Another was Grant Thorburn, subsequently immortalised as the hero of John Galt's novel *Lawrie Todd* (1830). Thorburn had joined the Friends of the People in Edinburgh; in 1794 he found it expedient to sail for America. An article in the *Scots Magazine* in 1809 entitled 'Answers to Queries concerning the United States of America', contained a reference to another Scottish refugee. Discussing the new American steamboats, the writer said:

> ... you will be amused to learn that the mechanist who super-
> intends the boat here is from the neighbourhood of Edinburgh,
> from the works they call something like the Kaltoun works:
> they say here he was one of those whom Downie and Watt
> had some concern with; however, he is here a very useful
> harmless man, and there is no danger of his setting the Delaware
> on fire.[23]

Many years later, in 1830, James Stuart went into the shop in Washington of one Kennedy, a 'theological bookseller'. Inside, he met Mr Kennedy and learned something of his history:

> I found he was from Paisley. When he was a young man he was attached to those political principles which sent Gerrald, Muir, Palmer, etc. to Botany Bay; and which were at that time (about the years 1793–4) sufficiently unfashionable. He had been induced to attend the meetings of the Edinburgh Convention, though not a member; but Mr. Kennedy's brother, now a senator in Maryland, was a member of the Convention; and they both thought it prudent, during the then reign of terror in Scotland, to emigrate to the United States.[24]

Another emigrant of the same period by compulsion rather than by choice was John Craig Millar, the son of Professor John Millar of Glasgow, married to the youngest daughter of Dr William Cullen. Mrs Fletcher had been very friendly with Mrs Millar and in her *Autobiography* she describes the departure of the couple:

> In the spring of 1795 our friends Mr. and Mrs. Millar took their departure for America, banished thither by the strong tide of Tory prejudice which ran so fiercely against Mr. Millar. He had joined the Society of "The Friends of the People." He lost his professional employment, and though a most able and honourable man, was so disgusted with the state of public affairs in Scotland that he determined to seek peace and freedom in the United States of America.[25]

Millar died within two years of his arrival in America and his widow returned to Scotland. In conversation with Mrs Fletcher, she described how, while they were living in Philadelphia, they had often met and conversed with President Washington.[26] John Craig Millar was clearly a man of intellectual ability. Another Scottish emigrant at this time of a similar professional type was John Maclean. Maclean was a physician and surgeon in Glasgow and had been associated with the reform movement in the city. He left for America early in 1795 and subsequently helped to maintain Princeton's strong Scottish link by joining its faculty. In October, 1795 he became professor of chemistry and natural history in the college and remained a leading member of the faculty until 1812.

Finally, it is to this period of political oppression in Scotland that America owes the arrival within her shores of one of her greatest ornithologists: Alexander Wilson. Before turning to ornithology, Wilson had already exercised his talents as a poet, and like Burns he had been an ardent enthusiast for the French Revolution and the rights of man. However, in May 1793, some satirical poems on local figures gained him a three months' jail sentence in Paisley, an experience which inspired him with a longing for the freedom that had temporarily disappeared from his own country. In May 1794, he sailed for America from Belfast. An incident on board ship, which he described in the letter he wrote home after his arrival in Philadelphia, suggests his feelings: '... Dr. Reynolds, who was tried and condemned by the Irish House of Lords, was discovered to be on board, and treated all the passengers and crew with rum-grog, which we drank to the confusion of despots, and the prosperity of liberty all the world over.'[27] A comment from a letter Wilson wrote to his father some years later, in November, 1798, might well stand as an epigraph for all those Scots who sought political asylum in America in the 1790s: 'men of all nations, and all persuasions and professions find here an asylum from the narrow-hearted illiberal persecutions of their own Governments.'[28]

The widespread republication in America of detailed accounts of the Scottish 'sedition' trials undoubtedly reflects considerable American interest in the Scottish political situation. Seen in relation to the steps taken in America to secure the rescue of Thomas Muir from Australia, that interest may be translated into sympathy and concern for the Scottish democrats.[29] It may be that American sympathisers were unaware of the admiration with which the Scottish liberals viewed the establishment of democratic principles in America, yet there is little doubt that most Americans would see in the repressive policies of the British government, symbolised by the trials, a reflection of the policies which they themselves had defeated only a decade before.

After the flurry of interest in the 1793–4 period, Scotland did not again force herself upon American attention until 1802–3. It was in 1802 that the event occurred which was to bring Edinburgh and Scotland back to the centre of the European stage—the foundation of the *Edinburgh Review*. The names of two of the three founders of the *Review*, and many of its chief contributors, are to be found among those of the young Whig lawyers in Edinburgh who experienced the exigencies of the period of political repression in Scotland which has been described. In estimating their aims and attitudes, including their attitude toward America, that background should always be kept in mind.

NOTES AND REFERENCES

1. Mrs Fletcher, *Autobiography*, p. 367.
2. Robert James Mackintosh (Ed.), *Memoirs of the Life of Sir James Mackintosh* (Boston, 1853), I, 8.
3. *North American Review*, XXXV (1832), 442–3.
4. Fagerstrom, 'Scottish Opinion and the American Revolution', *William and Mary College Quarterly*, 3rd Series, XI (April, 1954), 255.
5. *News from America*, p. 13.
6. *Information to Emigrants, Being the Copy of a Letter from a Gentleman in North-America* (Glasgow, n.d.) p. 16. The letter is by the Hon. William Smith, and is dated 11 June 1773; presumably William Smith, provost of the College of Philadelphia.
7. H. W. Meikle, *Scotland and the French Revolution* (Glasgow, 1912), p. 49.
8. Ibid., p. 56.
9. For details of the 'reign of terror', see Meikle, pp. 154–7.
10. Mrs Fletcher, *Autobiography*, p. 66. Henry Cockburn, *Memorials of his Time* (Edinburgh, 1856), pp. 147–8.
11. Meikle, p. 135. After a series of misadventures, Muir died in France in 1799.
12. John C. Fitzpatrick (Ed.), *The Writings of George Washington from the Original Manuscript Sources 1745–1799* (Washington, 1939), XXXI, 63. *The Gazette of the United States* was a more or less official paper published between 1789 and 1847. Washington was as good as his word to the Earl of Buchan. On July 10 1790, the *Gazette published a lengthy* advertisement for *The Bee*: 'Edinburgh, 1790. Prospectus of an Intended New Periodical Work, to be called The Bee, or Universal Literary Intelligencer. To be published weekly ... By James Anderson, LLD. FRS. FSAS.' Four days later, on 14 July, an even larger notice, with long extracts from Anderson's own elaborate prospectus, appeared. The notice ended with this comment apparently by Washington himself: 'No plan of a similar work that has come under our observation appears to be calculated on more philanthropic, useful and comprehensive principles; and, we most sincerely wish Doctor Anderson success in his undertaking. A republication of this article may merit attention from the friends of literature and of mankind.'
13. Ibid., XXXII, 58. From this period, Washington carried on a considerable correspondence with Anderson, mainly on agricultural topics. Another distinguished reader and admirer of *The Bee* was Thomas Jefferson. Jefferson received the first eleven volumes from James Anderson himself and subsequently wished to subscribe to the periodical. See *The Library of Thomas Jefferson*, V, 172–4.
14. Samuel Miller, *Memoir of Charles Nisbet*, p. 193.
15. *The Bee*, III (1791), 96.
16. The Earl of Buchan never lost faith in the efficacy of his prescriptions for the health of America. In 1805 he suggested to John Eliot, Corresponding Secretary of the Massachusetts' Historical Society, that he should arrange for the republication in Boston of all his writings on America contributed to *The Bee*. Eliot's rejection of the suggestion provides further evidence of the American circulation of the periodical: republication is unnecessary because 'The Bee is in every circulating library and every social library' (National Library of Scotland, Adv. Mss 22. 4. 16). In the end the Earl published most of his papers on America, and his correspondence with Washington and Jefferson in a pamphlet entitled *The Earl of Buchan's Address to the Americans at Edinburgh, on Washington's Birth-Day, February 22nd, 1811*. American material published in *The Bee* included two letters from Samuel Stanhope Smith, Witherspoon's successor as president of Princeton, to Charles Nisbet at Montrose. Written in November, 1784, and February, 1785, they give a lengthy and somewhat pessimistic account of the state of America after the Revolution. See *The Bee*, XII (1792), 41–5, 88–95, 225–33, 281–6.
17. Ross, *The Scot in America*, p. 354. Mott's *History of American Magazines* does not mention either periodical.
18. *The Scots Magazine*, LXV (1803), 136. The *DAB* states that Callender was regarded by Jefferson and other lovers of liberty as a man of genius suffering under persecution. Eventually even Jefferson himself was to be the subject of the journalist's abuse.
19. R. R. Palmer, *The Age of the Democratic Revolution*, II (Princeton, 1964), p. 472.
20. Miller, *Memoir of Charles Nisbet*, pp. 230–1.

21. Ibid., p. 234.

22. William J. Couper, *The Edinburgh Periodical Press* (Stirling, 1908), II, 160–1. Ross, *The Scot in America*, pp. 383–4. Ross confuses Tytler with another radical writer of the period, William Johnston, in his account.

23. *The Scots Magazine*, LXXI, pt 2 (1809), 821. *Kaltoun* is presumably a version of Calton.

24. Stuart, *Three Years in North America*, II, 41.

25. Mrs Fletcher, *Autobiography*, p. 71.

26. Ibid., p. 78.

27. Grosart (Ed.), *The Poems and Literary Prose of Alexander Wilson*, I, 60.

28. Ibid., p. 68.

29. The fact, however, that a pamphlet called *Look Before Ye Loup* (Leap), written in support of the government by one Brown, from Dundee, was reprinted in America, in Philadelphia in 1798, and again at Newburyport in 1805, suggests that at least some Americans saw potential dangers for their own social and political stability in the principles of the reformers.

A Selected Bibliography

This is not an exhaustive bibliography of all sources and secondary works consulted. Nor does it list every title alluded to in the text and notes. However, the list of manuscript and printed sources accurately embodies the range of material surveyed to furnish evidence of cultural relations between Scotland and America in the period 1750–1835. In the list of secondary works only such items as contribute more or less directly to the central topic are included.

MANUSCRIPT SOURCES

Correspondence of Robert Anderson. National Library of Scotland, Adv. Mss 22.4.16.
Correspondence of Hugh Simm. Princeton University Library.
Papers of Charles Steuart. National Library of Scotland, Mss 5025–46.

PRINTED SOURCES

BRITISH AND AMERICAN MAGAZINES AND PERIODICALS
The American Monthly Magazine and Critical Review, I (1817)–IV (1818–19)
The American Monthly Magazine, I (1829)–III (1831)
The American Museum, or Universal Magazine, X (1791), XII (1792)
The American Quarterly Observer, I (1833)–III (1834)
The American Quarterly Review, I (1827)–VIII (1830)
The American Review, and Literary Journal, I (1801)–II (1802)
The American Review of History and Politics, I (1811)–IV (1812)
The Analectic Magazine, I (1813)–XIV (1819); New Series, I–II (1820)
The Bee or Literary Weekly Intelligencer, I (1790)–XVIII (1794)
Blackwood's Magazine, I (1817)–XXXVIII (1835)

The Boston Weekly Magazine; Devoted to Morality, Literature, Biography, History, the Fine Arts, Agriculture, etc. etc., I (1802) III (1805)

The Casket, I (1826)–II (1827)

The Edinburgh Review, I (1802)–LX (1835)

The Knickerbocker; or New York Monthly Magazine, I–II (1833)

The Ladies' Literary Cabinet, Being a Miscellaneous Repository of Literary Productions, in Prose and Verse, I (1819–20), IV (1821)–V (1822)

The Literary Gazette, and American Athenaeum, II (1826)–III (1827)

The Literary Gazette: or, Journal of Criticism, Science, and the Arts. Being a Collection of Original and Selected Essays, I (1821)

The Literary Magazine, and American Register, I (1803)–VIII (1808)

The Monthly Magazine and American Review, I (1799)–III (1800)

The New York Literary Gazette, and Phi Beta Kappa Repository, I (1825–6)

The New York Magazine; or, Literary Repository, I (1790)–VI (1795); New Series, I (1796)–II (1797)

The North American Review, I (1815)–XL (1835)

The North Briton from No. I to No. XLVI Inclusive. 2 vols. London, 1769

The Port Folio, I (1801)–V (1805); New Series, I (1806)–VI (1808); New Series, I (1809)–VIII (1812); 3rd Series, I (1813)–VI (1815); 4th Series, I (1816)–XX (1825); Hall's 2nd Series, I (1826)–II (1827)

The Scots Magazine, I (1739)–XCVII (1826)

The Southern Review, I (1828)–VIII (1832)

The United States Review and Literary Gazette, I (1826)–II (1827)

BOOKS BY BRITISH AND AMERICAN TRAVELLERS

Bigelow, Andrew. *Leaves from a Journal; or Sketches of Rambles in North Britain and Ireland.* Edinburgh, 1824

Carter, Nathaniel Hazeltine. *Letters from Europe, Comprising the Journal of a Tour through Ireland, England, Scotland, France, Italy, and Switzerland, in the years 1825, '26, and '27.* 2 vols. New York, 1829

Colton, Calvin. *Four Years in Great Britain. 1831–1835.* 2 vols. New York, 1835

Dewey, Orville. *The Old World and the New; or, a Journal of Reflections and Observations Made on a Tour in Europe.* 2 vols. New York, 1836

Duncan, John Morison. *Travels through Part of the United States and Canada in 1818 and 1819.* 2 vols. New York, 1823

Griscom, John. *A Year in Europe. Comprising a Journal of Observations in England, Scotland, Ireland, France, Switzerland, the North of Italy, and Holland. In 1818 and 1819.* 2 vols. New York, 1823

Hall, Captain Basil. *Travels in North America in the Years 1827 and 1828.* 3 vols. Edinburgh, 1829

[Hamilton, Thomas.] *Men and Manners in America. By the Author of Cyril Thornton, etc.* 2 vols. Edinburgh, 1833

Irving, Washington. *Tour in Scotland, 1817, and other Manuscript Notes, by Washington Irving; Edited, with a Critical Introduction, by Stanley T. Williams.* New Haven, 1927

Melish, John. *Travels in the United States of America, in the Years 1806 & 1807,* and 1809, 1810, & 1811; Including an Account of Passages Betwixt America and Britain, and Travels through Various Parts of Great Britain, Ireland, and Upper Canada. 2 vols. Philadelphia, 1812

Silliman, Benjamin. *A Journal of Travels in England, Holland and Scotland, and of Two Passages over the Atlantic, in the Years 1805 and 1806.* 2 vols. New York, 1810

Stewart, Charles S. *Sketches of Society in Great Britain and Ireland.* 2 vols. Philadelphia, 1834

Stuart, James. *Three Years in North America.* 2 vols. New York, 1833

Wheaton, Nathaniel S. *A Journal of a Residence during Several Months in London; Including Excursions Through Various Parts of England; and a Short Tour in France and Scotland; in the Years 1823 and 1824.* Hartford, 1830

Willard, Emma (Hart). *Journal and Letters, from France and Great-Britain.* Troy, New York, 1833

Willis, Nathaniel Parker. *Famous Persons and Places.* New York, 1854

PAMPHLETS, LETTERS, JOURNALS, LITERARY WORKS, ETC.

Bell, Whitfield J., Jr. 'Scottish Emigration to America; a Letter of Dr. Charles Nisbet to Dr. John Witherspoon, 1784', *William and Mary College Quarterly*, 3rd Series, XI (April, 1954), 276–89

Bland, Theodorick. *The Bland papers: Being a Selection from the Manuscripts of Colonel Theodorick Bland, jr ... To Which Are Prefixed an Introduction, and a Memoir of Colonel Bland ... Edited by Charles Campbell.* 2 vols. Petersburg, Virginia, 1840–3

Brevoort, Henry. *Letters of Henry Brevoort to Washington Irving, together with other unpublished Brevoort papers, edited, with an introduction, by George S. Hellman.* 2 vols. New York, 1916

Britannia's Intercession for the Deliverance of John Wilkes, Esq.; from Persecution and Banishment. To which is added, a Political and Constitutional Sermon, and a Dedication to L—B—. Boston, n.d.

A candid enquiry into the causes of the late and the intended migrations from Scotland. In a letter to J——— R——— Esq., Lanark-shire. Glasgow, n.d.

Cockburn, Henry. *Memorials of His Time.* Edinburgh, 1856

Journal of Henry Cockburn; Being a Continuation of the Memorials of His Time. 1831–1854. 2 vols. Edinburgh, 1874

Creech, William. *Edinburgh Fugitive Pieces: with Letters, Containing a Comparative View of the Modes of Living, Arts, Commerce, Literature, Manners, etc. of Edinburgh, at Different Periods.* Edinburgh, 1815

Dinsmoor, Robert. *Incidental Poems, Accompanied with Letters, and a Few Select Pieces, Mostly Original, for their Illustration, together with a Preface, and Sketch of the Author's Life.* Haverhill, 1828

Erskine, David Steuart, Earl of Buchan. *The Earl of Buchan's Address to the Americans at Edinburgh, on Washington's Birth-Day, February 22nd., 1811.* Edinburgh, 1811

Fletcher, Mrs Eliza (Dawson). *Autobiography, with Letters, and other Family Memorials. Edited by the survivor of Her Family.* Boston, 1876

Grant, James P. (Ed.) *Memoir and Correspondence of Mrs. Grant of Laggan.* 3 vols. London, 1845

Griffin, Edmund D. *Remains, Compiled by Francis Griffin: with a Biographical Memoir of the Deceased by the Rev. John McVickar, D.D.* 2 vols. New York, 1831

Information to Emigrants, being the copy of a letter from a gentleman in North-America; containing a full and particular account of the terms on which settlers may procure lands in North-America, particularly in the provinces of New York and Pensilvania. As also, the encouragement labourers, mechanics, and tradesmen of every kind may find by going there to settle. To which is added observations on the causes of emigration. Glasgow, n.d.

[Leacock, John.] *The Fall of British Tyranny: or, American Liberty Triumphant. The First Campaign. A Tragi-Comedy of Five Acts, as Lately Planned at the Royal Theatrum Pandemonium, at St. James's.* Philadelphia, 1776

Miller, Samuel. *Brief Retrospect of the 18th. Century. Containing a Sketch of the Revolutions and Improvements in Science, Arts, and Literature during that Period.* 2 vols. New York, 1803
Memoir of the Rev. Charles Nisbet, D.D., Late President of Dickinson College, Carlisle. New York, 1840

Munford, Robert. 'The Patriots', *William and Mary College Quarterly*, 3rd Series, VI (July, 1949), 448–503

Neal, John. *American Writers, a Series of Papers Contributed to Blackwood's Magazine (1824–1825) by John Neal; Edited with Notes and Bibliography by Fred Lewis Pattee.* Durham, N.C., 1937

News from America. Letter I. From Alexander Thomson, late Tenant at Corker-Hill in the Parish of Paisley, now Proprietor of a Considerable Estate in Pensilvania. To a Gentleman near Glasgow. Glasgow, 1774

Rush, Benjamin. *The Autobiography of Benjamin Rush; His "Travels through life," together with his Commonplace Book for 1789–1813. Edited with Introduction and Notes by George W. Corner.* Princeton, 1948
Letters. Edited by L. H. Butterfield. 2 vols. Princeton, 1951

Stiles, Ezra. *Literary Diary, edited by Franklin Bowditch Dexter.* 3 vols. New York, 1901

Ticknor, George. *Life, Letters, and Journals of George Ticknor* (Edited by G. S. Hillard, and by Mrs. Ticknor and Miss Ticknor). 2 vols. Boston, 1877

Witherspoon, John. *The Miscellaneous Works of the Rev. John Witherspoon.* Philadelphia, 1803
An Address to the Natives of Scotland Residing in America. Being an Appendix to a Sermon Preached at Princeton on a General Fast. London, 1778

Wodrow, Robert. *The Correspondence of the Rev. Robert Wodrow. Edited from Manuscripts in the Library of the Faculty of Advocates, Edinburgh, by the Rev. Thomas M'Crie.* 3 vols. Edinburgh, 1842–3

SECONDARY WORKS

Adam, Margaret I. 'The Causes of the Highland Emigrations of 1783–1803', *Scottish Historical Review*, XVII (June, 1920) 73–89

Ahlstrom, Sydney E. 'The Scottish Philosophy and American Theology', *Church History*, XXIV (September, 1955), 257–72

Bell, Whitfield, J., Jr. 'Philadelphia Medical Students in Europe, 1750–1800', *The Pennsylvania Magazine of History and Biography*, LXVII (January, 1943) 1–29 'Some American Students of "That Shining Oracle of Physic"', Dr. William Cullen of Edinburgh, 1755–1766', *Proceedings of the American Philosophical Society*, XCIV (June, 1950), 275–81

Brown, Wallace. *The King's Friends; the Composition and Motives of the American Loyalist Claimants*. Providence, 1965

Butterfield, Lyman Henry. *John Witherspoon Comes to America; a Documentary Account Based Largely on New Materials*. Princeton, 1953

Carpenter, Frederic I. 'The Vogue of Ossian in America: A Study in Taste', *America Literature*, II (January, 1931), 405–17

Carus, Gustave. 'Robert Burns and the American Revolution', *The Open Court*, XLVI (February, 1932), 129–36

Charvat, William. *The Origins of American Critical Thought, 1810–1835*. Philadelphia and London, 1936

Clive, John and Bailyn, Bernard. 'England's Cultural Provinces: Scotland and America', *William and Mary College Quarterly*, 3rd Series, XI (April, 1954), 200–13

Cockburn, Henry. *Life of Lord Jeffrey. With a Selection from his Correspondence*. 2 vols in 1. Philadelphia, 1856

Collins, Varnum Lansing. *President Witherspoon, a Biography*. 2 vols. Princeton, 1925

Davis, Richard Beale. 'Literary Tastes in Virginia before Poe', *William and Mary College Quarterly*, 2nd Series, XIX (January, 1939), 55–68 *Intellectual Life in Jefferson's Virginia, 1790–1830*. Chapel Hill, 1964

Duffy, Charles. 'Thomas Campbell and America', *American Literature*, XIII (January, 1942), 346–55

Easterby, James Harold. *History of the St. Andrew's Society of Charleston, South Carolina, 1729–1929*. Charleston, 1929

Eisenhart, Luther P. 'Walter Minto and the Earl of Buchan', *Proceedings of the American Philosophical Society*, XCIV (June, 1950), 282–96

Fagerstrom, Dalphy I. 'Scottish Opinion and the American Revolution', *William and Mary College Quarterly*, 3rd Series, XI (April, 1954), 252–75

Finley, John H. *The Coming of the Scot*. London and New York, 1940

Gardner, Edgar S. *The First Two Hundred Years, 1747–1947, of the St. Andrew's Society of Philadelphia*. Philadelphia, 1947

Gower, Herschel. 'The Scottish Palimpsest in Traditional Ballads Collected in America', in W. E. Walker and R. L. Welker (Eds.), *Reality and Myth*, Nashville, 1964

Graham, Ian Charles Cargill. *Colonists from Scotland: Emigration to North America, 1707–1783*. Ithaca, New York, 1956

History of the Speculative Society of Edinburgh from its Institution in M.DCC.LXIV. Edinburgh, 1845

Insh, George Pratt. *The Scottish Jacobite Movement; a Study in Economic and Social Forces*. Edinburgh, 1952

Irving, Pierre Munroe. *The Life and Letters of Washington Irving*. 4 vols. New York, 1864

Leary, Lewis. 'Ossian in America; A Note', *American Literature*, XIV (November, 1942), 305–6

Leavelle, Arnaud B. 'James Wilson and the Relation of the Scottish Metaphysics to American Political Thought', *Political Science Quarterly*, 57 (1942), 394–410

Mathieson, William Law. *The Awakening of Scotland; a History from 1747 to 1797*. Glasgow, 1910

McCosh, James. *The Scottish Philosophy, Biographical, Expository, Critical, from Hutcheson to Hamilton*. New York, 1875

Meikle, Henry W. *Scotland and the French Revolution*. Glasgow, 1912

Morgan, James Henry. *Dickinson College; the History of One Hundred and Fifty Years, 1793–1933*. Carlisle, Pa., 1933

Mowbray, Paul Wheeler. *America Through British Eyes; a Study of the Attitude of the Edinburgh Review toward the United States of America from 1802 until 1861*. Rock Hill, South Carolina, 1935

Nolan, James Bennett. *Benjamin Franklin in Scotland and Ireland, 1759 and 1771*. Philadelphia, 1938

Orians, G. Harrison. 'The Romance Ferment after Waverley', *American Literature*, III (January, 1932), 408–31

Osterweis, Rollin G. *Romanticism and Nationalism in the Old South*. New Haven, 1949

Price, Jacob M. 'The Rise of Glasgow in the Chesapeake Tobacco Trade, 1707–1775', *William and Mary College Quarterly*, 3rd Series, XI (April, 1954), 179–99

Pryde, George S. *The Scottish Universities and The Colleges of Colonial America*. Glasgow, 1957

Riggs, Alvin R. 'The Colonial American Medical Student at Edinburgh', *University of Edinburgh Journal*, XX (Autumn, 1961), 141–150

Ross, Peter. *The Scot in America*. New York, 1896

Sachse, William Lewis. *The Colonial American in Britain*. Madison, Wisconsin, 1956

Schneider, Herbert Wallace. *A History of American Philosophy*. New York, 1946

Shepperson, George. 'Writings in Scottish–American History: A Brief Survey', *William and Mary College Quarterly*, 3rd Series, XI (April, 1954), 163–78

Shores, Louis. *Origins of the American College Library, 1638–1800*. Nashville, 1934

Sloan, Douglas. *The Scottish Enlightenment and the American College Ideal*. New York, 1971

Slosser, Gaius Jackson (Ed.), *They Seek a Country; the American Presbyterians, Some Aspects*. New York, 1955

Snow, Louis Franklin. *The College Curriculum in the United States*. Printed for the author, 1907

Spiller, Robert E. *The American in England, during the First Half Century of Independence*. New York, 1926

Strang, John. *Glasgow and Its Clubs: or Glimpses of the Condition, Manners, Characters, and Oddities of the City, during the Past and Present Centuries*. London and Glasgow, 1857

Trinterud, Leonard J. *The Forming of an American Tradition, a Re-Examination of Colonial Presbyterianism*. Philadelphia, 1949

Wellwood, Sir Henry Moncreiff. *Account of the Life and Writings of John Erskine, D.D., Late One of the Ministers of Edinburgh*. Edinburgh, 1818

Wertenbaker, T. J. *Early Scotch Contributions to the United States, being a Lecture Delivered within the University of Glasgow on 8th March, 1945.* Glasgow, 1945

Wright, Esmond. 'Education in the American Colonies. The Impact of Scotland', in E. R. R. Green (Ed.), *Essays in Scotch–Irish History* (London, 1969), 18–45

Index